Stranger Gods
Salman Rushdie's Other Worlds

In *Stranger Gods* Roger Clark offers an ambitious and wide-ranging study of Salman Rushdie's seven published novels, with a special focus on his earliest, *Grimus*, and his most powerful and provocative, *Midnight's Children, Shame,* and *The Satanic Verses.* Clark shows how Rushdie employs cosmology, mythology, and mysticism to structure otherworldly dramas that are fascinating in their own right, as well as crucial to the more worldly points Rushdie makes about literary tradition, history, ethnicity, and the politics of religion.

Clark's exploration of Rushdie's novels works on at least three levels. First, he clarifies and interprets Rushdie's often puzzling references to figures such as Loki and Shiva, settings such as the mountains of Qaf and Kailasa, and experiences such as the annihilation of the self and the temptations of the Muslim Devil, Iblis. Second, he demonstrates how otherworldly motifs work with or against each other, fusing or clashing with Dantean, Shakespearean, and other literary forms to create hybrid characters, plots, and themes. Finally, Clark argues that Rushdie's brutal assault on tradition and taboo is mitigated by his secular idealism and by his subtle homage to mystical ideals of the past.

This novel interpretation, which presents Rushdie's first five novels as a heterogeneous yet consistent body of work, will challenge and delight not only Rushdie scholars but anyone interested in comparative religion and mythology, iconoclasm, and the interplay of Western and Eastern literary forms.

ROGER Y. CLARK teaches in the Department of English at the University of British Columbia.

STRANGER GODS

Salman Rushdie's Other Worlds

Roger Y. Clark

McGill-Queen's University Press
Montreal & Kingston · London · Ithaca

© McGill-Queen's University Press 2001
ISBN 0-7735-2107-0 (cloth)

Legal deposit first quarter 2001
Bibliothèque nationale du Québec

Printed in Canada on acid-free paper

This book has been published with the help of a grant
from the Humanities and Social Sciences Federation of
Canada, using funds provided by the Social Sciences
and Humanities Research Council of Canada.

McGill-Queen's University Press acknowledges the
financial support of the Government of Canada through
the Book Publishing Industry Development Program
(BPIDP) for its activities. It also acknowledges the
support of the Canada Council for the Arts for its
publishing program.

Canadian Cataloguing in Publication Data

Clark, Roger Y. (Roger Young), 1960–
   Stranger gods: Salman Rushdie's other worlds
   Includes bibliographical references and index.
   ISBN 0-7735-2107-0 (bnd)

   1. Rushdie, Salman – Criticism and interpretation.
   I. Title.
   PR9499.3.R8Z63 2001   823'.914   C00-900611-7

This book was typeset by Typo Litho Composition Inc.
in 10/12 Baskerville.

Contents

Acknowledgments

I would like to thank the following people for their advice and support: Inder Nath Kher, Burkhard and Marie Anne Niederhoff, Thorsten Ewald, Kent Lewis, Jackie Tahara, Rob Edmonds, Ken Bryant, Mandakranta Bose, Vidyut Aklujkar, Graham Good, Bill New, Margery Fee, Mark Vessey, Aruna Srivastava, Joan Harcourt, Joan McGilvray and Noel Gates. I offer a special thanks to Ronald Hatch for his critical insight, stylistic advice and good cheer, my parents, William and Velma Clark, for their unflagging support, and my wife, Ruby Mah, for her patience and encouragement.

Works of A.S. Rushdie

		Abbreviation
*1975	*Grimus*	G
*1981	*Midnight's Children*	MC
*1983	*Shame*	S
1986	*The Jaguar Smile* (travelogue)	
1987	*The Riddle of Midnight* (documentary)	
*1988	*The Satanic Verses*	SV, the Verses
*1990	*Haroun and the Sea of Stories*	H, Haroun
1991	*Imaginary Homelands* (essays)	IH
1992	*The Wizard of Oz* (essays on the film)	
1994	*East, West* (short stories)	EW
*1995	*The Moor's Last Sigh*	M, the Moor
1997	*The Vintage Book of Indian Writing* (anthology)	
*1999	*The Ground Beneath Her Feet*	GB, Ground

* major novels

Time-Line:
History, Culture, and Rushdie's Fiction

Rushdie's novels are steeped in the culture and history of the Indian subcontinent. This includes one of the world's earliest and least understood civilizations (Harappa), diverse strands of Hinduism, Buddhism, Zoroastrianism and Islam, as well as the more recent incursions of England and the West. The following time-line puts names and dates to some of these cultural and historical currents, and shows how these are reflected, twisted, and otherwise transformed in Rushdie's fiction. The time-line highlights Hindu epics and mythology, Arabic and Persian milestones from the seventh to the sixteenth centuries, and subcontinental politics of the last eighty-five years.

Date	History and Culture	Rushdie's Fiction
2500–1700 BC	*Harappa*: civilization located in the Indus Valley, including the cities of Mohenjodaro and Harappa; their script remains a mystery; Ali Bhutto's family estate is near a site	*Shame*: Rani and Bilquis are exiled to the estates of Mohenjo and Daro by their husbands; the shawls knit by Rani are in a sense coded scripts condemning her husband, the authoritarian Iskander Harappa – a fictional version of Ali Bhutto

Date	History and Culture	Rushdie's Fiction
2000– 1500 BC	Indo-Aryans, an Eastern branch of Indo-European peoples, move into the sub-continent, bringing with them the myth and poetry of the Sanskrit *Vedas*; similar invasions from the north occur in Persia and Greece	*Ground*: The Parsi anglophile Sir Darius revels in the parallels between Hindu and Greek myth; his fascination echoes that of Orientalists such as Sir William Jones, who in 1786 first proposed a common root between Sanskrit and Greek
560– 480 BC	Buddha: enlightenment under a bodhi (peepul) tree near Benares; his "nirvana" is considered a "snuffing out" of desire, and is accompanied by a sense of freedom and bliss	*Midnight's Children*: Saleem enters a thoughtless "buddha-hood" under a bodhi tree; in this state he becomes a dog of war for the Pakistani generals, and, as a result, his self is almost snuffed out in a meaningless nirvana
400 BC– 400 AD	*Mahabharata*: world's longest poem about the battle between two North Indian families; contains within it the core story of *Bhagavad Gita*, in which Krishna (an avatar or incarnation of Vishnu) gives advice to Arjuna on the battlefield *Ramayana*: the poem follows the romance between Rama (another incarnation of Vishnu) and Sita; Sita is captured by the demon king Ravana and rescued with the help of the monkey king Hanuman	*Midnight's Children*: Saleem learns his family's stories from Mary, who sees Indian history in terms of the battles of the *Mahabharata*; Ahmed suffers extortion by the Ravana gang, and, in a reversal of Hindu myth, a monkey called Hanuman scatters his pay-off; in order to make Christianity more acceptable to Hindus, a priest tells Mary that Jesus was blue like Krishna *Shame*: Raza sees his child Sufiya as an avatar of his dead first son *Verses*: Gibreel's confused state of mind partly results from the stories about the Hindu gods his mother told him as a child; Gibreel stars in a film about a debauched Rama

Date	History and Culture	Rushdie's Fiction
42–8 BC	Virgil's *Aeneid* and Ovid's *Metamorphoses* both include the story of how the musician Orpheus journeys to Hell and tries to bring back his beloved Eurydice	*Ground*: after the death of his beloved Vina, the rock star Ormus tries to find her in his psychotropic underworld of music and drugs
6 BC–30 AD	Jesus Christ, son of Joseph and Mary: to Christians, Jesus is the son of God who died on the cross and saved the world from sin; Ahmadiyya Muslims believe Christ escaped from the cross and travelled to Kashmir	*Midnight's Children*: to impress the left-wing Joseph, Mary puts the poor baby (Saleem) in the place of the rich baby (Shiva); Mary also offers refuge and a grace of sorts to a world-weary Saleem; the drunken boatman Tai claims to have seen a bald and gluttonous Christ in Kashmir
300–1000 AD	Puranas: eighteen major collections of stories about the lives of the gods Shiva: the erotic-ascetic god of destruction and creation; he dances the dance of death and rebirth Vishnu: complex god of many forms and incarnations, including Rama and Krishna Krishna: an incarnation of Vishnu, he is beloved for his childhood pranks, taste for butter, and flirtation with female cowherds Kali: an often terrifying form of the Divine Mother, she scourges the world's evil and wears a necklace of skulls	*Grimus*: Eagle's sexual intercourse with Media on Mount Calf reworks that of Shiva and Parvati on Mount Kailasa; as Shiva, Eagle destroys the novel's setting and replaces it with another *Midnight's Children*: Saleem sees his story as another Purana; General Shiva procreates wildly and violently, signalling the nation's overpopulation and nuclear capacity; in frenzied devotion, Shiva worshippers topple land reclamation tetrapods and inadvertently kill the pro-birth control gynecologist Dr Narlikar *Shame*: the possessed Sufiya acts like Kali by scourging Pakistan and beheading her victims

Date	History and Culture	Rushdie's Fiction
		Moor: the Hindu fundamentalist Mainduck is seen in terms of a violent Vishnu or "Battering Ram"
570–632	Muhammad: founder, exemplar and prophet of Islam; his life and practices are described in "Reports" called Hadith	*Verses*: Gibreel has serial dreams which supply an irreverent account of Muhammad's life, including the "satanic verses incident" mentioned in some Hadith
610	Koran: first revelation to Muhammad of the 114 surahs or chapters (arranged from longest to shortest); Muslims believe the Koran is the word of God revealed to Muhammad by the angel Gabriel; the Koran does not directly mention the "satanic verses incident"	*Midnight's Children*: Ahmed dreams of reorganizing the Koran; Saleem hears what he thinks are angelic voices *Verses*: Chapter 2 reworks the incident in which Satan tricks Muhammad into thinking that his words are those of Gabriel, after which Muhammad repudiates these "satanic verses"
622	Hegira: Muhammad escapes Mecca and finds safety in Medina; in 630 he returns triumphantly to Mecca; the Hegiran calendar starts with the flight to Medina	*Verses*: "Mahound" leaves Jahilia (Mecca) in Chapter 2 and returns in Chapter 6 *Shame*: Rushdie titles the penultimate chapter, *In the Fifteenth Century*, according to the Hegiran calendar
800–1100	*The Prose Edda*: stories about Norse gods such as Loki and Odin; they include the story of the apocalypse of Ragnarok, in which Loki and his monstrous crew set fire to heaven and earth, and Odin sacrifices himself beneath	*Grimus*: Deggle renames himself "Lokki"; Grimus sees himself as a mystical Odinic figure, and sacrifices himself under his own giant ash tree; Eagle destroys Grimus's realm; Eagle and the prostitute Media become the pri-

Date	History and Culture	Rushdie's Fiction
	Yggdrasil (the giant ash tree which is shaken by the eagle and which harbours the primordial couple)	mordial couple who appear to survive the apocalypse
1001	Approximate (and fanciful) date for *Arabian Nights* or *The Thousand and One Nights*; there are numerous collections of these varied, interconnected stories from the Middle East and India, all framed by the following story: betrayed by his wife, King Shahriyar decides to kill each morning the woman he spends the night with; Scheherazade tells the king such fascinating stories that after 1001 nights he marries her	*Midnight's Children*: Saleem sees himself as Scheherazade, writing in order to stave off death by meaninglessness; the fiery, lecherous Ahmed drinks bottles full of gin/ djinn; Saleem communes telepathically with the 1001 magical children born in the first hour of Indian Independence *Haroun*: Haroun and Rashid get their names from Haroun al-Rashid of the *Nights*; Rashid's stories restore democracy in Kashmir and unite Rashid with his estranged wife
11th c.	*The Ocean of Story* by the Sanskrit Kashmiri poet Somadeva: real and fantastic stories collected from earlier sources; there are 124 chapters or "waves"; the stories are intertwined and often tangential to the narrative line	*Haroun*: From Kashmir, Haroun and his father reach the moon, which contains a huge ocean of stories that flow into one another; Haroun then stops the Cultmaster from plugging the source of stories and from poisoning the ocean *Moor*: Bombay is seen as an ocean of human stories
11–12 c.	*Ruba'iyat*: quatrains by the poet and astronomer Omar Khayyam (1048–1131) from Nishapur in northeastern Persia; Khayyam ponders the uncertainty of human knowl-	*Shame*: the protagonist Omar Khayyam Shakil is raised in the mansion of Nishapur; he ponders the frightening and uncertain wonders of the cosmos, displaying a fearful inter-

Date	History and Culture	Rushdie's Fiction
	edge and fortunes; the hedonistic and Sufi elements may seem incongruous yet both suggest the desire to escape worldly suffering	est in the depths of the stars; somewhat like his namesake, he is a hedonist strongly influenced by scientific knowledge (he becomes a famous immunologist)
1177	*The Conference of the Birds*: a book-length poem by the Persian Farid ud-Din Attar (c. 1142–1220); in it thirty (*si*) birds (*murgh*) are led by a bird-guide (the Hoopoe) to the Impossible Mountain of Qaf, where they hope to find the great king of birds, the Simurgh; at the summit they find that the king they sought lies within them; the birds attain mystical unity and annihilation	*Grimus*: the protagonist's entire journey is modelled on Attar; the antagonist's name, "Grimus," is an anagram for "Simurg," and suggests a twisted egocentric mysticism *Midnight's Children*: old Aziz sahib dies happily after conversing with thirty species of birds; Aadam joins the doomed Free Islam Convocation in order to unify Muslims and Hindus; Saleem hopes to play the Hoopoe by uniting Indians in his *Midnight Children's Conference*; Saleem reaches the age of thirty and writes thirty chapters *Shame*: Omar's mothers take away Omar's screen of Qaf at the beginning, and fly away to the Impossible Mountains at the end *Verses*: Allie longs to climb Everest and the impossible mountain of Gibreel's love (at twenty-nine thousand feet, Everest is just shy of thirty) *Haroun*: two Hoopoes convey Haroun to the moon, where he helps to bring unity and love to the divided inhabitants

Date	History and Culture	Rushdie's Fiction
1221	Nishapur sacked by the Mongols; Nishapur was home to the scientist and poet Omar Khayyam as well as to the mystic and poet Farid ud-Din Attar	*Shame*: Omar Khayyam Shakil is born in the mansion of Nishapur, and is chased back to it in the novel's final scene of cataclysmic destruction; Omar is trained in science yet witnesses the beauties and horrors of the mystic realm
1310–14	*The Divine Comedy* by Dante Alighieri: Virgil takes Dante into the Inferno and then up the island mountain of Purgatory; since the pagan Virgil cannot reach the higher Christian truths, Beatrice shows Dante the wonders of Paradise	*Grimus*: Eagle is guided by Virgil Jones into the inferno of his mind and then up the island mountain of Calf; Media shows him to the peak *Midnight's Children*: Saleem and his fellow Pakistani soldiers descend into a jungle version of Hell *Verses*, *Moor* and *Ground*: Chamcha, the Moor and Ormus all plummet to their own versions of Hell
1492	Columbus reaches the Caribbean, supported by King Ferdinand and Queen Isabella of Spain Jews expelled from Spain Boabdil, the last Muslim ruler in Andalusia, surrenders the Alhambra in Granada, reportedly shedding a tear as he looks back; this marks the end of the *reconquista*, in which Christian Spain regains its lands from the Muslims	*East, West*: the short story, "Christopher Columbus and Queen Isabella of Spain Consummate Their Relationship," is set amid the expulsion of the Jews and the defeat of the Muslims in Granada *Moor*: in a villa in Andalusia, the modern day Moor soliloquizes on the past greatness of Boabdil and the Alhambra; Rushdie parallels the expulsion of the Moors and Jews from Spain with the rejection of Muslims in India; Belle wins back the family business in Cochin, a *reconquista* which

Date	History and Culture	Rushdie's Fiction
		earns her the nickname Queen Isabella
1497	Vasco da Gama: Portuguese explorer who makes the first sea voyage from Europe to India, spurring interest in the spice trade	*Moor*: Aurora da Gama's Portuguese Goan family gets its riches from the spice trade
1526	Babur begins Moghul rule by defeating the Sultan of Delhi; later Moghul emperors Akbar, Jehangir, Shahjahan and Aurangzeb expand the empire to include most of the subcontinent; Shahjahan builds the Taj Mahal in memory of his wife Mumtaz	*Shame*: Babar becomes a fighting hero of the Baluchi tribespeople *Midnight's Children*: Saleem evokes the power and beauty of Jehangir's Kashmir, and hopes to honeymoon with Padma in this earthly paradise; Nadir Khan and Mumtaz (later Amina) find love in her basement, their "Taj Mahal"
1600	British East India Company established; starting in Surat and other coastal locations, the English gradually take control of the subcontinent from the waning Moghuls, the Marathas and the French; after the 1857 rebellion, often called "The Mutiny," the Crown takes direct control, thus beginning The British Raj (which ends in 1947)	*Midnight's Children*: Saleem goes to an English-style school in Bombay; Sir William Methwold's departure mimics the transfer of power from England to India (his sunset gin and tonics become the fire-water djinns of Ahmed's decadence) *Verses*: Chamcha finds his Indian self despite his desire to become thoroughly British *Ground*: the Anglophile Sir Darius pretends to have earned a law degree from Cambridge

Date	History and Culture	Rushdie's Fiction
1603	*Othello; the Moor of Venice* by William Shakespeare: the bitter Iago uses sinister innuendo to drive the war hero Othello into a jealous rage, in which he kills his wife and then himself	*Verses*: an embittered Chamcha whispers satanic verses into the ears of his friend, the great movie-star Gibreel; these verses drive Gibreel to murder his lover and then himself
1789	French Revolution: popular revolt against the *ancien régime*, followed by the Reign of Terror, in which the guillotine speeded up the execution of those formerly in power	*Shame*: Raza Hyder's regime is brought to an end by the extreme violence of the possessed Sufiya, who is a mix of the Beast, Kali with her necklace of skulls, and Madame Guillotine with her basket of heads
1915	Mahatma Gandhi returns to India from South Africa and leads civil disobedience campaigns until 1947	*Midnight's Children*: the novel opens in 1915 with Dr Aadam Aziz returning to India from Germany; Aadam's wife Naseem does not understand what Gandhi intends by bringing the country to a halt, to "mourn, in peace, the continuing presence of the British"
		Moor: Francisco takes part in the Home Rule campaign of Gandhi and the Congress Party
1919	Amritsar massacre: in a brutal application of the Rowlatt Act prohibiting demonstrations, the British General Dyer has his soldiers fire on a large crowd of peaceful protesters, killing over 300 and injuring over 1000	*Midnight's Children*: we see the massacre from the Indian perspective of Dr Aadam Aziz; when Naseem asks where he has been (and thinks the blood all over his body is mercurochrome), he says "Nowhere on earth"

Date	History and Culture	Rushdie's Fiction
1924	*A Passage to India* by E.M. Forster: a novel set during the British Raj of the early twentieth century; after being acquitted of molesting Stella, the Muslim Dr Aziz goes off to live in a princely state in central India, as far as possible from the British; in the 1984 film he ends up in Kashmir	*Midnight's Children*: the novel starts in Kashmir with the Muslim Dr Aadam Aziz, who accepts Western science yet rejects Western Orientalist notions of superiority; Aadam is not personally betrayed by the British, yet witnesses first-hand the Amritsar Massacre and struggles to reconcile East and West; he returns to Kashmir at the end of his life
1939–40	*The Master and Margarita* (suppressed for at least thirty years in Russia): a novel by Mikhail Bulgakov; the Devil descends on Moscow and narrates Chapter 2	*Verses* (still banned in Islamic countries and India): the Devil descends on England and Arabia; his narrative voice is least disguised at the beginning of Chapter 2
1940	The Muslim League, allegedly speaking for Muslims in the subcontinent, declares an independent Pakistan as its goal; historical accounts seldom emphasize the aim of Sheik Abdullah's Muslim National Conference, which is to keep Muslims within a unified subcontinent	*Midnight's Children*: the Muslim League lies behind the death of the Hummingbird (Sheik Abdullah) and the destruction of his Free Islam Convocation
1945–7	Communal violence; Partition of India from East and West Pakistan: Britain makes a hasty retreat, conceding to the vision of a partitioned subcontinent; millions killed in violence between Hindus, Muslims and Sikhs; Hindus	*Shame*: in Delhi Mahmoud protests communal violence by playing a Hindu-Muslim double bill; his cinema is boycotted and blown up *Midnight's Children*: communal violence is represented in Delhi by the Muslim mob that

Date	History and Culture	Rushdie's Fiction
	flee to India and Muslims flee to West and East Pakistan	attacks Lifafa Das and by the gang named after the Hindu demon Ravana; the Calcutta riots are described succinctly as "four days of screaming"
1947	Independence of India and Pakistan at midnight on August 14–15; Nehru, first Prime Minister of India, gives a famous speech about India's "tryst with destiny"	*Midnight's Children*: of the first 1001 magical children born, Saleem and Shiva are born closest to midnight and hence have the greatest powers; Nehru sends Saleem a special letter of high hopes
1956–8	Pakistani dictatorship sets in; Ayub Khan imposes military rule, taking power from Iskander Mirza and his Republican Party	*Midnight's Children*: a naive Saleem helps his uncle Zulfikar and General Ayub plot a coup
1959	*The Tin Drum*: German novel in three parts by Günter Grass; a magic realist work emphasizing the solipsistic perspective of Oskar, who refuses to grow and who comments on the course of twentieth-century Germany history	*Midnight's Children*: the three parts of the book chronicle in magic realist fashion the solipsistic vision Saleem has of his magical self and of his influence over events in sub-continental history, including the rise of Pakistani militarism
1962	India-China border war: China deflates Indian confidence by taking Aksai Chin, a region scarcely populated yet strategic to the Chinese since it lies on the western route between Xinjiang and Tibet	*Midnight's Children*: China's successful assault coincides with the magical children's assault on Saleem as leader of the Midnight Children's Conference; Saleem notes how Indian optimism is deflated and how Indian citizens of Chinese descent are interned

Date	History and Culture	Rushdie's Fiction
1965	India-Pakistan war: battles fought to Pakistan's advantage in the Rann of Kutch (east of Karachi) and to India's advantage in the greater conflict; tank and air battles near Sialkot in northern Pakistan	*Midnight's Children*: Saleem feels that the official version of the Rann skirmish is so unreliable that he decides to relate a ghost-story version instead; Saleem loses his family and becomes amnesiac as a result of the bombing in northern Pakistan
1971	Bangladesh Independence: East Pakistan (later Bangladesh) elects the separatist Awami League, thus constituting a slim majority in a parliament once dominated by the West Wing; the West Wing tries to stop the East from seceding; Indian troops enter the struggle on the East's side and swiftly prevail in Dhaka	*Midnight's Children*: The chapters "The Buddha" and "Sam the Tiger" chart the course of the civil war; in a dog-like amnesiac state of subservience to the West Pakistani military, Saleem helps sniff out East Bengal separatists ("enemies of the state") in Dhaka; traumatized by the war and his conscience, Saleem flees into the purgatory of the Sundarbans Jungle; he returns to a liberated Dhaka
1975–7	The Emergency: Indian Prime Minister Indira Gandhi suspends parliament in a doomed bid to retain power; forced sterilizations and slum clearings	*Midnight's Children*: the Widow (Indira Gandhi) sterilizes the Midnight's Children, who represent the diverse voices of India; Saleem's wife Parvati dies in the slum-clearings
1977–8	Zia ul-Haq takes power from Ali Bhutto in his "Fair Play" military coup; Zia postpones elections and implements Islamic Law	*Shame*: Raza takes power from Iskander in his "Fair Play" coup; Raza professes to be a fair umpire, and declares Iskander's leftist politics to be against Islam

Date	History and Culture	Rushdie's Fiction
1979	Ali Bhutto executed by hanging	*Shame*: after his hanging, Iskander haunts Raza in the form of a devil in his left ear
1985	Air India bombing: Flight 182 from Vancouver (via Toronto) to London explodes off the coast of Ireland, killing all 329 passengers (156 Canadians, 122 Indians; 187 Hindus, 18 Sikhs; 125 under the age of 21); a number of West Coast Canadians fighting for a Sikh nation in the Punjab are still under investigation by the Royal Canadian Mounted Police	*Verses*: the Canadian Sikh terrorist Tavleen girds herself with explosives and leads her less fearless band in a hijacking; not receiving what she wants, she executes passengers and blows up the plane; a prototype of the religious extremist, Tavleen foreshadows Ayesha and the Imam, who both lead their followers into death
1988	Zia dies in a plane crash and Benazir Bhutto wins the national elections Fatwa of Ayatollah Khomeini delivered on Valentine's Day: "I inform all zealous Muslims of the world that the author of the book entitled *The Satanic Verses* – which has been compiled, printed and published in opposition to Islam, the Prophet, and the Koran – and all those involved in its publication who were aware of its content, are sentenced to death. I call on all zealous Muslims to execute them quickly, wherever they may be found, so that no one else will dare to insult the Muslim sanctities. God willing, whoever is killed on this path is a martyr";	*Shame*: in this 1983 novel Raza (Zia) is killed by knives in an elevator, and the "Virgin Ironpants" (Benazir Bhutto) takes his place as national leader *Verses*: Chapter 4 contains a ten-page attack on Khomeini, portraying him as a xenophobic zealot who smashes clocks (to stop progress and return to the days of Muhammad), who snaps his fingers and commands the archangel to fly him to his homeland, who takes on the traits of a flying demon or witch, and who devours his people for the sake of his revolution; the novel contains hints of backlash: there are warnings about a script containing the same subject matter as the offending Chapters 2 and 6;

Date	History and Culture	Rushdie's Fiction
	the next day Rushdie goes into hiding under the protection of Scotland Yard	the Madame of a brothel says that mimicking the prophet's wives will be dangerous but good for business; Mahound executes the poet Baal, who parodies and satirizes him and his God; Salman Farsi, the scribe who distorts Mahound's words, flees for his life
1992	Destruction of mosque at Ayodhya: in northern India Hindu fundamentalists tear down the sixteenth-century Mosque of Babur, believing it to be built on a site sacred to the god Rama; about 1,000 people die in rioting	*Moor*: Mainduck heartily agrees with the decision to tear down the Mosque of Babar; Abraham (representing Muslims) and Mainduck (representing Hindus) fight a turf war in the streets of Bombay; Mainduck is called "the Battering Ram"

Stranger Gods

1 A Jungle of Books

Let it suffice now for me to repeat the classic dictum: The Library
is a sphere whose exact centre is any one of its hexagons and
whose circumference is inaccessible.

Borges, "The Library of Babel"[1]

Readers find in Rushdie a bright ocean of crisscrossing stories, a paper labyrinth of crosscultural references, and a world of transreligious trouble. If we leave aside for the moment the challenge of his tightly woven metafictional style, his work remains extremely demanding, presenting as it does an overwhelming variety of allusions – from the most inane pop trinkets of movieland to the most contentious points of Islamic theology. Not surprisingly, most readers have difficulty following everywhere he goes. This is less true, however, of the political and historical directions he takes. For instance, in *Midnight's Children* he supplies dates and places, and he makes it pretty clear how he feels about secularism, dictatorship, and the unreliability of historical accounts. Even when he cloaks his political figures in fabulous guises and gives them names like the Widow, Razorguts, and the Cultmaster, it takes little guessing (or slight information) to see that he is alluding to Indira Gandhi, Zia ul-Haq, and Ayatollah Khomeini. This translucency is not apparent, however, when it comes to what I call *other worlds*, that is, to the overlapping realms of cosmology, mythology, and mysticism. Here his allusions are more diverse than his political ones (which tend to stay within the subcontinent and Britain), yet they are seldom defined and rarely explained in relation to each other. As a result, readers are left guessing, without an adequate foundation on which to build their own interpretations.

This is where the present study will come in handy, for in it I give background information on Rushdie's often puzzling references to figures such as the Norse Loki, settings such as the Hindu Mount

Kailasa, and episodes such as the temptations of the Muslim Devil Iblis. I also hazard explanations about the way in which otherworldly
motifs work with or against each other, fusing or clashing to shape
character, plot, and theme. Finally, I suggest that Rushdie's notorious
iconoclasm – his brutal assault on tradition and taboo – is mitigated
somewhat by his secular idealism and by his subtle homage to mystical ideals of the past. Rushdie posits a fragmented self in a chaotic
universe, yet he also hints at a mystical ideal of unity, a secular salvation that strives to exist beyond dogma or ideology.

I am well aware that in dealing with Rushdie's volatile mix of
magic and realism, history and metafiction, tradition and rebellion,
there can be no final reckoning, no final formulating or fixing on a
pin. This is especially the case with his first four novels, which are rife
with paradoxes and ambiguities, and hence are miraculously im-
mune to the critic's scalpel. Each murderous attempt to dissect them
fails, for the layers of their meanings multiply. Worlds upon worlds
open before our eyes, and we are left dumbfounded in the mirrored
halls of a labyrinth not unlike that of Borges' famous Library, *"whose
exact centre is any one of its hexagons and whose circumference is inaccessible."* We are left in a critical space which – to borrow from John Keats
– frustrates the rational philosopher yet delights the chameleon poet.

Rushdie's finest points are often his most arcane, frequently owing as
much to cosmology as to geography, as much to mythology as to politics, as much to mysticism as to the plight of the cross-cultural self.
For instance, in describing Saleem's odyssey through the Sundarbans
Jungle in *Midnight's Children* Rushdie gives us more than eerie man-
grove swamps or tirades against the horrors of war. He also blends in
elements from cosmology, mythology, and mysticism, using these to
magnify his points about war and those indoctrinated to fight it. The
wall of trees on the edge of the Sundarbans becomes the gate to a
strange world of the afterlife; the wall becomes a permeable border
leading from this world of destruction and karma to the next world of
death and consequences. Saleem glides his boat through this wall
into a jungle hell reminiscent of *Heart of Darkness* and *Apocalypse Now*,
a purgatory like that in Dante's *Comedy*, as well as an afterlife inhabited by nymphs who are not quite Muslim *houris* or Hindu *apsaras*.

It is crucial to know that in this episode Rushdie is revisiting the
1971 war in Bangladesh, and it is helpful to know that Saleem exem-
plifies the postcolonial outsider and the fluid postmodern self travelling amid multiple layers of metafiction. Yet readers also need to
know about epics, mystical journeys, and figures from Muslim and
Hindu myth. For Saleem has been brainwashed by Pakistani gener-

als who tell him that if he fights the secessionist Bengalis he will enjoy eternal bliss with four beautiful *houris* girls in a Muslim Heaven. In following these promises, Saleem literally and figuratively becomes a dog of war for the generals. Since Rushdie despises militarism and fundamentalism, and especially any combination of the two, he devises a spirit-devouring punishment for his wayward hero: instead of swimming in bliss with *houri* nymphs in a Muslim Heaven, Saleem dissolves into an emptiness that seems to be the work of *apsara* sirens in a Hindu Hell (one must remember that Saleem's greatest fear is meaninglessness and dissolution). The worldly or political moral – those who kill by the sacred sword die by the sacred sword – is closely tied to the cosmic settings of Heaven and Hell and to the mythic figures of *houris* and *apsaras*. Yet Rushdie does not stop there: he adds further depth and ambiguity to this episode by including at least three mystical elements. First, the birds in the treetops sing to God, just as long ago Saleem's great-grandfather conversed with thirty species of birds before his mystical death, and just as not so long ago his sister's hypnotic nightingale voice sang Saleem and his soldiers into battle. Second, Saleem's canine amnesiac state is likened to that of Buddha, and his near dissolution in the arms of the disrobing nymphs parodies mystical annihilation, be it Buddhist *nirvana*, Hindu *moksha*, or Sufi *fanah*. Third, the magical tidal wave that sweeps Saleem out of the jungle operates with a vague redemptive logic. Thus Rushdie not only uses cosmology and mythology to structure his Sundarbans setting and drive home his point about the religious advice of generals; he also leaves us with puzzles that can only be appreciated by using the paradoxical logic of mysticism.

This cursory look at the Sundarbans episode intimates the richness and complexity of Rushdie's other worlds. In the above instance cosmology is used to construct an afterlife setting into which the protagonist journeys. Elsewhere cosmology takes other forms and meanings: in *Shame* and the *Verses* hellish topographies shift and grow, germinating in the mind and branching out across entire nations; in *Grimus* the action takes place on a mountain that conforms to Dante's Purgatory, Attar's Qaf, and Shiva's Kailasa, all of which dissolve in a strange mystical and sexual eschatology. To understand such cosmological operations, readers need to be familiar with a wide variety of otherworldly terrain – with divine mountains circled by mystical birds, a cosmic ocean of stories, a mobius Hindu universe of worlds within worlds, Shiva's cosmic cycles of destruction and creation, the Hebrew Garden of Eden, the Greek Hell guarded by a three-headed dog, and so forth.

This cosmic diversity is matched by a mythic manifest so long that, to speak hyperbolically, it would keep Joseph Campbell and Mircea Eliade busy for several reincarnations. For instance, in *Grimus* we find superimposed on the mythologized quests of Dante and Attar the Norse myth in which Loki and Odin battle for dominion over the world. In *Grimus* and *Midnight's Children* we find different Shivas, the former an "erotic ascetic" whose lovemaking portends eternal destructions and creations, and the latter a whore-murdering general whose brutal copulations signal overpopulation as well as India's entry onto the nuclear stage. Rushdie's use of myth is too diverse to catalogue, yet it remains important to underline from the onset its metamorphic, inconstant nature. Thus in *Midnight's Children* Vishnu takes the form of a benign blue Jesus and in the *Moor* that of a belligerent Battering Ram (Ram or Rama is an incarnation of Vishnu). Throughout Rushdie's oeuvre we find the strangest of deific transmogrifications: we find djinns in gin bottles and on top of clouds; we find devils both satanic and Promethean; we find goddesses who nourish the nation, tempt believers away from a one true God, or cast the world into darkness. As if all these mythic dramas taking place on all these cosmic stages were not enough, Rushdie adds invisible mystical meanings to them, perturbing or inspiring readers with visions of a supernatural abyss, demonic possession, Odin's occult communion with the giant Ash, a yogic swan who lives in two worlds at once, and, most important of all, thirty birds who become one with God.

One of the reasons why it is so hard to get a fix on Rushdie's fiction is that his dissident visions of the universe either fuse or clash, depending on the point he is making at the time. For instance, in *Grimus* he fuses other worlds to make his point about the free play of dimensions, while in *Midnight's Children* he sets other worlds on a collision course to make his point about communal tension in the subcontinent. Fortunately or unfortunately, there is no polestar to guide readers across the purple hazes and the lightning-streaked cumulus of his star-crossed heaven. There are, however, four overall points I would make, points which act less like polestars than bobbing beacons to the wandering bark.

First, Rushdie consistently attacks the notion that beliefs relating to cosmology, mythology, and mysticism – that is, to such things as Heaven and Hell, gods and demons, visions and possessions – should be used to determine political or social policy. In his essay " 'In God We Trust'," he argues that his secularism makes sense in terms of Indian history of the last half-century: "After the terrible communal killings of the Partition riots, it was plainer than ever that if India's remaining Muslims, Sikhs, Buddhists, Jains, Christians,

Jews and Harijans (untouchables), as well as the Hindu majority, were to be able to live together in peace, the idea of a godless State must be elevated above all of the 330 million deities" (IH 385). He is equally aware that such secularism does not sit well in Islamic countries: "we see in Christianity a willingness to separate Church and State, and [an] admission that such a separation is possible and maybe even desirable. In the world of Islam, no such separation has ever occurred at the level of theory. Of all the great sacred texts the Qur'an is most concerned with the law, and Islam has always remained an overtly social, organizing, political creed which, again theoretically, has something to say about every aspect of an individual life" (IH 380). Despite this acknowledgment, Rushdie champions a secularism he considers latent in Pakistani Muslims. This is contentious enough (Pakistan was after all conceived as a Muslim state), yet he goes one big step further: he judges seventh-century Arabia and contemporary Iran according to the dictates of his secular conviction. And the more the objects of his satire are resistant to his secular vision, the more caustic he gets. The result is almost inevitable: death threats and a decade of playing mouse to the cat of fundamentalist rage.

Second, Rushdie's novels from *Grimus* to the *Verses* follow a hell-bound trajectory. I often think of these first four novels in terms of Yeats's widening gyre, that is, in terms of a situation that starts off relatively controlled – the falcon in the range of the falconer – and then gets more and more out of control as the falcon moves further and further from the centre, until mere anarchy is loosed upon the world and the Beast steers the bird toward some vague doom. In *Grimus* other worlds are more or less held in check, in a sort of eclectic and shifting pattern reminiscent of Eliot's *Wasteland* and *Four Quartets*. Yet *Grimus's* hints of death by water, and of the Devil striding toward a burning city of the apocalypse, project themselves wider and wider: in *Midnight's Children* General Shiva and the terrifying Widow stalk Saleem and threaten to drain him of all conviction and meaning; in *Shame* the rough Beast slouches toward the innocence of Sufiya, raping her and scourging the nation; and in the *Verses* the Devil turns London into an inferno, Chamcha into a Devil, and Gibreel into a murderous schizophrenic.

My third point is that Rushdie's first five novels are radically different from his last two. The first five are chock-full of otherworldly references and allusions, and in all but *Haroun* the otherworldly takes deep root in the world. Figures like Kali and the Devil wreak destruction, and inexplicable events tied to myth and mysticism permeate the narratives. Of course, Rushdie questions many of these otherworldly figures and events, often suggesting that they are a function of indoctrination, fear, desperation, or diseased minds. Yet this skepticism clashes with the ongoing eruptions of the sacred and the diabolic. It also paradoxically highlights the idea that the otherworldly is a force to contend with, that it cannot be rejected out of hand – as is seen most clearly in the cases of Aadam Aziz, Omar Khayyam, and Mirza Saeed, all characters who believe *against their own wills* in the presence of God, the Devil, and angels. All of this differs from the *Moor* and *Ground*, where other worlds are either metaphorical or ineffectual.

Speaking positively, one could say that these last two novels do not contain the sacrilege and horror, the apocalyptic diabolism of *Shame* and the *Verses*. Maybe the last thing this world of Ayodhya riots and Luxor massacres needs is another Rushdie Affair. Yet this does not change the fact that his latest novels lack any profound or provocative religious challenges. Alternatively, one could argue that it is not so much that they do not contain the same amount of religiously charged polemic; it is rather that they do not offer the engaging psychological and philosophical perplexities that people find interesting in a postmodern, postcolonial writer such as Rushdie. They do not offer the same kinds of labyrinthine puzzles and paradoxes that are built into the struggles of his characters – or that explode into a world at once magical and real.

Fourth, Rushdie's use of other worlds can be disturbing or insulting to those who believe in sacred ideas that never change. At times his iconoclasm leads him to attack sacred structures and beliefs in a way that can infuriate not just Muslims but also Hindus, Sikhs, and Christians. I must, however, qualify this last point, for while he is iconoclastic in many ways, he also builds powerful myths and awe-inspiring cosmologies into his fiction, and he often promotes the mystical over the material – although never the orthodox over the revisionary. For instance, in *Grimus* the hero smashes an altar and then rapes the goddess venerated at that altar. Taken out of context, these actions underscore desecration and violation – purely negative forms of iconoclasm. Yet, taken in context, they illustrate the moment at which the spell of iconic or revered structures is broken, after which the seeker is free to continue along the pathless path of a spiritual odyssey. Or, as Whitman says in *Song of Myself*, "I tramp a perpetual journey … No friend of mine takes his ease in my chair, / I have no chair, no church, no philosophy."[2]

Like Borges's Library of Babel, Rushdie's oeuvre has many centres and many circumferences, all depending on what angle one sees it from. It is to this profusion of books that I now go, with the proviso that the following overview is meant to be reductive, to intentionally avoid complexity and ambiguity. Later the picture will get fuzzier, as I explore the convolutions which make his novels some of the most problematic ever. What follows also supplies a sketch of Rushdie's earliest years and of several aspects of religion, literature, and politics that will come up in the next chapter, *When Worlds Collide*, and in the chapters on the novels themselves.

Ahmed Salman Rushdie was born in Bombay on June 19, 1947 to Anis Ahmed Rushdie, a businessman from Delhi, and Negin Rushdie (née Butt), a schoolteacher from Aligarh. The fact of their being a Muslim family in the newly partitioned subcontinent enters his fiction in diverse ways. For instance, Rushdie's father, Anis Ahmed, seems to have suffered a fate similar to that of Ahmed in *Midnight's Children*: both are hounded by a supposedly secular post-Independence Indian government. According to Sameen, the eldest of Salman's three sisters, there "were questions about my family's loyalty to India: as Muslims who *hadn't* left." She notes that there "were court cases" and the "government took over my father's properties" – a situation reworked with humour in *Midnight's Children*, when Ahmed's testicles freeze in sympathy with his assets which have been frozen by the government. Sameen also says they were "conscious of being a Muslim minority in India."[3] This larger sense of alienation works into every novel Rushdie writes and is especially evident in the *Moor*, where the Hindu fundamentalist Mainduck responds to the 1992 destruction of the mosque at Ayodhya by saying that when "such alien artifacts disappear from India's holy soil, let no man mourn ... If the new nation is to be born, there is much invader-history that may have to be erased" (*m* 364). Sameen notes with irony that since their father Anis "had all these cases against him, no Hindus were to be trusted, really, although my father's best friends were Hindu." She adds diplomatically, "There were certain things our parents never said out loud, certain things we knew we *mustn't* mention to anybody."[4]

Religion and story-telling were also preoccupations in Rushdie's family. In addition to being a great storyteller, his father knew classical Arabic and Persian, and worked on interpreting the Koran.[5] There seems to be something of him in the Ahmed of *Midnight's Children*, with his intention of re-organizing the Koran. (Ahmed's temper and drinking habits may also be borrowed from Anis.[6]) There also seems to be something of Anis in *Haroun*'s Rashid, with his endless narratives, his great "Ocean of Notions." Rushdie's mother was also a great source of stories. She may even be one of the progenitors of

Mary in *Midnight's Children's*, who is Saleem's main source of family history. Negin's "tales were rooted in real life [and it] was she, according to Rushdie, who was 'the keeper of the family stories.'"[7]

Salman's maternal grandfather was a minor Urdu poet, which is interesting in that it connects Rushdie to a great tradition of poetry and music which runs through much of the cultured Muslim world from Morocco to Bangladesh. Like Dr Aziz in E.M. Forster's *A Passage to India*, who is both a medical doctor and a lover of Persian verse, Dr Butt seems to combine the hard sciences with a poetic tradition that includes the epics of Rumi and Attar as well as the shorter lyrical poems of the *ghazal*, which are extremely popular among the Muslims of the subcontinent. Dr Butt also seems "to have been unusually enlightened for his time": Hamilton notes that though a "medical doctor, he had seen to it that his daughters got an education, and he never required them to observe purdah."[8] There may thus be something of him in Dr Aziz, in *Midnight's Children*, who breaks with tradition and passes his Westernized ways to his daughter. Interestingly, Dr Butt helped in his daughter's divorce and urged that "her new marriage contract should give her the right to divorce"[9]; in *Midnight's Children*, Dr Aziz helps his daughter Amina hide her first husband, and puts up no resistance to her second marriage. Further traces of Rushdie's doctor-poet grandfather can be spied in *Haroun*, where he takes both technical and poetic form in the figures of Butt the bus driver and Butt the mechanical bird – both linked to Attar's Sufi bird who leads his flock to mystical unity.

Muslims like his father and grandfather are, according to Rushdie, part of a subcontinental Muslim tradition that is more lenient than it has become in recent years. In his lively and wide-ranging collection of essays, *Imaginary Homelands*, he contends that the Pakistani dictator Zia ul-Haq's Islamic regime was in a sense foreign to the Muslims of South Asia: "To be a believer is not by any means to be a zealot. Islam in the Indo-Pakistani subcontinent has developed historically along moderate lines, with a strong strain of pluralistic Sufi philosophy; Zia was this Islam's enemy" (*IH* 54). While Rushdie may have a tough time getting this argument accepted in Pakistan, certainly his Bombay family once lived along moderate lines.

Equally germinal to Rushdie's development as an English-language writer is that Anis and Negin Rushdie spoke to their children in both Urdu and English, and allowed them to read whatever they wanted: "Low culture was not perceived to be a threat. The little Rushdies were let loose on Reader's Paradise, with no restraints. Sameen says, 'They thought, As long as they read, that's terrific. Let them find what they want.'"[10]

It is in these early years in Bombay that Rushdie writes his first story, on which Hamilton makes the following comment: "Salman's Sunday-morning outing to the cinema was the high point of his week, and it is no surprise that the first story he attempted, at the age of ten, was movie-based. Its title was 'Over the Rainbow,' and it featured 'a talking pianola whose personality is an improbable hybrid of Judy Garland, Elvis Presley and the "playback singers" of the Hindi movies.'"[11] The cinema element of this story is worth noting, for it reflects the importance of movies at the time when he was growing up: Hollywood was influential, yet he was also living in the nation's film capital during the 1950s, a golden decade for a Bombay (or Bollywood) that "was by numerical criteria the largest film centre of the world."[12] The film element in "Over the Rainbow" also anticipates Rushdie's many later references to film – as in the scene where Saleem witnesses his mother having an affair in a café, then mocks her indirect kiss (Amina drinks from her glass and passes it to Nadir), and finally censors the scene by tearing himself from the window. A book could be written on Rushdie's use of film techniques – especially the cutting, splicing, panning, zooming, and censoring of *Midnight's Children* and the *Verses*.

Rushdie was also exposed to a serious English education, starting with the English-language school he went to in Bombay. In 1961 he was sent to Rugby, the school for boys which serves as the setting for Thomas Hughes's *Tom Brown's Schooldays* (1857). In the *Verses* we see an alienated young Chamcha, whose difficulty in eating a kipper is drawn from Rushdie's real-life experience of feeling very much out of his element at Rugby.[13] A fish out of water indeed! Yet long before that anti-colonial reminiscence, Rushdie was writing against colonial attitudes: while still at the famous school for boys he wrote a story called "Terminal Report," which Weatherby says "featured a conservative, conventional hero – such as he had once been – transformed by his experiences into an aggressive, radical fellow whenever he encountered racial prejudice."[14]

From Rugby he went to King's College, Cambridge, where his father had received his law degree years before. The fact that he took his master's degree in Islamic History (1968) may partly account for his countless references to Islamic religion, culture, and history – from the obscure allusion to the Muslim Antichrist Deggial in *Grimus* to the more overt references in *Midnight's Children*, where Saleem feels he is having revelations *à la* Muhammad. His interest in the subject matter edges into dangerous sarcasm in *Shame*, and explodes into full-blown irreverence in the *Verses*, with its kaleidoscopic reimagining of Muhammad's personal thoughts and feelings.

Before and after finishing at Cambridge, Rushdie visited his family, who moved in 1964 to Karachi. The political problems between his family's old and new countries erupted into open conflict in 1965 and 1971, and these wars form the essential backdrop to chapters 23 through 26 in *Midnight's Children*. Not surprisingly, the Indo-Pakistani fighting pulled at Rushdie's sense of identity: "I didn't particularly feel India was my enemy, because we'd only very recently come to Pakistan. And yet if somebody's dropping bombs on you, there is really only one reaction that you can have toward them, which is not friendly."[15] He also feels that as a writer he belongs to both and neither country: "In Pakistan there is suspicion because *I'm* Indian and in India because *I'm* Pakistani. Both sides wish to claim me. Both sides find it hard that I *don't* reject the other side."[16] This comment of course precedes the *Verses*, after which fame is replaced by infamy, and both sides no longer found it so difficult to reject him!

In Pakistan Rushdie also had difficulties with censorship, which may partly explain his antagonism to the religious side of Pakistani culture in both *Midnight's Children* and *Shame*. After travelling to Pakistan overland via Iran in 1968, he encountered restrictions that would be particularly irritating to a young liberal Londoner of the late 1960s: "Before production could begin [on a televised version of Edward Albee's *Zoo Story*] there had to be a series of 'censorship conferences.' An Albee remark about the disgustingness of pork hamburgers was seized on by the censors. 'Pork,' they said, is a 'four-letter word.'" Rushdie argued that Albee's hamburger remark was "superb anti-pork propaganda" and should stay. " 'You don't see,' the executive told me ... The word 'pork' may not be spoken on Pakistan television. 'And that was that.' He also had to cut a line about God being a colored queen who wears a kimono and plucks his eyebrows."[17] While such experiences with censorship appear to have left him feeling bitter, he supplies a good-humoured account of being required (as an actor in Albee's play) to use a knife that was not retractable, and of the background noise provided by chants of an Urdu-speaking crowd which had marched on the TV station.[18]

He then settled permanently in London, working as a copy-writer for *Ogilvy and Mathur*, and acting on occasion at the Oval Theatre. He also started writing a novel, *The Book of the Pir*. A *pir* is an Islamic spiritual master or *sheik*, and, according to Hamilton, the manuscript "featured a Muslim guru, in some unnamed Eastern land, who gets taken up by a military junta and installed as the figurehead President of its corrupt regime. It was a strong enough plot, but it was written in what the author calls 'sub-Joyce.' After being rebuffed by various literary agents ('It couldn't even achieve *that!*' Rushdie says of it), the book was set aside, and Rushdie decided to go back to advertising."[19] Weatherby comments that, after finishing the novel, he "decided its experimental style made it 'totally incomprehensible' to the general reader, and he abandoned it. He was still trying to find his own style forged by his experiences in both East and West."[20]

In 1970 Rushdie met his first wife, Clarissa Luard, and shared her parent's vacated flat near Eaton Square. It was here that he wrote *Grimus*, which he entered in the Gollancz science-fiction contest. It did not win, probably because it deals with other worlds of myth and religion rather than with anything one might (even freely) associate with science, or with the types of cosmographies found in *Star Wars* or *Star Trek*. While the novel contains intergalactic journeys and a race of extraterrestrial stone frogs, the characters have heavy mythological and mystical associations, the setting is a strange fusion of four cosmographies, and the structure derives mainly from a Sufi mystical journey. Weatherby surmises that "probably the judges didn't know what to make of this attempted literary flight masquerading as science fiction." He adds that critics "liked it even less than the judges."[21] While *Grimus* is at times stilted, it nevertheless has much of interest to those who enjoy following epic journeys or speculating *à la* Borges about multiple versions of reality.

In *Grimus*, Rushdie conflates four otherworldly schemas, the most important being that of Attar's *Conference of the Birds*, a long poem written in the Sufi idiom of twelfth-century Persia. Attar's flight of thirty birds toward mystical unity and annihilation on Mount Qaf supplies the model for Eagle's journey up the Mountain of Calf, which is a false or Golden Calf version of the sacred mountain. Eagle climbs beyond Calf to Attar's Impossible Qaf, a mountain which symbolizes the obliteration of the self and a union of disparate realities. Rushdie conflates Attar's union and annihilation with Dante and Beatrice's lift-off from Purgatory, Shiva and Parvati's near-cataclysmic intercourse on Mount Kailasa, and the Norse apocalypse of Ragnarok. As I argue in chapter 3 "Worlds Upon Worlds," the novel contains other such conflations, all of which serve to emphasize the main ideals of iconoclasm, multidimensionality and the infinite trajectory of the soul. While the novel is riddled with skepticism and a Kafkaesque sense of the absurd, it is also intensely idealistic – not far from Whitman when he says to his cosmic spirit, "*When we become the enfolders of those orbs, and the pleasure and knowledge of every thing in them, shall we be fill'd and satisfied then? / And my spirit said No, we but level that lift to pass and continue beyond.*"[22]

The ideal of eternal flight across a heterogeneous yet somehow unified universe works in the fantastic conflated worlds of *Grimus*, yet the same notion has a hard time flying – or even getting off the ground – in the history-laden world of *Midnight's Children*. In this profuse masterpiece, which won the Booker Prize and the twenty-five year Booker of Bookers, Rushdie retraces the lines of twentieth-century history and geography, and puts into a myriad of perplexing refractions the religious and cultural traditions that bring people together and tear them apart. In chapter 4, "The Road From Kashmir," I argue that the chronologies of Saleem's life and subcontinental history are not the only things that lend the novel form: Rushdie also makes clever use of a mythic cycle which starts with a fall from the Eden of Kashmir and ends with a potential return to Kashmir. This cycle incorporates many diverse otherworldly elements which also give the work a measure of structural integrity, prominent among these being the Hindu figures of Shiva, Parvati, Padma-Sri-Lakshmi, and Durga.

While the Hindu figures work into *Midnight's Children* profusely and problematically, the otherworldly schema that functions most coherently is again that of Attar. More subtly than in *Grimus*, the *Conference* is woven into the novel with surprising consistency, even when it takes comic or inverted form. The paradigm of the thirty birds first surfaces when old Aziz sahib converses with his thirty species of birds and slips into mystical senility in the Edenic garden of Kashmir. His son Aadam Aziz then falls from this primal happiness, only to embark on a quest to unify a divided, fallen world. Aadam joins the Hummingbird's doomed Free Islam Convocation and passes his ideals of subcontinental unity on to Saleem, who more conspicuously plays the role of Attar's bird-guide (the Hoopoe) at the helm of his fractious Midnight Children's Conference. Whether or not Saleem, his Conference, and India itself will regain the symbolic unity of old Aziz Sahib's Kashmir remains uncertain. While Saleem is himself pessimistic, Rushdie subtly links the *Arabian Nights'* magic number 1001 with the age of both Saleem and the post-Raj subcontinent (30), and with the 30 chapters or pickle jars Saleem fills with his rambling, spicy stories. Since Saleem's predecessor, Scheherazade, obtains her freedom after telling 1001 tales, Saleem and his beloved subcontinent may also find some measure of freedom in his "thirty jars and a jar," (*MC* 461), that is, in the ineffable après-tale which symbolizes more than the sum of its parts.

In *Shame* Rushdie narrows his focus from the subcontinent to Pakistan, schematizing the life of three families rather than expanding on the lives of one. Shorter than *Midnight's Children*, *Shame* chronicles the frightening emotional landscape of the doctor Omar Khayyam Shakil, as well as the political careers of Iskander Harappa and Raza Hyder, fictional versions of Ali Bhutto (d.1979) and Zia ul-Haq (d.1988). In regard to the two latter figures, Rushdie's main argument is that Iskander's authoritarianism paves the way for Raza's religious dictatorship. Rushdie also narrows his otherworldly focus – from the scattering of mythology in *Midnight's Children* to *Shame*'s cause and effect dynamic in which worldly repression gives rise to the otherworldly revolt of the Beast. Hence my chapter title, *An Other World Strikes Back*.

Like Saleem, Omar ponders the wide wheels and shifting gears of the cosmos – both the wonders of the Greek-influenced Persian universe and the menacing abyss of history that lies in the basement of "Nishapur," the family mansion named after the city where both Attar and Khayyam lived before its sacking in 1221. Whereas Saleem retains vestiges of his early idealism to his bittersweet end, Omar's visions are overwhelmed by sinister forces: not only do his three witchy mothers remove from his life an exquisite screen depicting Qaf and its thirty birds; they also work in concert with the Beast, Kali, and Madame Guillotine to wreak vengeance on the patriarchal world around them – a world that very much includes Omar the opportunistic pedophile. The novel reaches deeper and deeper into a heart of darkness, as Omar's child-wife Sufiya is possessed and raped by the Beast, and Omar is brought face to face with the horror he feared but vaguely in his youth.

Rushdie's second, third, and fourth novels constitute a loose trilogy, starting with the subcontinental setting and imminent doom of *Midnight's Children*. Rushdie then moves on to *Shame*, with its Pakistani setting, its satanic possession of Sufiya, and its cosmic retribution. The trilogy ends with *The Satanic Verses*, in which characters travel back and forth from India to England, and in which all the main characters are possessed, destroyed, or otherwise manipulated by the Devil. The three novels are also linked in terms of cause and effect dynamics. In *Midnight's Children* Saleem and his fellow Muslim soldiers are punished by pagan and Hindu forces for obeying leaders who mix religion and politics. This same dynamic spills into *Shame*, where Raza's militaristic piety is punished by a strange fusion of the Beast and Kali. *Shame* and the *Verses* also share a peculiar dynamic in which the Devil and his pagan female birds stage assaults on the one male God of Islam. While in both novels the Beast possesses innocent victims and triumphs over Attar's God/Qaf, the distinctions are equally telling. In *Shame* the Beast is the fearsome product of political, sexual, and religious repression. One might even say that Raza's imposition of *God* and *Islamic Submission* creates the *Beast* and *Pagan Rebellion*. In the *Verses*, on the other hand, the Beast does not *surface* from this world as much as he *invades* this world, using humans as pawns in his cosmic chess game with God.

The Satanic Verses remains an immensely problematic novel. Understandably, many find it difficult to get beyond the Rushdie Affair, which includes protests, fatal riots, book-burnings, attacks on translators (one fatal), the 1989 death threat of Ayatollah Khomeini, and Rushdie's subsequent life in hiding – a decade under the protection of Scotland Yard. In chapter 6 I suggest that much of the controversy is based on unfounded views about the novel – views Rushdie himself has failed to clear up, perhaps for fear of creating even greater hardship for himself. The main issue he has sidestepped is his almost obsessive interest in diabology, a predilection that harks back to *Grimus*'s enigmatic figure of Deggle-Lokki, who is modelled on the Devil, the Muslim Antichrist, and the Norse trickster who leads his demonic crew against the gods. In the *Verses* Rushdie pushes the role of the Devil to a dangerous extreme: he allows a satanic narrator to swoop in and out of a text that is charged with demonic revisions of cosmology, antireligious rhetoric, and the increasingly hellish visions of a schizophrenic who half-believes he is an archangel. Moreover, the conclusion highlights tragedy and the triumph of cosmic evil: in a masterfully designed triple parallel, Chamcha/Satan/Iago drives Gibreel/Adam/Othello to murder Alleluia/Eve/Desdemona. Yet the scenario is not all dark: the confluence of Shakespeare's pathos and Attar's symbolism (seen in Sufyan and in Allie's yearning to climb Everest) hints at a deeper ideal of unity and love.

Rushdie's writing from this point takes a number of directions. He publishes several eloquent defences of the *Verses*, the delightful children's tale *Haroun and the Sea of Stories*, the celebrated collection of essays *Imaginary Homelands*, a British Film Institute volume on *The Wizard of Oz*, a collection of fine short stories *East, West*, and two novels: *The Moor's Last Sigh* and *The Ground Beneath Her Feet*. He also co-edits a fiftieth anniversary anthology, *The Vintage Book of Indian Writing (1947–1997)*, has a feud with John le Carré, and makes surprise appearances in venues as diverse as the Jerry Springer Show and a U2 concert in front of 85,000 fans. In recent interviews he stresses that he is, as his latest novels suggest, turning more and more to the West for his subject matter. Not that he will not write about the subcontinent anymore; just that for the time being he has said what he has to say about it. Quite understandably, he wants to write about the country and the culture he has lived in since his days of Rugby and Cambridge, and since his decision to call England home in the mid-seventies.

In chapter 7 I examine his three latest novels, although in less detail than the first four. *Haroun* is relatively unproblematic: in it Rushdie skilfully conflates Attar's journey to Qaf with the Sanskrit poet

Somadeva's Ocean of Stories. Likewise, the *Moor* and *Ground* are not as difficult to interpret as his earlier novels – at least not in terms of the other worlds in them, which Rushdie shuts down rather than opens up. One might even say that he becomes antagonistic to other worlds, using them less to bring out the perplexities of his characters than to show how dangerous or ridiculous he thinks they are. In *Ground* there is a great deal of talk about alternate dimensions, yet the one dimension that breaks through to ours lacks all force; it appears designed more to prove the superiority of a secular, non-religious philosophy than to explore conflicting views of the universe.

Rushdie's uncompromising worldly slant first surfaces in a short story, "The Harmony of the Spheres," published one year before the *Moor*. When the narrator of the story concludes that the occult drove the protagonist to madness and that afterwards "there has been no intercourse between the spiritual world" and his own (EW 144), Rushdie appears to signal a shift away from his earlier strategy, where he is skeptical about religion yet gives it wide scope in the minds and hearts of his characters.

While the *Moor* and *Ground* on occasion rework myth in striking ways, the vast, overlapping fields of cosmology, mythology, and mysticism are not used extensively and do not present anything like the ontological and epistemological challenges we find in his earlier fiction. This is not to say that Rushdie has given up exploring the grand unities and dire pitfalls of the spiritual universe. Yet after the many backfirings of the *Verses*, he may be tired of putting himself so deeply into the exploration of belief and disbelief, the mystical and the diabolic.

2 When Worlds Collide

> If this world is not to our taste, well, at all events there is Heaven,
> Hell, Annihilation – one or other of those large things, that huge
> scenic background of stars, fires, blue or black air. All heroic
> endeavour, and all that is known as art, assumes that there is
> such a background, just as all practical endeavour, when the
> world is to our taste, assumes that the world is all. But in the
> twilight of the double vision a spiritual muddledom is set up for
> which no high-sounding words can be found; we can neither act
> nor refrain from action, we can neither ignore nor respect Infinity.
>
> Forster, *A Passage to India*[1]

There is no obvious way to do an introduction to the myriad of other
worlds in Rushdie's fiction, except perhaps to do a second introduction, a second run through that library of permutating letters, that
jungle of books which changes with every reading.

In attempting to give context to his work, one could start anywhere
from the dawn of Vedic poetry to the latest postmodern transmutation
of myth. Yet what seems constant in his finest writing is a love of the
metamorphic and inconstant, which, when applied to what Forster calls
"those large things, that huge scenic background of stars, fires, blue or
black air," becomes a questioning of fundamental truths as they have
been formulated by the great religions and myths of the past. Rushdie's
queries into the nature of the universe lead him to juxtapose one cosmic
system with another, and to question the balance within any one system. In *Shame* the narrator proclaims that the cosmic battle for domina-
tion is far from over: "Forget left-right, capitalism-socialism, black-
white. Virtue versus vice, ascetic versus bawd, God against the Devil:
that's the game. *Messieurs, mesdames: faîtes vos jeux*" (s 240). Rushdie's
fiction – and especially *The Satanic Verses* – enters this game in the deepest, most dangerous way imaginable; for in all of his first four novels he
revisits the conundrums of theodicy, weighing the forces of good and
evil, of order and chaos, and he also throws in new systems which operate by other rules. For instance, in *Shame* he pits the Devil against God in
a number of ways, yet he also brings in the goddess Kali, suggesting a
cosmic alliance between the Devil of the Middle East, who operates
largely within (and against) monotheism, and a goddess from the polytheistic universe of Hinduism.

In his radical questioning of the epistemologies found in overarching systems, Rushdie resembles what Borges calls "the heresiarch" or "arch heretic who questions all before him, and particularly all forms of established dogma." In her work *The Unresolvable Plot* Elizabeth Dipple adds that for Borges "reality itself is an infinite *mise-en-abyme* [sic] that cannot be traced to any secure source and requires a brilliant heresiarch to demonstrate its infinite resonances."[2] Rushdie also calls to mind the hammer-wielding philosopher Friedrich Nietzsche, the dark visionary Edgar Allan Poe, as well as the hell-bound Charles Baudelaire of "Le Voyage":

Nous voulons, tant ce feu nous brûle le cerveau,
Plonger au fond du gouffre, Enfer ou Ciel, qu'importe?
Au fond de l'Inconnu pour trouver du *nouveau!*
> – Baudelaire, *Les Fleurs du Mal*[3]

We wish, so long as this fire burns the brain,
To plunge to the depths of the abyss, Hell or Heaven, what does it matter?
To the depths of the Unknown to find something *new!*
> (translation mine)

Rushdie's journeys into dark, dangerous realms are on occasion harrowing, especially in *Shame* and the *Verses*. Yet they are not without their consolations and moments of grace. His fiction is also full of wonder, emotional warmth, sensuality, and a sense of humour which is as irrepressible as it is inimitable. He counters the sense of being lost in a meaningless universe with a sense of being liberated by an eclectic, iconoclastic mysticism. His position is difficult to get hold of, for while he hints at an esoteric unifying perspective, a "huge scenic background" that gives the cosmos meaning, he also questions every act of magic or revelation that would give substance to such a vision.

Paradoxically, Rushdie has become something of an icon of that most iconoclastic of forms, postmodern metafiction. Given his metafictional style, his sense of the metamorphic self, and his extensive use of metaphysical realms, one might even call him a *metacist*. *Meta* signals a strategy of displacement, a tendency to place at a distance *from, beneath, above*; Rushdie constantly puts a metafictional distance between believing and doubting his narrator's stories, between the habitual personalities of his characters and the selves into which they metamorphose, and between worldly and metaphysical versions of reality. These multiple gaps destabilize the self and render doubtful any explanation it might advance about truth or about the very act of attempting any such explanation.

Rushdie's metafiction and magic realism go hand in hand, for both serve as levering devices to distance one belief system from another. In his comments on magic realism, Jean-Pierre Durix notes that much of "the pleasure produced by Rushdie's work" derives from his "play on verisimilitude" and from his "adept juggling with different levels of 'reality'."[4] Stephen Slemon notes that "the characteristic maneuver of magic realist fiction is that its two narrative modes never manage to arrange themselves into any kind of hierarchy." He calls magic realism "a binary opposition between the representational code of realism and that, roughly, of fantasy ... the ground rules of these two worlds are incompatible, neither one can fully come into being, and each remains suspended, locked in a continuous dialectic with the 'other,' a situation which creates disjunction within each of the separate discursive systems, rending them with gaps, absences and silences."[5] The liberating term *magic realism* can become reductive, however, unless one assumes that the dialectic between realism and the magical other is also a "polylectic" between realism and many other magical versions of reality. Such a multiple process offers an endless array of conflicting directions, imperfectly aligned contours, and puzzling gaps. It dooms to obscurity any integrated or systematic vision of the universe, as well as any attempt to relegate specific versions of reality to such categories as *true* or *false, high* or *low.*

One could complain that adding further magical worlds or *modes* to Slemon's dialectic progressively replaces meaning with conundrum, unity with fragmentation, certainty with doubt. One might argue that Rushdie merely replaces solid (or at least integrated or referential) versions of the universe with an infinity of slippery versions, an ocean of divergent narratives. This of course assumes that there was solidity, integration or referentiality to begin with – a difficult proposition in many cases. On the other hand, one could argue that Rushdie only mirrors the eclectic nature of our times, and that his writing suggests a sort of narrative democracy – not a two- or three-party system, but rather a parliament with many independents. What I say here applies, however, only to Rushdie's first five novels; in his sixth and seventh he takes a rather dogmatic stand, one which precludes support for multiple religious beliefs and urges readers to vote, so to speak, only for the Atheist Party.

The license Rushdie allows himself in exploring myth, religion and metaphysics in his first five novels remains based on the conviction that no one, himself included, has a monopoly on the truth about whatever might lie beyond this world of practical experience – what I call our common four-dimensional world (I am of course assuming here that the three dimensions of space, along with the fourth dimen-

sion of time, are not themselves illusions.) In this Rushdie resembles
the Byron of *Don Juan*, for whom the question of the afterlife remains
a mystery which is superseded by the story of our present lives:

> The path is through perplexing ways, and when
> The goal is gained, we die, you know – and then –
>
> What then? – I do not know, no more do you –
> And so good night. – Return we to our story[6]

This type of skeptical and self-skeptical stance is less pronounced in
Rushdie's latest two novels, for there he comes close to proselytizing
in an antireligious vein – as if he actually *knows* there is no afterlife.
Yet to insist on this later Rushdie would be to ignore his earlier self-
critiquing metafiction as well as the majority of his finest creations:
Aadam Aziz tortured by "a God in whose existence he could not
wholly disbelieve" (*MC* 12); Saleem lost in mystical visions amid a
battlefield of gods, demons, angels and djinns; Padma with her stubborn belief in witches who can make people invisible and in mothers
who can keep a moral watch over their daughter's dreams; Omar the
trembling cosmographer who fears the monstrous forces that eventually devour him; Raza hounded by the puritan angel at his right ear
and the socialist demon at his left; Chamcha growing horns he does
not believe in; Gibreel sprouting the invisible wings of an angel and
being flown from one demon-infested realm to the next; and Allie
with her icy visions of angels on the peak of Everest.

Rushdie's extensive use of other worlds in his first five novels fits
with his aim of responding less to his own doubts than to the beliefs
of the South Asians he writes about. As recently as 1992 he says that
his aim has been "to develop a form which doesn't prejudge whether
your characters are right or wrong ... a form in which the idea of the
miraculous can coexist with observable, everyday reality." This coexistence of the miraculous and the mundane explicitly includes religion: his fiction has always "been shaped by the everyday fact of
religious belief in India – not just Muslim, Hindu, Buddhist and Sikh,
but every belief."[7] While he claims that he lost his belief in "God,
Satan, Paradise and Hell" at the age of fifteen, and that his "sense of
God ceased to exist long ago" (*IH* 377, 417), he nevertheless finds it
impossible to talk about human beings without talking about religion: "It did not seem to me, however, that my ungodliness, or rather
my post-godliness, need necessarily bring me into conflict with belief.
Indeed, one reason for my attempt to develop a form of fiction in
which the miraculous might coexist with the mundane was precisely

my acceptance that notions of the sacred and the profane both needed to be explored, as far as possible without pre-judgement, in any honest literary portrait of the way we are" (*IH* 417).

In the area of belief Rushdie is difficult to tie down. It is not just that he inhabits Aadam Aziz's middle ground between belief and disbelief and that he agrees with Khayyam that "To be free from belief and unbelief is [his] religion"[8]; it is also that he swings from one side to the next. He sometimes calls himself an atheist, yet he also expresses a strong interest in religion and in the existence of the spirit. While his attacks on orthodoxy appear relentless, his fiction is also rife with heavens, hells, angels and djinns, and he returns again and again to the mystical symbology of Farid ud-Din Attar. At one moment he affirms "the two central tenets of Islam – the oneness of God and the genuineness of the prophecy of the Prophet Muhammad" (*IH* 430), and the next moment he retracts this affirmation.[9] To this apparent mass of contradictions one might add his admission that religion and mysticism have had a growing influence on him. In 1990 he writes, "I have been engaging more and more with religious belief, its importance and power, ever since my first novel used the Sufi poem *Conference of the Birds* by Farid ud-din Attar as a model" (*IH* 430).

The *Verses* marks the peak of his engagement with belief and disbelief, after which he relinquishes serious and problematic exploration. One thing that remains constant in his novels, however, is the idea of transcendence or spiritual flight, which, not surprisingly, he explains very broadly as "that flight of the human spirit outside the confines of its material, physical existence." He claims that "all of us, secular or religious, experience [it] on at least a few occasions" (*IH* 421). Flight also represents "the imagining spirit" which is "*at war* with the 'real' world" in which "centres cannot hold" (*IH* 122).

It is this notion of flight and unity which makes most sense of his otherwise puzzling obsession with the mystical poetry of Attar. It also explains his related interest in the *ghazal*, a Persian and Urdu form of poetry and music which highlights the separation between the human lover and his beloved, as well as between the human soul and the Divine. Exemplified in the singing of Saleem's sister, the ghazal is "filled with the purity of wings and the pain of exile and the flying of eagles and the lovelessness of life and the melody of bulbuls and the glorious omnipresence of God" (*MC* 293–4). Like tragic love, the *ghazal* is all the more potent because the love it speaks of cannot be realized; it is, like Attar's Impossible Mountain of Qaf, impossible in this world.

One could argue that Rushdie's notion of transcendent flight cannot be compared to that of Attar or other Sufis since that of Rushdie is too loaded down with materialism, sexuality, plurality and doubt. Yet Sufism in its most poetic and iconoclastic form insists neither on an unswerving monotheism nor an explicitly religious sentiment. While some Sufis follow strict definitions and codes of belief and behaviour, others have more in common with Hindu and Taoist mystics, who by and large see dogma as a limitation imposed by humans, not God. A helpful comparison of Sufism and Hinduism can be found in *Hindu & Muslim Mysticism*, in which R.C. Zaehner observes that Hindu mystics have operated within a framework that encourages mysticism, whereas Sufis have often been forced to hide their revelations. For this reason metaphor is all the more indispensable, since it obscures what remains unacceptable to the orthodox. By using Sufism in secular and irreverent contexts, Rushdie follows in the Sufi's, rebellious footsteps. That is, he is breaking established or orthodox patterns. Yet he also creates a brand of mysticism – if in fact it can be called that – which is more iconoclastic and permissive than what Attar or most Sufis would allow. Although anyone who has read the famous Sufi poet Jalal ud-Din Rumi would see that Sufism is not only about whirling in a dance of atoms and stars, Rushdie combines Rumi's subversive and humorous vision with an even deeper and more anguished sense of doubt, which makes him closer to skeptics like Khayyam than to believers like Attar or Rumi. And were Attar still living, he would most probably disapprove of Rushdie's fiction, given that he condemned his contemporary Omar Khayyam for hedonism.[10]

Rushdie may not be compatible with most mystics or theologians, yet he feels free to take Sufi notions and use them for his own narrative aims. Here at least he is consistent, for he is always attacking what he calls "the bogey of Authenticity," the purist notion that one must refrain from altering the paradigms of culture and religion. He insists that "it is completely fallacious to suppose that there is such a thing as a pure, unalloyed tradition from which to draw. The only people who seriously believe this are religious extremists" (*IH* 67). This view works itself out in a thousand and one different ways in his novels, most pointedly in *Shame*'s attack on the sanctification of family stories, in the *Verses*'s portrait of the Imam who smashes clocks so that ancient religious versions of reality cannot be further transformed, and in *Haroun*'s figure of the Cultmaster, who tries to poison and plug the flow of narratives in the moon's great ocean of stories.

Orthodox Muslims might shudder at Rushdie's distortion of Attar, yet they might also approve (however reluctantly) of the opposition he sets up between Qaf's abstract transcendental divinity and the violent, deceptive figure of the Devil. The dynamic between these two is involved and paradoxical, one complicating factor being that both Qaf and Satan are elusive by nature: the Mountain of Qaf cannot be located, just as God cannot be defined; and the Prince of Darkness slides surreptitiously in and out of this world. Also problematic is the way Rushdie sometimes suggests that God is a dictator and Satan a rebel hero. Yet he also reinverts this Romantic inversion: the possessions and coercions of his Devils go a long way in nullifying any of their Promethean rhetoric. In addition, his many eulogies to Attar's Simurg and Qaf go a long way in compensating for his occasional portrait of a limited, anthropomorphic God.

In *The Sacred and the Profane* Mircea Eliade argues that a *hierophany*, an eruption of the sacred, "allows the world to be constituted, because it reveals the fixed point, the central axis for all future orientation."[11] I cannot help seeing this in terms of Forster's cosmic background, and in terms of a fixed star which makes sense of the heavens, the sort of star which Shakespeare writes of in sonnet 116, "whose worth's unknown although his height be taken." In Rushdie's fiction, this kind of "sighting" or sacred eruption provides but momentary orientation, for it is inevitably accompanied by darker and more chaotic eruptions. For instance, Saleem initially hears angelic voices, yet these turn into a cacophony of fallen angels and drunken djinns; Omar initially sees the screen of Qaf, but this is taken from his field of vision, after which he ponders the heavens and the depths of the earth only to find intergalactic monsters and a frightening abyss; Gibreel in his dreams hears the voice of Gabriel yet the reader cannot help but hear the voice of Satan. What begins as a liberating orientation, a meaningful vision of the universe, most often turns into a nightmare.

If Rushdie were strictly a magic realist writer, eruptions from some other world would not be as disruptive and problematic as they are. For magic does not necessarily reverberate into the cosmos, does not necessarily reach toward Shakespeare's "edge of doom," Yeats's "blood-dimmed tide" or Attar's blissful annihilation. When writers introduce a magical or inexplicable event into a framework of realism this does not force them into an established otherworldly realm. Yet religion does. When writers introduce a religious symbol or motif this brings with it an entire cosmic system, a prefabricated universe dominated by figures such as Satan or Shiva and by ideas such as Apocalypse or Grace.

It may be that writers who seek to break free from conventional conceptions cannot simply ignore conventional models. My reading of Rushdie's novels does not rest on this idea; nevertheless, it would appear that the writer who would be an iconoclast cannot deliver the attack merely through magical moments that contradict a realistic vision of the universe. For ancient otherworldly systems orient the individual and constitute the world in a psychologically, culturally and historically responsive way. Often learnt in childhood, they have psychological impact even after the rational mind has rejected them. In terms of ontology and epistemology, they are well-rounded and cannot be dismissed easily or quickly, if at all. In order to fully challenge an established cosmic system or orientation, it may be necessary to respond to it with an equally weighty or developed orientation. For instance, in questioning the notion of an afterlife in Paradise or Hell, a plot involving reincarnation may be more effective than one involving a unique setting inhabited by souls of the departed dead. Even if one does not believe in any particular version of the afterlife, there is nevertheless a power structure based on usage, indoctrination and precedence. There is a sort of "Common Law of the Unknown" which makes mythology and religion carry more weight than cosmologies which never gained adherents or which appear to be freshly hatched from the imagination. While Vonnegut's *Slaughterhouse-Five* may shake up our view of America, the aliens in that novel are unlikely to shake our view of the afterlife.

Rushdie may not believe – or fully disbelieve – in the other worlds he includes in his fiction, yet he knows that these have been employed for centuries and that they consequently reside and reverberate deep inside the minds of his readers. In *The Study of Literature and Religion* David Jasper observes that when people ask themselves fundamental questions, the language used is still steeped in cosmological settings and mythological figures: "The story of Eden and the figure of Satan remain alive in our emotions, and in the textuality of theodicy they continue to address the problem of suffering and evil in God's world, however dead their 'theory.'"[12] Rushdie understands that "theory" has been undermined by skepticism and other theories. Nevertheless, he brings it alive again and again by creating characters who believe in the otherworldly and by describing events which corroborate their belief. For instance, in *Midnight's Children* Padma's belief in witchcraft is validated when Parvati makes Saleem invisible. Even when characters such as Aadam Aziz, Omar or Chamcha reject religion, they are indelibly marked by the very belief structures they reject.

In his first five novels, Rushdie questions, yet never entirely dismisses, the notion that different epistemologies can be marshalled into a heterogeneous yet coherent view of the universe. These novels can thus be situated between what Lonnie Kliever calls *monotheistic polysymbolism*, which is associated with modernity and with the view that diverse systems contain universal meanings, and *polytheistic polysymbolism*, which rejects this universality. According to Kliever, *polytheistic polysymbolism* "celebrates the variousness and many-sidedness of all expressions of culture and religion. But it decidedly rejects the monotheistic ideal of a fundamental unity underlying and integrating this heterogeneity. Thereby it calls into question modernity's sense of centered self, integral universe, and historical destiny. In short, this rival form of polysymbolic religiosity appears to be polytheistic and postmodern."[13] This polytheistic polysymbolism comes very close to what some people find impossible to accept in Rushdie. His most ardent detractors are staunchly monotheistic and repeatedly blame him for promoting a fragmented vision of God's universe. In addition, Rushdie's novels from *Grimus* to the *Verses* increasingly reflect the "historical dislocation," the "apocalyptic pessimism" and the "rising tide of occultism" which accompanies the ontological and epistemological chaos of Kliever's polytheistic polysymbolism.[14] Yet despite this, Rushdie's fiction also suggests some very positive and unifying perspectives. Idealistic or desperate, he returns again and again to Attar's unity and annihilation, Shiva's endless cycle of worlds, Somadeva's Ocean, and other religious paradigms of infinite contextuality and creativity. This tension between chaos and a hidden cosmic order remains one of his fiction's most challenging aspects – be it contradictory or paradoxical.

One of the problems in trying to weigh the fragmenting and pessimistic against the unifying and optimistic is that each novel has a different mix of these elements. *Grimus* and *Haroun* are rather overt in their mysticism and in their depictions of a triumphant and unifying multidimensionality. *Midnight's Children* and the *Verses*, on the other hand, suggest unity in an esoteric manner, the occult and the apocalyptic taking on ever more dire proportions. *Shame* is the darkest of Rushdie's novels in this respect, for in it the protagonist is both alienated from a unifying mystical perspective and overwhelmed by the most fearsome of his nightmares. The ending of *Shame* brings to mind what Dante and Virgil see at the end of *Inferno*, where Satan uses his three mouths "like a grinder / with gnashing teeth he tore to bits a sinner"[15] – the sinner in this case being Omar. The important difference here is that readers of *Inferno* move on the *Purgatory* and *Paradise*, whereas readers of *Shame* have nowhere to go; they can only shudder to think of Omar's fate in the maw of the Beast.

In "Religion and Literature in a Secular Age: The Critic's Dilemma," Theodore Ziolkowski argues that the lack of a "unified faith" and an "epistemological field" deriving from such a faith leads to a critical dilemma: "the general secularization of Western culture has produced a new problem for literary interpretations because there is no longer a unified faith – what structuralists would call an epistemological field – that provides an automatic context of understanding for the literary work."[16] Rushdie gives this dilemma unprecedented sharpness, for he not only breaks open the Western treasure horde of religious systems and epic narratives, but also, adds a bewildering mix of Hindu and Islamic systems, creating an intercultural clash of realism and multiple *hierophanies* such as fiction has seldom seen.

Rushdie may disorient his readers with an alienating series of displacements, yet he also leads them on exciting explorations which hold out the possibility of a hidden orientation, a shifting field of meanings. He disturbs those who would find solace in some vague mystical promise, yet he also suggests that multiple versions of reality do not necessarily imply the absence of meaning.

In exploring the meaning of Rushdie's many worlds, I borrow from a variety of sources and I suggest numerous parallel texts and traditions. Yet in finding sources and parallels for a global writer such as Rushdie there is no end. I would therefore like to finish this introductory chapter with two interpretive possibilities which are not fully covered in the body of my text: the fluid epistemologies of Hinduism and Taoism.

Parameswaran, Kanaganayakam, Aklujkar and Goonetilleke supply insight into Hindu aspects of Rushdie's work, yet no one has yet published a detailed analysis of his oeuvre from a Hindu point of view. Throughout this study I suggest various ways in which Rushdie makes intriguing use of Hinduism, yet I do not pretend to cover the subject in any of the scope or profundity it deserves. For instance, Rushdie's cosmological speculations echo those of the earliest Hindu scripture of *Rig Veda*, in which the poet says that only the being who lives in the highest heaven knows from whence this universe arises – "or perhaps he does not know."[17] Rushdie also has much in common with the much more recent tantric subversions of K.D. Katrak's *Underworld* (1979) and with the angst-ridden mystical conundrums of Arun Joshi's *The Last Labyrinth* (1981). The Bhakti tradition might also provide insight into Rushdie's mix of reference and rebellion, allusion and alienation, given that it works both with and against orthodoxy.

Wendy O'Flaherty's various studies of Hindu myth supply insight into two key questions raised by Rushdie: What does it mean to exist in this or any world? and, What does it mean to arrive at a confident reading of any story? Her comments on the *Yogavasistha* are particularly

helpful in appreciating Rushdie's shifting and oneiric narrative structures: "If Vasistha can plunge into the page and come face to face with
the monk in his own story, as [the Vedic god] Rudra can go into his
dream and wake up the people who are dreaming him, we cannot rest
confident in our assumption that our level of the story is the final
one."[18] In her analysis of the stories of Lavana and Gadhi, she asks,
"Why could there not be a woman, say, dreaming that she was a king
dreaming…? In fact, this cannot happen in our text. For the Hindu, the
chain stops with the Brahmin, the linchpin of reality, the witness of the
truth. To the extent that the Brahmin represents purity and renunciation, he is real, safely outside the maelstrom of *samsara* and illusion.
Our confusion about our own place in the frames of memory, one con-
tained within another like nesting Chinese boxes, is shared by Lavana
until the very end of his tale. But to Gadhi, who is, after all, a Brahmin,
the god who pulls the strings is directly manifest and takes pains to
open his bag of tricks right from the start; moreover, he returns three
times at the end to make sure that Gadhi has understood his lesson
properly."[19] In *Midnight's Children*, *Shame* and the *Moor* there is no
Brahmin or god who enlightens Saleem, Omar or the Moor about the
meaning of their lives. In the *Verses* there is no one even remotely similar to a holy man or deity who might inform Gibreel about the nature
of the strange and dark journey he takes from one reality to the next.
Rather, his strings are pulled without his knowledge by Chamcha,
whose strings are in turn pulled without his knowledge by the satanic
narrator. While in *Grimus* Eagle learns the meaning of his quest from
three separate sources (Deggle, Virgil and then Grimus), in the *Verses*
Gibreel remains puzzled to the very end of his increasingly miserable
existence. Gibreel's universe is not like O'Flaherty's "mobius universe," whose final level is the "transcendent continuum" called
God.[20] It is rather a downward, chaotic, splintering spiral whose final
level is madness and suicide.

Another religious tradition which might offer useful points of comparison is Taoism. The writer Chuang Tze (third century B.C.) is of
particular interest, since he posits an ineffable Being yet refuses to insist on such things as the afterlife. Like Rushdie, Chuang Tze sees the
self as an indeterminate entity which cannot possibly grasp the pa-
rameters of its own reality. In the *Verses* Rushdie appears to borrow
from Chuang Tze, for Gibreel's notion that he is part of Gabriel's
dream echoes Chuang Tze's parable in which a man wonders
whether he previously dreamt he was a butterfly or whether he is
now a butterfly dreaming he is a man.[21] Much of the import of
Chuang Tze's parable lies in the parable of the shadow which precedes it, in which the shadow cannot understand itself since the con-

tours of its existence depend on the body which casts it. This body in turn depends on outside forces to do what it does, which in turn depend on outside forces to do what they do, ad infinitum. Rushdie's fiction in general, and Gibreel's predicament in particular, suggests that since the self is dependent on an infinite number of unknown factors, it cannot construct a coherent, encompassing framework or ideology. One might be tempted to read a postmodern or deconstructive stance into Chuang Tze's ontology and epistemology. Yet his understanding of displacement leads to a joyful acceptance of change and identity transformation, an acceptance which works in his philosophical system because he maintains a deep belief in the Tao or Way which guides and helps everything under Heaven. Rushdie on the other hand repeatedly asks the disturbing question, What if there is no such Way which gives hidden meaning to the transformations of the self? In *Midnight's Children* Saleem can only hope there is a spiritual meaning in the annihilation of his Midnight Children's Conference, and in *Shame* and the *Verses* the protagonists are unable to escape from an increasingly nightmarish universe. In *Shame* Omar ends up in the stomach of the fearsome Beast he has dreaded since childhood, and in the *Verses* Gibreel dreams he is a tortured archangel. Gibreel wonders if the archangel is "the guy who's awake and this is the bloody nightmare. His bloody dream: us" (*sv* 83). Rushdie pushes his readers even further into Gibreel's dilemma by hinting that this archangel is the Fallen Angel, and that Gibreel's oneiric existence is a function of Satan's perverted, violent imagination.

Rushdie's fiction can be especially disconcerting to those who believe (or want to believe) that the forces of the universe exist in a meaningful harmony, whether presided over by the laws of karma and *samsara*, by a God who precludes chaos and meaninglessness, or by the ideal of a mystical oblivion which projects the self beyond the suffering of this world. His last two novels seem to give up this disturbing exploration of what Forster calls "a spiritual muddledom," and fall back instead on the notion that religion is a waste of time. Yet the first four express a keen interest in the conflict between belief and nonbelief, including the conflict between the divine and the satanic forces within any given otherworldly system – or number of systems. As we shall see in the upcoming chapter on *Grimus*, the notion of many systems, of worlds upon worlds, obsesses Rushdie from the very start of his literary career.

3 *Grimus:* Worlds upon Worlds

The Library is unlimited and cyclical. If an eternal traveler were to
cross it in any direction, after centuries he would see that the
same volumes were repeated in the same disorder (which, thus
repeated, would be an order: the Order). My solitude is
gladdened by this elegant hope.

Borges, "The Library of Babel"[1]

The notion of an unlimited library which can be crossed many times
and in many different ways helps to conceptualize the labyrinth
that is Rushdie's first novel. *Grimus* has a complex yet recognizable
structure, an architectonic logic which contrasts with the tangential
meanderings of *Midnight's Children* and the confusing dream-
within-dream convolutions of the *Verses. Grimus* has a much more
definable shape, although this does not mean that it can be summed
up easily or viewed from any one angle. Often the reader feels like
Flapping Eagle, the protagonist who threads his way through a series of dimensions only to find that the end of his journey is the start
of his next.

To say that *Grimus* makes use of the journey motif is to understate
the case. Topographically, the novel most resembles Dante's *Comedy,*
for Eagle journeys through the forest of the world, descends into his
own personal hell (with a man called Virgil as his guide), struggles
up an island mountain in the sea, and then (accompanied by a
woman) appears to soar into another world. Eagle also resembles
Dante's version of Odysseus, whose wanderlust denies him the final
resting place Homer gives him.

Like Borges's "eternal traveler," Eagle journeys for centuries. Yet
unlike that traveller, he find no final Order. After traversing the
world till the age of 777 and after refusing to stay in the town of Calf
(the novel's Ithaca), he drowns, resurfaces, then dies another time
(both sexually and physically), only to rise on the wings of the Phoenix and the Simurg. At the end of the novel Eagle is both of these

birds, yet he is also Shiva, the Hindu god who has sex with Parvati on Mount Kailasa yet refuses to call that goddess wife or that mountain home.

In *Grimus* Rushdie at once subverts and adds to, undermines, and overworks the epic mode. If one imagines a line extending from Homer and Dante to the subversions of Joyce's *Ulysses*, one might see in *Grimus* a continuation of this line. For just as the epic journey becomes in Joyce a one-day odyssey through the pubs and brothels of Dublin, so in Rushdie literary tradition is turned on its head: the novel's epic guide Virgil Jones spends much of his time in a brothel; the demonic antagonist Nicholas Deggle becomes a cheap side-show conjuror; and the hero Flapping Eagle traipses through a farcical world. *Grimus* heaps epic figures and motifs into uneasy and highly metafictional juxtaposition, approaching the conventions of the epic at multiple angles, as if taking a run at them from Borges's various angles of disorder.

At once subverting and extending the epic journey, *Grimus* is a novel to reckon with, less for its use of language or depiction of character than for its fusion of cosmological settings, its mix of diverse epics and mythologies, and its tension between mysticism and iconoclasm. The novel is also postcolonial in the sense that it moves from European to non-European structures (from Dante and Norse myth to Attar and Hindu myth) and it posits a marginal figure who moves to the centre of power for the sole purpose of destroying this power.

While the dialogue in *Grimus* is at times wooden and its protagonist is as much a vehicle as an engaging character, the novel nevertheless offers a brilliantly realized ideal: the aim of the heroic journey is to break free of conventions and prejudices, to verture into an open, spiritually charged plurality. This point is bolstered by an impressive conflation of figures, landscapes and scenarios deriving principally from four sources: Attar's *Conference of the Birds*, Dante's *Divine Comedy*, Hindu mythology relating to the god Shiva, and the Norse *Voluspá* (also titled *Prophecy of the Seeress*, the *Voluspá* gives an overall account of Germanic cosmology and makes up the first book of *The Poetic Edda*). Rushdie weaves these different sources into a plot which goes like this: Virgil (the mystic) and Deggle (the demonic trickster) work in strange partnership so that Eagle (the iconoclastic hero) can climb the mountain and destroy the dimension maintained by Grimus (the God-like tyrant). After Eagle frees the island-mountain from Grimus and his selfish use of the God-object (the Stone Rose), the novel opens out yet further into a vague infinity, into an open-ended scenario implying any number of future patterns or dimensions. This is, of course, a simplification, yet it highlights the epic journey motif which dominates the novel, and it insists on the novel's iconoclastic – need I say paradoxical? – pattern-breaking pattern.

MYSTICAL JOURNEYS

While Dante's epic journey to the depth of Hell and to the peak of Purgatory dominates topographically, the main model for Eagle's journey remains the flight to Qaf in Attar's *Conference*. For Calf Mountain is an iconic, *golden calf* version of Attar's Qaf or Kaf, the mountain which is at once very far from, and very close to, the human heart. In *The Conference of the Birds* the Hoopoe tells his flock that "beyond Kaf's mountain peak / The Simorgh lives, the sovereign whom you seek, / And He is always near to us"[2]. Likewise, God is very far (He is nowhere to be seen) and very near (in the Koran He is said to be closer than the jugular). In *Mystical Dimensions of Islam* Annemarie Schimmel points out that the Q in *Qaf* "is mainly connected with the concept of *qurb*, 'proximity,' and the *qaf-i qurb*, the 'first letter,' or 'Mount Qaf,' of proximity, becomes a rather common expression – especially since this mountain is regarded as the station at the end of the created world, the place where man can find true proximity, *qurb*, on his way toward God (who, since Attar, has sometimes been symbolized by the Simurgh). Another combination is that of *q* with *qana'at*, 'contentment': the perfect Sufi lives, like the mythological bird, in the Mount Qaf of *qana'at*." [3] At the end of *Grimus* Eagle realizes the "*qurb* of proximity" by journeying to the peak of the mountain and by uniting with the infinite spirit which is at once within him and beyond any conception he might have about God or the soul. This type of mystical experience differs from the experience of the egomaniacal Grimus, who controls the mountain below him like a god manipulating people for his enjoyment – at times killing them for his sport. In Grimus's warped mind, mysticism consists in predicting and prescribing rather than allowing the infinity of God to overwhelm the self. Grimus sees Qaf as a "model for the structure and workings of the human mind" (G 232), yet he forgets the love and selflessness which lie at the heart of Sufi idealism.

In addition to Qaf there is one other fundamental componenet of Attar's mystical scheme: the figure of the Simurg. Schimmel calls it the "mystical bird that, according to Islamic tradition, lives on the world-encircling mountain Qaf and that became the symbol of the divine" in Attar's poetry.[4] At times the Simurg of Persian myth takes on a fairly concrete shape: Anthony Mercantante defines this form of the

Simurg as "a gigantic bird whose wings were as large as clouds," adding that it "sat on the magical tree, Gaokerena, which produced the seeds of all plant life." When it moved, "a thousand branches and twigs of the tree fell in all directions." Rushdie by and large employs Attar's less figurative Simurg, which Mercantante calls "a symbol of the godhead."[5] The only time Rushdie's Simurg takes on anything like a concrete form is when Koax foresees "the imminent clash of the Eagle, prince of earthly birds, and the Simurg, bird of paradise, wielder of the Stone Rose" (*G* 197). It is essential to note that Grimus sees himself as the Simurg – "Grimus" is an anagram of "Simurg" – and that this is precisely the type of egomania Rushdie attacks in the novel. Eagle is not only on a quest to destroy the definitions and boundaries Grimus imposes on the otherworldly mountain and those who live on it; he is also on a quest to defeat the desire to play God.

Eagle's mystical, iconoclastic journey begins on a mesa near the re-vivified city of Phoenix. This name fits with the initial American Southwest locale, with Rushdie's many ornithological references, and with the novel's cyclical cosmology – represented initially by the Phoenix and eventually by Shiva. When Rushdie writes that the city "had risen from the ashes of a great fire which had completely destroyed the earlier and much larger city also called Phoenix" (*G* 24), he subtly foreshadows the destruction and re-creation of Calf Mountain. One also suspects that Eagle's early name, Born-from-Dead, is meant to describe Shiva as well as the Phoenix, for the Hindu god creates new universes once he has destroyed old ones.

It seems appropriate that a novel which ends with cosmic annihilation would begin with an act of rebellion and iconoclasm: Eagle's sister Bird-Dog rejects the xenophobic rules of her Axona culture by daring to leave the confines of her homeland. In doing so she defies the taboo of the Whirling Demons. These imaginary spirits are reputed to surround the Axona Plateau, and they appear designed to keep Axonans in their isolation and on their moral high ground. The Demons represent alien, demonized cultures and as such they anticipate the "Foreign devilments," the "Devil things from abroad" and the "items from hell" in *Shame* (*S* 99), as well as "the evil thing" and "the alien nation" so despised by the Imam in the *Verses* (*SV* 206). Bird-Dog's successful descent through the feared realm of the Demons proves they are merely fabrications of an ethnocentric culture. As she puts it, "They're nothing at all but air" (*G* 19).

From a feminist perspective it might seem heartening that Rushdie kicks off his iconoclastic fiction with a *femme rebelle*. Yet Bird Dog suffers the fate of many other Rushdie would-be heroines; she is domesticated by Grimus, just as in *Midnight's Children* the Brass Monkey is domesticated and her voice co-opted by a militaristic patriarchy, and just as in *Shame* Rani and Bilquis are put under what amounts to house arrest by their husbands. Bird-Dog's name anticipates her fate, for she goes from living the free life of a bird to the chained life of a dog. Rushdie is true to epic and chivalric tradition here (feminists might add "falsely true"), for it is the male hero who rescues the female.

Nevertheless, Bird-Dog starts the pattern of rebellion against fixed patterns of culture and morality. She also, albeit unintentionally, leads her brother to the man on the mountain who attempts to perpetuate a spiritual hierarchy which makes slaves out of everyone, male or female.

Before Eagle can destroy Grimus's hierarchy, he must go through a number of tests. These do not come so much in the form of outer perils – the wolves or Malebranche of *Inferno* – but in the less tangible form of stubbornly held concepts or icons that stop the mind from ascending to a freedom beyond fixed forms. The first of these concepts is that of cultural hierarchy: the Whirling Demons that his sister prompts him to defy. Others are suggested by the various roles Eagle plays or the personalities he assumes in the 777-year course of his life on earth. By the time he is ready to leave for another world, he has played so many parts in life that his self has become "nameless as glass." He has become "Chameleon, changeling, all things to all men and nothing to any man. He had become his enemies and eaten his friends. He was all of them and none of them. ... Contentment without contents, achievement without goal, these were the paradoxes that swallowed him" (G 31–2). In becoming "all things" and "nothing," Eagle displays a less exuberant version of Keats's "poetical Character," which "has no self – it is every thing and nothing – It has no character ... What shocks the virtuous philosopher, delights the chameleon Poet. It does no harm from its relish of the dark side of things any more than from its taste for the bright one; because they both end in speculation."[6] Eagle is certainly more of a chameleon poet than the unnamed man he meets on the cliff. When he asks this man what he is doing, the man "called back – and each word was the word of a different being: – I am looking for a suitable voice to speak in" (G 32). The man's anxious mental searching is depicted metaphorically as a physical reaching: "As he called, he leaned forward, lost his balance and fell." In contrast, Eagle displays something of Keats's *negative capability*, that is, the ability to remain "in uncertainties, Mysteries, doubts, without any irritable reaching after fact & reason."[7] Most important to the novel's epic design, Eagle's early efforts to accept the mysteries in the world and in himself train him to keep an open mind. This openness will eventually allow him to confront the bizarre, dislocating dimensions of Calf Mountain without him losing his psychological balance.

Eagle's empty, open state throws light on the novel's third epigraph, in which Ted Hughes's trickster, Crow, appears as "his own leftover." In another poem from Hughes, Crow's "footprints assail infinity" and he makes a conscious choice to be used "for some everything."[8] Rushdie may have had Hughes's fine feathered friend in mind when writing the end of *Grimus*, for Eagle eventually enters a vague and infinite realm of "some everything," a realm represented in part by the infinity of Attar's Qaf and by Shiva's infinite destructions and creations. Yet for the time being Eagle's emptiness makes him more like Attar's bird-pilgrim, who enters an ontological void where he professes to "neither own nor lack all qualities," as well an epistemological void in which "All claims, all lust for meaning disappear."[9]

Eagle's ability to alter his fundamental conceptions makes him ready to ascend Calf, the island mountain which is as different from the contemporary world as is Dante's island mountain of Purgatory from fourteenth-century Italy. The Dantean elements of Eagle's quest are not immediately apparent, for it is the sinister Deggle and not the benevolent Virgil who initially serves as guide into the other world of the afterlife. Rushdie may be suggesting that, since Dante's Satan lives at the centre of the Earth, the devilish Deggle is best suited to lead Eagle down to this centre, seen metaphorically as a hole in the ocean which leads to the afterlife. Certainly the Devil is the one who traditionally urges people to kill themselves. In any case, Deggle has taken centuries to find his escape route from this world, and with his advice Eagle drowns and successfully surfaces in "that other sea, that not-quite-Mediterranean" (*G* 37).

His journey echoing those in Dante and T.S. Eliot, Eagle drifts up from the nursery rhyme "hole in the bottom of the sea" only to bump into the rocking chair of a strange, poetry-quoting man named Virgil Chanakya Jones. Virgil's last name, Jones, may emphasize his commonness or mediocrity (he might be seen as a bumbling, pedestrian version of the great classical poet) or may emphasize his Britishness, in which case he is, like Rushdie, something of a hybrid of Indian and English origins.

As Margery Fee suggested to me, Virgil's surname may also refer to Sir William Jones (1746–1794), the Orientalist scholar who identified the link between Sanskrit, Latin and Greek. This makes sense, given Virgil's interest in language and in both English and Indian culture. His middle name refers to a "very able and unscrupulous brahman adviser"[10] in Mauryan Empire India (321–185 B.C.). In *Grimus* Rushdie sees this historical Chanakya as a great ascetic, and in the *Verses* he sees him as a man whose detachment is so great that he "could live in the world and also not live in it" (*G* 133, *sv* 42). Virgil fits this description since he lives on Calf Island yet is philosophically detached from it, and since he practices the art of tantra, which is both sexual (or worldly) and mystical (or otherworldly).

At this stage in the novel Virgil's Englishness prevails, and in some ways he resembles the absent-minded poetry-quoting stereotype of the British schoolmaster. His abstruse poetics at first seem irrelevant, but one soon sees that they are very much part of the novel's game. This is particularly the case when Virgil throws out a quote from T.S. Eliot's *Four Quartets*, which Rushdie also includes in the novel's first epigraph: "Go, go, go, said the bird." Virgil calls this a "literary reference," a "piece of self-indulgence" (*G* 52), yet his words are metafictional markers drawing the reader's attention to an important explanation. So far, Rushdie has not made it clear how readers should interpret the otherworldly Mountain of Calf, a realm which operates not so much according to laws of physics as to those of metaphysics. Virgil apologizes for his literary indulgence after telling Eagle that he must have realized, because of his "acceptance of immortality, for instance," that the world is "no simple, matter-of-fact place": the world is both "what it appears to be and not what it appears to be" (*G* 51).

In explaining his worlds upon worlds philosophy, he borrows Eliot's notion that knowledge based on any one mode of perception "imposes a pattern, and falsifies."[11] In order to see the other worlds around him, Eagle must enter a "consciousness" that stays constant "in the shifts between the dimensions" (*G* 72). This is of course very similar to Eliot's "still point of the turning world," a point antithetical to "fixity," and one which allows the soul to "dance." Just as Eliot's dance at the still point of the turning world leads to a release "from action and suffering" and "from the inner / And the outer compulsion,"[12] so Eagle's cultivation of "consciousness" and his dance with Media lead to what Virgil calls "the way out" (*G* 72). This could mean both an escape from his own inner compulsions (symbolized by Khallit, Mallit and Axona) and from the outer compulsions of Grimus's tyrannical dimension. From beginning to end, both Eliot's poem and Rushdie's novel focus on the attempt to break free of old patterns – or, as Eliot puts is, "To become renewed, transfigured, in another pattern."[13]

Rushdie's Calf also echoes Borges's notion (placed in a footnote to "The Library of Babel") that "all solid bodies are the superimposition of an infinite number of planes."[14] Virgil comments that "an infinity of dimensions might exist, as palimpsests, upon and within and around our own, without our being in any wise able to perceive them" (G 52–3). Determined to experience these palimpsest dimensions come hell or high water, Eagle plunges into a psychological version of Dante's Inferno: "As the unknowable swept over me, I went all but mad. Hallucinations ... I thought they were hallucinations at first, but gradually they gained the certitude of absolute reality and it was the voice of Virgil Jones that came drifting to me like a dream. The world had turned upside down; I was climbing a mountain into the depths of an inferno, plunging deep into myself" (G 69–70).

Much about Eagle's internalized Inferno derives from *The Divine Comedy*, which can be seen as both a journey across a cosmic topography and as an exploration into the hell, purgatory and heaven of the spirit. Throughout this stage of their voyage, Eagle and Virgil feel uncertain, as do Dante and Virgil when they are in front of the city of Dis and when they reflect on their dangerous encounter with the Malebranche.[15] The situation of Eagle and Virgil is even more precarious, however, for while Dante's Virgil counts on the support of the omnipotent and benevolent Being above Purgatory, Virgil Jones does not trust Grimus, who skillfully manipulates (rather than helps) the people below him.

The two menacing figures Eagle meets in his inner hell seem to come from a Batman comic or maybe a Road Runner cartoon, yet they represent serious psychological, cultural and philosophical dichotomies. Deriving from Eagle's childhood memories of life in a culture of dos and don'ts, truths and falsehoods, Khallit and Mallit embody the polarity of Axonan thought. More specifically, they take the form of cantankerous twins who engage in endless arguments about morality and mortality. They pretend to *resolve* these arguments, but instead merely *revolve* them by flipping a coin. With each flip, the Road Runner canyon walls move toward Eagle like two sides of a vice. Left alone, he would die in this polar mindscape, but fortunately Virgil performs his dervish-like dance of unity, his "Weakdance," which makes the two *extrapolations* return "to the shreds of energy they had once been" (G 79). (I return to Virgil's mystic dance in the section below, "The Devil and the Dervish.")

The next stage of Eagle's spiritual journey resembles Cantos V to VII of Dante's *Inferno* as well as Valleys Five and Six of Attar's *Conference*. Cundy spells out several parallel with *Inferno*, noting that Cantos V to VII give rise to Chapters 24 and 25, in which Virgil and Eagle enter a tunnel, Eagle defeats Axona, and both characters return from their journey within a journey. She also notes the important correspondence between the point at which Eagle and Virgil reach "the edge of the Forest of Calf" and thus enter "alternative states," and the point at which the questing Sufi goes beyond the tree line and enters a world without forms.[16]

An important parallel between *Grimus* and Attar's *Conference* occurs when Virgil and Eagle find themselves on a raft, moving "from anywhere to nowhere across the infinite sea ... Towards infinity ... where all paradoxes are resolved" (G 82). Their isolated yet unified condition resembles that of the pilgrim soul in Attar's Valley of Unity, a "place of lonely, long austerity" where the "many ... are merged in one."[17] After they drift in this fifth Valley, becoming one with the sea "where all paradoxes are resolved," they return to a state of confusion, which corresponds to the sixth Valley, that of Bewilderment. Attar also implores the pilgrim to wake and scourge the evils inside him, to "encourage them, and they will swell / Into a hundred monsters loosed from hell."[18] Likewise, Virgil tells Eagle that he must "leap" the obstacles that lie within him, for "Lurking in the Inner Dimensions of every victim of the fever is his own particular set of monsters. His own devils burning in his own inner fires" (G 84).

This torture turns to questioning, as Eagle follows in the footsteps of Attar's bird-soul who has lost "both key and door." Awaking from a dream, Attar's pilgrim cries out, "Was it a dream, or was it true?" He also asks, "Who am I?" and admits to himself, "I have no certain knowledge any more."[19] In similar fashion, once Eagle returns from "the infinite sea," that is, once he realizes he is still on the mountain slope, he not only questions where he is but also what it means to be in one place and not another: "Flapping Eagle awoke with a splitting headache. The words *where am I?* formed on his lips for a second time on Calf Island; he dismissed them with a wry twist of his mouth. Where is anywhere? he asked himself" (G 90). The first time Eagle asks "*Where am I?*" he has just landed on Calf Island (G 40) and he has not yet been lectured by Virgil on the perplexing subject of infinite dimensionality. Now that he has listened to Virgil and has experienced one of these strange dimensions within him, he is prepared to consider the wider question, What does it mean to be anywhere?

Eagle's most radical and explosive self-questioning takes place in the temple of his mind, a temple he desecrates in iconoclastic frenzy. While his actions may seem extreme, one must remember the psychological framework within which Rushdie is situating his iconoclasm. For in attacking the devotee of Axona and in raping the iconic goddess, Eagle works himself free from the dichotomous, puritanical and xenophobic ideas that were inculcated in his subconscious during his earliest, most impressionable years. He derives the instrument of his attack, "the bone of K," from a surreal dream, a taboo-breaking trip into a hallucinatory dimension. In this bizarre dream his sister tosses Eagle a bone, lifts her skirt, and challenges him to bury the bone. When Eagle enters her surrealistically enlarged womb, she runs away, and he then chases her down the womb's cave-like mouth (*G* 71). Eagle uses this same "bone" to defeat the weapon-wielding devotee of Axona, who might be seen as both Axona's *altar-ego*, in that he protects Axona's altar, and Eagle's *alter-ego*, in that he stands for that part of Eagle which fears and defends an object of worship. Here the *object* is a goddess; later it will be the Stone Rose. Both objects can be seen as icons which must be smashed before the spiritual pilgrim can reach the formlessness of the soul. For the "bone of K" is the *os* (French for *bone*) of K, K-*os*, Chaos, and it garners much of its destructive power from Eagle's revolt against Axonan notions of ethnic and ethical purity. It literally and metaphorically flies against all the hierarchies of good and bad, deific and demonic, which are embedded in a socioreligious hierarchy of *us* and *them*, *good insiders* and *bad outsiders*. Eagle uses the deepest, most primal, creative and destructive part of him to break through the deepest taboos inside him. And his revolt is successful, for it cleanses "the guilt and shame that possessed some hidden part of [his] mind" (*G* 89).

When Eagle attacks the devotee with the bone, the result is "Chaos," "a hole," a "turbulent disarrangement in the structure of the dimension" (*G* 89). Rushdie revisits this idea in *Midnight's Children*, where Aadam Aziz's secular rebellion makes him "unable to worship a God in whose existence he could not wholly disbelieve," after which Aadam experiences a permanent alteration and enters "a hole" (*MC* 12). Aadam's refusal to follow orthodox practices does not, however, correspond to a stage in any mystical progression. Rather, it is the beginning of his fall into a divided existence, one which ends ambiguously when he carries a lock of Muhammad's hair into a shrine dedicated to the Hindu god Shiva (*MC* 277–8). Eagle's attack on the devotee and the goddess, on the other hand, is a necessary iconoclastic or "icon-breaking" stage on a journey which ends with the implosion of Grimus's dimension, with Eagle's identification with Shiva, and with the ascent of Eagle and Media into various possible heavens or new dimensions.

The hero's quest also involves rejecting the notion of a fixed place or home. His momentary "urge to fit in, to be accepted" in the town of K, and to abandon his "long-time search," derives from "the natural condition of the exile," who yearns to escape from the psychological state in which he can only put "down roots in memories" (*G* 122, 107). The theme of a fluid self resulting from the exile's (or immigrant's) dislocation crops up in many of Rushdie's essays, "Imaginary Homelands" providing the most notable example. The comments of the narrator in *Shame* are equally appropriate to Eagle's condition. This Rushdean narrator says that roots and gravity are conservative myths "designed to keep us in our places" (*s* 86). He proposes that we replace these myths with "flight," which is applicable to Eagle's name, and "freedom," which is applicable to Eagle's final state – for he leaves behind him the confines of Grimus's Calf and he journeys on the drumbeat of Shiva into a new cosmos.

Eagle eventually realizes that his desire to strike roots in K is "a coming home ... to a town where he had never lived." His desire is founded on the "persuasive" voice in his head which tells him that he knows himself and that because he has a fixed self he can fit in somewhere. Yet the concepts of self-knowledge and of a fixed self are exactly those Rushdie is contesting. Eventually, Eagle sees that his desire to have a fixed abode is a by-product of his falling into "the Way of K," that is, into a false philosophy of permanence (*G* 106, 122, 164).

Initially, however, he is lured by the notion of belonging in K, a strange town in which the citizens are under the dual influence of the Grimus Effect and the Doctrine of Obsessionalism. When Grimus's hold on the island weakens, the townsfolk start to see that the obsessive interests on which they base their lives are meaningless once their minds are opened to other ways of looking at reality. Ignatius Gribb created the Doctrine of Obsessionalism and is thus hardest hit: when "the Inner Dimensions [are] unleashed upon him," they scald "his nerve-centres, burning out the synapses of a brain which could not accommodate the new realities invading it." Eagle on the other hand can accommodate "new realities" because he has already confronted his inner demons and has already learned to accommodate what Virgil calls "the shifts between the dimensions" (G 180, 72).

The hero's infatuations with Elfrida and Irina do, however, make him momentarily like Attar's princess in the Valley of Bewilderment, who thinks highly of divine love but feels entangled in the snares of earthly love. She has "read a hundred books on chastity" yet she remains frustrated: "And still I burn – what good are they to me?"[20] In Sufi terms, the princess is not necessarily wrong to pursue earthly love, since this love partakes of divinity (God is the divine Lover) and frees the soul from preoccupation with the self (the self being the Sufi's main obstacle). Eagle's passionate love for Elfrida and Irina momentarily forces him to think about something besides himself. Such an outward focus is necessary after his intense preoccupation with his own spiritual struggles, that is, after his dangerous descent "into the depths of an inferno, plunging deep into [him]self," and after confrontation with his "own devils burning in his own inner fires." Eventually, however, Eagle sees Elfrida and Irina as Circe-like impediments, as "witches weaving their spell, binding him in silken cords" (G 70, 84, 147). Because they keep him in Calf and because they are possessive, Elfrida and Irina remain antithetical to the free-spirited Media, whose uninhibited and unconditional love helps him set himself and the island free.

While Deggle and Virgil are trapped on the lower levels of the otherworldly mountain by Dantean convention (Deggle's demonic associations and Virgil's pagan ties preclude their ascent), Eagle and Media pass through Grimus's "gate" and journey up to Grimushome, a labyrinthine mansion situated near the peak. Reaching Grimus' elitist realm, they enter a sterile "Heaven" presided over by an egomaniacal "God." The proof of Grimus's selfish tyranny lies in his domestication and enslavement of Bird-Dog, Eagle's erstwhile free-spirited sister. Eagle decides that he must destroy this power which can reduce the spirit (a bird) to a slave (a dog). He accomplishes this by transforming Calf into Qaf, that is, by reconstructing the Island without the Stone Rose (G 252), the instrument which Grimus uses to maintain control over the island and its inhabitants. One should note that the journey which starts with Bird-Dog, and with Eagle's desire to find his sister, is successful not so much because Eagle finds her, but because he finds and recuperates the freedom of the younger Bird-Dog in another female lover, the prostitute Media.

Media is the perfect match for Eagle because she, as her name suggests, can lend herself to many forms. In this sense she is an archetypal woman who both complements and magnifies the power of the Hindu god Shiva. When Media tells Eagle she's "a woman who can cope with [him]" (G 187), one can see what Rushdie is getting at in terms of Hindu myth: she is the primal energy and matter which allows itself to be transformed into various forms of existence.

I shall return to Shiva on several occasions below, yet here I want to note that the final stages of Eagle's journey also have strong elements of Germanic myth – especially Odin's fall from power and the survival of the primordial couple.

Grimus resembles Odin, who is "the master of arcane ('runic') wisdom, poetry, and magic,"[21] and who communes with Yggdrasil, the giant or cosmic tree which is his "strange source of arcane wisdom." In the crisis before Ragnarok, Odin undergoes a bizarre ritual eye-poking under Yggdrasil and he communes "necromantically with his preserved head."[22] Grimus's death beneath his giant tree echoes this. There are also two important related parallels. First, Grimus's discovery of the elixir of immortality reworks Odin's discovery of the mead of wisdom, which "is hidden in the other world, in a place difficult to get to, but Odinn manages to obtain it, and from then on it is accessible to all the gods."[23] Second, Grimus' last-ditch efforts to save Calf from dissolution rework Odin's efforts to forestall the cataclysm of Ragnarok, which Odin "foresees and tries to stave off by increasingly desperate and deviant expedients."[24] While Grimus attempts to garner some Odinic brand of immortality or wisdom by sacrificing himself under his giant ash-tree, his "martyrdom" remains an egomaniacal and ugly spectacle.

Grimus's importance is in any case superseded by that of Eagle and Media, who in this Germanic context become the primordial couple who weather Ragnarok inside the trunk of Yggdrasil.[25] In both Germanic myth and *Grimus*, a magician figure dies without ever attaining control over the destiny of his world, yet a human couple find new life in the next world. Destiny "is hidden in the subterranean well into which Yggdrasill's roots plunge,"[26] yet neither Odin nor Grimus plumbs this depth successfully. While Grimus foresees what Koax calls "the imminent clash of the Eagle, prince of earthly birds, and the Simurg, bird of paradise, wielder of the Stone Rose" (*G* 197), he is powerless to determine the outcome of this clash. He wants the Rose to captivate Eagle's imagination, yet Eagle destroys it instead.

Eagle and Media are free, not so much because they destroy Grimus's tyranny but because they refuse to inherit the esoteric machinery which makes such tyranny possible. Grimus uses the Crystal of Potentialities to isolate individual lives, or *lines*, from their many potential *"line[s] of flux"* (*G* 235), and he chooses the *lines* that will fulfill his esoteric and egomaniacal Plan. The culminating aspects of his Plan involve his martyrdom and the perpetuation of Calf by his lookalike, Eagle. Yet Eagle rebels against the *line* chosen for him. Refusing to follow in Grimus's footsteps, he destroys Grimus's esoteric machinery and thus makes it possible for Media, himself, and everyone on the mountain below them to choose their own paths.

The bed on which Eagle and Media make love is at once the place where Attar's birds reach union and annihilation on the Impossible Mountain of Qaf, where Dante's pilgrim flies with Beatrice from the mountain of Purgatory to the spheres of Heaven, where Shiva makes love with Parvati on Mount Kailasa, and where the primordial couple of Germanic mythology survive inside the trunk of Yggdrasil. The fate of Eagle and Media remains neatly outside the text, although some kind of continuity seems likely given that Islamic, Christian, Germanic and Shaivite cosmologies all point to postcataclysmic realms.

THE DEVIL AND THE DERVISH

The success of Eagle's quest to destroy Grimus's tyranny depends on assistance given him by two figures who are in many ways opposite: Deggle, who is vain, sarcastic, and occult; and Virgil, who is self-deprecating, ironic, and mystical. Deggle's character is extremely elusive, deriving as it does from the slippery personalities of Loki and the Devil. Virgil Jones is a less elusive character, yet he too has various antecedents: he is a blend of Dantean guide, Sufi mystic and tantric guru. Despite their differences Deggle speaks for them both when he expresses his hope that Eagle will succeed in destroying the Rose: "One thing is certain, he told himself, if Flapping Eagle doesn't get to Bird-Dog and [destroy the Rose], I'm stuck here for life" (G 99). Deggle and Virgil both help Eagle reach and destroy the Rose: Deggle points Eagle to the "gate" or "hole" in the ocean which leads to the other world of Calf, and Virgil points him to the "gate" which leads to Grimus and his Rose. While Deggle partially resembles the Mephistopheles figure in the *Verses,* who *"always wills the Bad, and always works the Good"* (sv 417), and while Virgil both wills and works the good, the moral polarity they represent is subsumed in the larger cosmic drama that the two characters help bring to an implosive climax. Just as Virgil, Eagle and Liv form a front of "weakness, ignorance and hate, united against their will" (G 205), so Deggle and Virgil become unwilling partners in an alliance against Grimus's tyranny.

Deggle's mix of playfulness and cruelty suggest affinities with "the Trickster" Jeffrey Russell describes in his study *The Devil: Perceptions of Evil from Antiquity to Primitive Christianity:* "The curious figure of the Trickster, the spirit of disorder, the enemy of boundaries, is also related to the divine, but his functions are too ill defined to make it possible to equate him with the principle of evil. He is sensual, childish, foolish, sometimes ugly and cruel, but he is also lighthearted and funny. Sometimes his opposition to the gods entails a creative attempt to help man, as when Prometheus steals the gods' fire. The fundamental characteristic of the Trickster is the upsetting of order; as in the myth of chaos, order upset can release creative energies as well as destroy established values."[27] In general terms Deggle is a Trickster, yet in specific terms he is a blend of Loki and the Devil. Rushdie makes the parallel between Deggle and the Germanic god Loki explicit when Deggle renames himself "Lokki," referring vaguely to "the old Norse and so forth" (G 34–5). Deggle is less overt about his scheming than the crude Loki of the *Lokasenna,*[28] yet he resembles Loki when he steers Eagle to the gate in the ocean. In the *Voluspá* Loki steers a ship over the ocean, bringing with him the dark forces which create the violent apocalyptic scenario – wherein "Trembles the tow-ering tree Yggdrasil" and "screams the eagle."[29] The tree in front of Grimus's mansion vaguely calls to mind the Persian Gaokerena,[30] yet it is explicitly referred to as the Norse "Ash Yggdrasil" (G 230). The name "Flapping Eagle" is particularly relevant here, given that from "the time of its emergence (that is, from the time that the world was organized by the gods), Yggdrasill was threatened with ruin: an eagle set out to destroy its foliage, its trunk began to rot, and the snake Nithhogg began gnawing at its roots."[31] In rough terms one can equate the gods (especially Odin) with Grimus, the eagle with Flapping Eagle, and the snake with Deggle.

The struggle between Grimus and Deggle also parallels that be-tween Odin and Loki. While Loki does not directly kill Odin, he mates with the giantess Grief Boding, who then gives birth to the wolf Fenrir, the snake Mithgarthsomr and the guardian of the under-world, Hel. These three "children" oppose Odin and the gods[32] and eventually Fenrir kills Odin.[33] Perhaps most important is the fact that the drama pitting Deggle against Grimus ends in cataclysm, just as the battle between Loki and Odin ends in Ragnarok, the Norse equiv-alent of the Apocalypse. Also, much of what these opposing charac-ters stand for is superseded by the creation of a new island, which Eagle reconstructs in *Grimus* and which rises "from out of the sea" at the end of the *Voluspá*.[34]

Deggle is a mix of the Loki who propels the world toward Ragnarok, and the Devil or Antichrist who drives the world toward the Day of Judgement. As attested by Virgil's diary, Deggle's life parallels that of the Devil cast from Heaven. Indeed, one can read the diary as a minia-ture version of cosmic history and politics, which starts when Grimus brings a dead bird of paradise (the Phoenix? the Simurg?) to the grave-yard in which Virgil, working as a gravedigger, discovers the Stone Rose. Given that Grimus's coercion and egomania destroy the beauty of the Rose, the Simurg and Qaf – all of which symbolize God – it is ap-propriate that a bird symbolizing the spirit and Heaven lies dead in Grimus's hands. Rushdie makes a strong yet subtle point when he has Grimus demonstrate immediate proficiency in his handling of the Rose. Virgil and Deggle, on the other hand, lose consciousness when they first try to use it (G 208). This makes sense in that a mystic (Virgil) excels in exploring the soul rather than controlling external things, and a devil (Deggle) remains fundamentally alienated from any God-like power which can connect and shape an infinity of dimensions. Deggle's belief "that the power in Grimus's possession should be de-stroyed" (G 158) may result from an envy of Grimus's ability to control the Rose, and this envy may prompt his subsequent philosophical objection to the Rose's power. After Deggle breaks the stem from the Rose (G 26), Grimus and Virgil cast him from their company and condemn him to wander over the face of the earth, much like the Satan of mythology, and very much like the Satan in the epigraph of *The Satanic Verses*.

Rushdie stresses Deggle's satanic traits when he describes him as a "wickedly-smiling conjurer" who has a sorcerer's "*malin* talent," and when he dresses him in "dark svelte finery, ring-laden and perfumed, with a rose in his buttonhole" (G 36, 26). The rose may be a symbol of his defiance, of his belief that the Stone Rose ought to belong to him. Other details suggest a satanic bent, as when "he was feeling very angry with himself, and, therefore, with the universe" (G 97). In addition, the name Deggle resembles "Devil." After the sly conjuror lets "drop some dark conversational flower" (probably some *fleur du mal!*) from his "saturnine lips," the decadent Livia Cramm cries out in admiration: "*Ain't that the Deggle himself talkin' to you*" (G 27).

Another clue to Deggle's satanic identity can be seen when one recognizes that the name "Deggle" refers to the Muslim Antichrist. "Deggle" bears an unmistakable resemblance to *Deggial* or *ad-Dajjal*, which literally means "the deceiver" or "the impostor."[35] The use of this name goes back some way in European literature; for instance, in William Beckford's *Vathek* (English translation, 1786) we find a fear that "the Deggial, with his exterminating angels, had sent forth his plagues on the earth."[36] In his notes to Beckford's Gothic novel, Peter Fairclough defines *Deggial* as "the Mohammedan version of Antichrist; he has one eye and on his forehead is written the word, 'Infidel.' Traditionally he will destroy the whole world except Mecca but will himself be slain by Jesus at the gate of the church at Lydda in Palestine."[37] The Deggle of Rushdie's novel also seems to think of himself as "a kind of saviour" or "popular messiah" (G 215), which may be an echo of the Muslim notion that the Jewish people "will mistake [ad-Dajjal] for the true Messiah."[38]

Deggle can be quite closely linked to *ad-Dajjal* as the Antichrist who appears "shortly before Jesus returns to earth at the end of time," and who seeks "to lead people into disbelief, or to the practice of a false religion."[39] Deggle precedes Eagle in his confrontation with Grimus and he has a clear interest in the occult, which is often considered false religion: the sly conjuror shares Livia Cramm's interest in "the tarot, the scriptures, the cabbala, palmistry, anything and everything which held that the world was more than it seemed." This shared interest in a spiritual world does not, however, produce a communion of souls. Rather, Deggle appears to be the one who murders Livia (G 26, 31).

Deggle's role in the cosmic drama of *Grimus* deserves attention in its own right, yet Deggle also anticipates the most problematic of all of Rushdie's constructions, the satanic narrator of the *Verses*. Deggle changes his name to Lokki, and, in light of his subsequent assertion that he has become the descendant of his "illustrious ancestor Nicholas Deggle" (*G* 35), one might see *their* descendant in turn as the trickster-ish, sinister, elusive Satan of the more recent novel. Both satanic conjuror and satanic narrator foreground an important question of theodicy: what motivates evil? In the *Verses* the satanic narrator refers to *Othello*, saying that unlike Iago he will furnish the reason behind his evil deeds. Although he does not give us the reason directly he hints that his bitterness derives from his jealousy of the favoured Archangel Gabriel (*SV* 424–5). In *Grimus* Eagle tells Deggle that he would "love to know what motivates" him, to which the "wickedly-smiling conjurer" responds, "perhaps I don't like your friend Sispy [Grimus] very much either. But then, perhaps I do" (*G* 36). As a Satan-figure, Deggle is attracted to Grimus's God-like power and he understands Grimus's desire to control others. The difference between Deggle and Virgil in this regard is treated symbolically: after Grimus's gate is destroyed, they choose opposite directions or paths. Deggle climbs toward the peak while Virgil walks down to the beach (*G* 250). Their choices suggest that while Deggle is still lured by the power which resides at the top of the mountain, Virgil refuses to give Grimus and his hierarchical view of the universe any more importance than Grimus has already given it.

Deggle's aim may be to reach the peak of Calf, yet everything else about him suggests a downward, hell-bent direction. And while Virgil remains content to stay on the beach, everything about him – including his sexuality – points upwards. In directing Eagle to the peak of Calf, Virgil of course wears the mantle of Dante's famous guide, yet he also wears the coarser cloth of the Sufi and Hindu mystics.

Virgil's role as a Sufi guide (a *sheik* or *pir*) surfaces most clearly when Eagle encounters Khallit and Mallit, who are two "extrapolations" that the extraterrestrial Gorf Koax has "set" in his mind. Khallit and Mallit argue back and forth in Eagle's head, their absurd debate applying ever more insidiously to Eagle's immortal condition: "Suppose a man deprived of death. Suppose him wandering through all eternity, a beginning without an end. Does the absence of death in him mean that life is also absent? – Debatable, said Mallit. He flipped the coin. Yes, he said" (*G* 78). Their "debate" becomes absurd because it seems meaningless or arbitrary (questions are answered by flipping a coin) and because their arguments aggravate the anguish Eagle feels at not knowing his place or fate in the universe.

Khallit and Mallit throw irreconcilable opposites at Eagle and then make his survival depend upon reconciling them. Eagle does not so much need a resolution of, or solution to, these opposites as he needs a *dis*solution; he needs a response enabling him to dissolve or dis-solve the sadistic puzzle, a respose that refuses to admit the puzzle's very axiom of polarity. Luckily for him, his guide Virgil knows all about such a dis-solution. In his experimental days he used the Stone Rose to reach "the planet of the Spiral Dancers," where he learned a dance which transcends the logic of opposition and dichotomy. He explains to Eagle that the "scientist-poets" of that planet "elevated a branch of physics until it became a high symbolist religion" in which they found "a harmony of the infinitesimal, where energy and matter moved like fluids" (*G* 75). Although Virgil learns his Weakdance and his religion of Spiral Unity from the scientist-poets, Rushdie is clearly borrowing from the theory and practice of the Sufi brotherhoods, commonly referred to as "the whirling dervishes." In their ecstatic *sama* dances the dervishes imitate the whirling of atoms and celestial spheres. Energy becomes a unifying plane on which worldly and oth-erworldly spaces converge. In her introduction to the *sama*, Eva de Vitray-Meyerovitch quotes from the famous Sufi poet, Jalal ud-Din Rumi, more commonly known as Rumi: "Oh daylight, rise! atoms are dancing / The souls, lost in ecstasy, are dancing / To your ear, I will tell you where the dance will take you. / All the atoms in the air and in the desert, / Let it be known, are like madmen. / Each atom, happy or miserable, / Is in love with the Sun of which we can say nothing."[40] Rushdie employs such a notion when he has Virgil dance his way into primal matter – Rumi's "atoms" – and dissolve the di-chotomous construction in which Eagle is trapped.

Schimmel's discussion of the *sama* is also helpful in understanding Virgil's rescue of Eagle. She starts by noting that the ecstatic bliss of union with God can be called *instasy* instead of *ecstasy*, "since the mystic is not carried out of himself but rather into the depths of him-self, into 'the ocean of the soul,' as the poets might say."[41] This notion of an interior ocean associated with the ecstasy of union comes into the novel when, after Virgil dances the Weakdance, the two float on a raft "from anywhere to nowhere across the infinite sea." This "sea" is clearly inside them in a shared dimension rather than around them on the mountain slope. Virgil's "Strongdance" corresponds to the moment of unity, and his "Weakdance" to the moment of falling "back into the Primal" (*G* 82, 75). These two phases might allude to Attar's *union* and *annihilation* as well as to the *second turn* and the *third turn* of the *sama* dance. The Turkish poet Mehmed Tchelebi ex-plains that the Sufi mystics, called "lovers," "turn a second time until they disappear." At this point God declares, "You have known My Unity through your own experience." The third turn corresponds to Attar's annihilation and to Rushdie's "falling back into the Primal": Tchelebi's lovers attain *"absolute Truth," "complete annihilation* and *death," "complete disappearance* and *death,"* at which point God exclaims, "Peace be on you, oh lovers! / In dying you have liberated yourselves from death. By the annihilation you have found ... the path toward Me."[42]

In rescuing Eagle, Virgil takes the form of a whirling dervish, an apt counterpart to the divisive Whirling Demons which divided the world between Axonans and foreigners, between *us* and *them*, and which formed the deep polarity in Eagle's mind (represented by Khallit and Mallit). Through his Sufi dance of unity Virgil is able to turn these demons to dervishes, healing the primal rift in Eagle's psyche. This unifying process takes place when the coin's dichotomous "decisions" – landing on one side then the other – are replaced by its continual spinning, forever mixing the two sides in eternal rotation – very much as the fixed and polarized moon is brought into a spinning unity in *Haroun*.

Virgil's mystical whirlwind counteracts the spinning action of the coin Khallit and Mallit use to inflict the anguish of opposites on Eagle. Ensconced in the poles of their own logic, Khallit and Mallit fear the force of Virgil's dervish dance of unity: "Mallit looked up. – It can't be, he said. – But it is, it is, cried Khallit. The whirlwind came closer and closer. – Fascinating paradox, said Mallit. – Fascinating, said Khallit doubtfully" (G 79). In his *sama* dance of unity, Virgil comes as close as possible to the unifying presence of God and hence to the dissolution of dichotomy into unity. From this position, he is able to make Khallit and Mallit return "to the shreds of energy they had once been. On the planet of the Spiral Dancers, people would have said: – they danced the Weakdance to the end."

Just as Bird-Dog found that the Whirling Demons which represented the Other were "nothing at all but air," so Eagle finds that the dangers posed by Khallit and Mallit do not exist once they are replaced by a more unified way of thinking, which is in this case exemplified by Virgil and his Sufi dance of unity.

In addition to teaching Eagle the Weakdance, Virgil leads the way to a tantric sexuality which prefigures Eagle's final union with Media. Indeed, it is Virgil's whoring that first brings Eagle to the brothel where he meets Media, the prostitute who will help him enter into the role of the ithyphallic Shiva. Rushdie names the prostitute Kamala Sutra, which is appropriate since she contorts herself into a sexual position described in the *Kama Sutra*. And given that Eagle is climbing Calf Mountain it makes an equal sort of comic sense that she demonstrate the "climbing-up-the-mountain position." Rushdie also alludes to the sacred and symbolic genitalia of Shaivism when Virgil observes that Calf Mountain "is rather like a giant *lingam* weltering in the *yoni* that is the Sea" (*G* 156, 55–6). Rushdie then shifts into a more subtle mode of allusion when Eagle takes on Shiva's "erotic-ascetic" aspect, that is, Shiva's ability to remain sexually aroused without climaxing: Eagle remains balanced "between denial and consummation, standing at the peak, from which the only direction was down" (*G* 172). Finally, Eagle and Media take on the aspects of Shiva and Parvati, whose intercourse threatens the very structure of the cosmos. In her book *Shiva: The Erotic Ascetic* Wendy O'Flaherty observes that Shiva's raised phallus "is the plastic expression of the belief that love and death, ecstasy and asceticism, are basically related."[43] Eagle's union with Media clearly links love and death, for in making love they terminate their existence in Grimus's dimension. Rushdie thus manages to conflate Sufi and Shaivite motifs, for, as noted above, Tchelebi's "lovers" also attain mystical annihilation or *"complete disappearance* and *death."*

Although Deggle and Virgil are opposite in many ways, they both help Eagle destroy Grimus's dystopic Calf. It makes sense for the devilish Deggle to help Eagle journey through the lower regions of the cosmos and for the mystical Virgil (and Media, the more elevated Beatrice-Parvati figure) to aid him in his ascent to the higher realms. Rushdie may be suggesting here that while good and evil are major factors in the soul's journey, they are less important than the transcendental, liberating union which lies, at least in theory, beyond moral dichotomy. This appears appropriate to the Sufism in the text, given that Sufi poets suggest that purity and impurity are not as important as mystical experience. Attar claims that "Islam and blasphemy have both been passed / By those who set out on love's path at last,"[44] and Sana'i declares, "If you were really a lover / you'd see that faith and infidelity / are one."[45] The Hindu tantric element in the text – by which I mean the use of sexuality to attain mystical experience – also suggests that traditional morality is not as important as spiritual liberation.

Another way of looking at Rushdie's subordination of orthodox morality is to situate it in a Romantic context, one in which fixed values are often casualties in the war against dogma, against any hierarchy that is imposed on the landscape of the human imagination; or, as Blake puts it in *The Marriage of Heaven and Hell*, "The man who never alters his opinion is like standing water, & breeds reptiles of the mind."[46] This is especially appropriate since Khallit and Mallit are like torturing demons extrapolated from deep in Eagle's mind. In this sense Virgil acts as the river that runs through it.

THE STONE ROSE: DEUS IN MACHINA

Eagle's battles with the demons inside him are only a prelude to his greater battle with Grimus, who uses the Stone Rose to manipulate everyone on the mountain below him. Grimus's selfish behaviour does not, however, mean that the Rose is in itself a coercive machine. Indeed, it starts off as a wonderful Object that has strong associations with the mystic's God: combining elements of mysticism, the occult and science fiction, the Rose is capable of linking dimensions and hence of opening people's minds to new realities. Yet Grimus's megalomania makes of it a dangerous God-Object, a supradimensional machine which lets the finite self manipulate dimensions as if it were God.

In creating a plot in which a God-Object must be destroyed, Rushdie is not proposing that God must be destroyed. Rather, he is suggesting that God as an Object or a definable Entity must be destroyed. This is not because the idea of such an Object is bad, but because the Object itself is likely to be abused. The notion of an unattainable or mystical God, one which cannot be manipulated to further personal agendas, remains entirely valid. Indeed, such a notion is consistent with Virgil's initial poetic, mystical, liberating use of the Rose.

In explaining the nature of the Rose to Eagle, Virgil begins by noting that Koax took "Conceptualism" to its fullest extent, opening a door to an infinite and not merely theoretical arena of dimensions. Taking the ultra-Cartesian notion, "*I think therefore it is*," Koax postulated "that anything of which such an intellect could conceive *must therefore exist*" (*G* 66). Koax's "conceptualization" of endless dimensions eventually nonplussed the Gorfs because it destroyed the possibility of reaching a final "ordering" of reality, a goal highly prized by the interstellar race of rational stone frogs. In what appears to be an attempt to minimize the damage he wrought, Koax "conceptualized an Object" which could structure or "order" disparate, runaway dimensions (*G* 66). Following Koax, the Gorfs then "created the Objects which linked the infinity of Conceived and Inconceivable Dimensions." The Gorfs continue to hope that such Objects, with their "elements" beaming "directly to the planet Thera," will help them order, or account for, the universe (*G* 244–5).

Koax's conceptualization of open-ended dimensions constitutes a revolt against those who use the free-thinking mind and then restrict the arenas within which this thinking can operate. Given that the *Gorfs* from *Thera* are, anagrammatically, *Frogs* from *Earth*, Rushdie may be suggesting a human propensity for unfeeling, hyper-logical, constrictive rationality. In light of his echo of Descartes's famous *je pense donc je suis*, one might conclude that the Frogs refer to the French, yet any such allusion is clearly meant to be playful rather than insulting.

While the Gorfs might be faulted for their cold and at times controlling rationality, they must be credited for not interfering with any other dimension (or "endimions" anagrammatically) and for refusing to use the Objects to coerce others into accepting their rational way of life. Enforcing a variant of Star Trek's Prime Directive (according to which Federation members are enjoined never to interfere with the cultural and internal affairs of other cultures or species), the Gorfs punish Koax for his meddling, for his "gross Bad Order": "banned from Thera," he "stands or falls" with Grimus's dimension (*G* 245). The Gorfs also warn against Grimus's use of the Rose to conceptualize his subdimension of Grimushome. Dota, the Master Anagrammari or chief Gorf, argues that a place "is either part of an Endimions or it is not" and that to conceptualize a place *"which is both a part of an Endimions and yet secret from it could stretch the Object to disintegration-point"* (*G* 244–6).

Dota's title, Magister Anagrammari, calls to mind Magister Ludi in Hermann Hesse's *Magister Ludi or The Glass Bead Game*. In his introduction to that novel, Theodore Ziolkowski comments that Hesse "depicts a future society in which the realm of Culture is set apart to pursue its goals in splendid isolation, unsullied by the 'reality' that Hesse had grown to distrust." The rise of Nazism and other events disillusioned Hesse about the value of "any spiritual realm divorced wholly from contemporary social reality" and of "a life consecrated exclusively to the mind."[47] Likewise, Grimus creates Calf in a splendid isolation and lives in a mental isolation. Grimus's re-arrangement of the planes of the Rose and Dota's Divine Game of Ordering may also owe something to the Game which gives rise to Hesse's title.

In writing about the infinite dimensionality established by Koax Rushdie may also have had Borges's "The Library of Babel" in mind. Borges's fantastic realm contains books with every possible permutation of letters. His narrator hopes that if "an eternal traveler" (Flapping Eagle fits this description) were to cross the library in any direction, "after centuries he would see that the same volumes were repeated in the same disorder (which, thus repeated, would be an order: the Order)."[48] The narrator bases this principle of Order on the repetition of the given disorder of the library. Yet what if he were given other libraries or disorders? What if he were given an infinite number of other libraries, including libraries in which books floated from one shelf to the next and letters resembled black fish that swam in oceans of white paper? Borges's narrator and Koax are both fascinated by the notion of permutations, yet Koax derives an anarchic pleasure from the notion of an infinity of dimensions, that is, from the notion that there are always more dimensions beyond any given number of dimensions in which permutations can be located. For this reason Koax's name may be a skewed version of "Kaox" or "Chaos," although the K may also allude to the Simurg's *Kaf*, or perhaps even Shiva's *Kailasa* – which would be appropriate, given the dissolution implicit in Attar's mystical annihilation and the entropy implicit in Shiva's cosmic destructions. In any case, while Koax does not seem bothered by the implication that an infinity of dimensions makes one increasingly unimportant in the ever-expanding schemelessness of things, Borges's narrator is unnerved by what might exist beyond the library.

One might also compare the Stone Rose to Borges's "perfect compendium" and Grimus to Borges's elusive librarian who has read the compendium and is "analogous to a god."[49] Grimus would no doubt applaud such a deification, yet he would also gloss over the notion that it highlights hubris and the egomania of dictatorship rather than wisdom and the selflessness of Sufi mysticism (which he exploits for less than it is worth). For Grimus believes that to "be wise and powerful is to be complete," and he thinks that he has honed to perfection "the faculties which add potency to wisdom" (*G* 232). Yet in exercising this "potency" for his own ends, he destroys this "wisdom." In the ways of mysticism he has much to learn from Sufis and Taoists.

The same type of infinite dimensionality that Rushdie explores in *Grimus* crops up fifteen years later in *Haroun and the Sea of Stories*. Haroun sees in the currents of the moon Kahani (Hindi for "Story") "a liquid tapestry of breathtaking complexity." In this Ocean Haroun sees "all the stories that had ever been told" as well as those "that were still in the process of being invented." The Ocean of the Streams of Story "was in fact the biggest library in the universe" (*H* 72). Both *Grimus* and *Haroun* posit infinite permutations and both depict a scenario in which the protagonist defeats a megalomaniac who tries to impose a specific pattern on what is otherwise a metamorphic realm of possibility. Eagle takes this victory furthest, for while Haroun and company *restore* the flow of story-streams into the Ocean, Eagle, as Shiva, *becomes* the Ocean that contains an infinity of potential stories.

The order Grimus imposes on Calf and the rationalization for this order are undermined when Eagle refuses to use the Rose in Grimus's coercive and self-aggrandizing manner. His refusal implies that an interdimensional God-like power either should not exist or should not be accessible to finite beings. Rushdie may be speculating about a universe without a personal God when he has his Eagle ask an assembly of Gorfs if it is possible to conceptualize a dimension without an Object. He receives the following response: "A long pause, in which I felt complex arguments flashing between the assembled Gorfs. – *We cannot be sure*, said Dota. *For us, the answer would be No, since the very existence of the Endimions relative to us is a function of the Object. But for a dweller in the Endimions* ... a mental shrug-form followed." Because the Gorfs think structurally, they cannot imagine a dimension without an ordering mechanism such as the Rose. Dota, however, concedes "that he could conceive of a Dimension-dweller devising such a Concept" (G 246, 251). Having no Object or having a hidden, unattainable, transcendent Object (a Supradimension or a transcendent God) suggests the possibility of living in dimensions that are not constantly manipulated as if from above or outside. This seems to be the only God Rushdie can countenance, and this iconoclastic deity may lie behind his numerous parodies of an anthropomorphic god, from the comic phantasm of Aadam's anger in *Midnight's Children* to the bumbling myopic "Guy Upstairs" in the *Verses*.

In *Grimus* Rushdie suggests that if dimensions must have Objects, then such Objects ought to remain hidden or they will be subject to selfish manipulation. As is intimated in Virgil's diary, the Rose initially appears to be hidden, inactive or dead – a status symbolized by the dead bird of paradise and by the Rose's location in the forest next to the cemetery (G 208). Virgil brings the Rose from the cemetery into the world and he uses it to fly to the far-off (but mystically near) planet of the Spiral Dancers. Later, he uses the esoteric knowledge he finds on that planet to free Eagle from Khallit and Mallit. Grimus, on the other hand, makes the Rose the instrument of his ego. In so doing, he reduces reality to a game and he reduces the lives of others to fictions, to entities which have no free will. He is "so far removed from the pains and torments of the world" that he sees death as "an academic exercise" (G 236). Grimus' detachment remains a degradation of Attar's notion that the universe – and everything within it – is irrelevant once one reaches mystical union with God: "If you should see the world consumed in flame, / It is a dream compared to [mystical union], a game; / If thousands were to die here, they would be / One drop of dew absorbed within the sea; ... If all the worlds were swept away to hell, / They'd be a crawling ant trapped in a well; / If earth and heaven were to pass away, / One grain of gravel would have gone astray; ... And if the nine revolving heavens stop, / Think that the sea has lost a single drop."[50] Grimus takes these analogies and does what is the death of all mysticism: he takes them literally. He takes a literary conceit and turns it into a personal, materialistic, egotistical conceit.

In order to appreciate the degree to which Grimus abases the Rose, one must first see the spiritual heights it represents. The Rose brings to mind Dante's Blessed Rose (which is a meeting-place of souls or human dimensions) and evokes the mystical symbology of Persian and Turkish poetry. The novel's bird and flower imagery – the Eagle and the Rose – work particularly well together in light of this Islamic poetry, in which the rose "reveals divine beauty and glory most perfectly" and the nightingale, "symbol of the longing soul, is once and forever bound to love it." Schimmel adds that "the numberless roses and nightingales in Persian and Turkish poetry take on, wittingly or unwittingly, this metaphysical connotation of soul-bird and divine rose."[51] One might argue that Eagle as nightingale destroys rather than adores the Rose. Yet he destroys the Cracked Rose, that is, the Rose as a ruined and coercive tool, not the Rose as an instrument of creation and mind-expansion. It is in destroying the Cracked Rose that Eagle restores the Rose's unlimited potential, just as it is in destroying Grimus's Calf that he restores Attar's Qaf.

Given Rushdie's use of Eliot's *Four Quartets*, the Stone Rose might also be seen in terms of the rose which takes on increasing importance towards the end of that poem. Eliot concludes by affirming that "All manner of thing shall be well / When the tongues of flames are in-folded / Into the crowned knot of fire / And the fire and the rose are one." In *Grimus* Eagle's passionate union with Media accompanies the destruction of the dysfunctional God-Object (the Cracked Rose) and replaces it with the fire of their deified union. Thus the Rose eventually becomes what it should be according to Eliot (and we might assume, according to Eliot's chief source, Dante): replete with sensuous and spiritual beauty.

In her insightful interpretation of *Grimus*, Uma Parameswaran notes that Borges's Aleph is "the object or abstraction through which one can control the Dimensions" and that his Zahir, "though literally a rose, is also 'the shadow of the rose and the rending of the veil.'" She adds that "Rushdie uses the Dance of the Veils in the final denouement; he combines the qualities of Aleph and Zahir in his rose: the Aleph gives a miraculous vision of the universe and the Zahir eclipses everything." Curiously, Borges's Aleph "is in the basement of a house, and the Rose is in a secret room; the narrator arranges various objects in the room as instructed and gets a vision. The Rose in *Grimus* is a set of stone slabs that can be arranged and aligned in different ways. Among the many things that the narrator sees in the Aleph are 'all the ants in the world' and a 'beach along the Caspian Sea'; Eagle, during his 700-year travel sees 'A beach on which a maiden had been staked out naked, as giant ants moved up her thighs,' (*G*. p. 32)." Finally, she observes that, like Rushdie, Borges uses Arabic and Persian allusions – in particular, he alludes to a Persian who "speaks of a bird which is somehow all birds."[52]

Rushdie's use of the Rose, the Simurg and Qaf demonstrate interest in a mystical God, one which is not definable or subject to manipulation. A deep and recurrent strain of his thinking is summed up in Virgil's following aphorism: "If there were no god, we should have to invent one [and] since there is a Grimus, he must be destroyed" (G 101). Rushdie is not attacking the notion of a mystical God who is forever beyond human conception; rather, he is suggesting that most people fail to understand or benefit philosophically from the notion of such a God. Instead, people create an anthropomorphic, finite or otherwise manipulable God. They then realize the limitations either of this God or of those who take advantage of "Him." They eventually feel they must destroy this imperfect conception.

SHIVA: CYCLES OF DEATH AND REBIRTH

The death of Grimus and the continuing journey of Eagle and Media in the closing pages of the novel open wide the doors of cosmological and narratological speculation. Prior to his confrontation with Grimus, Eagle states, "I must know that a way back exists: a way back to the place, world, dimension, whatever, that I came from" (*G* 192). Eventually, he abandons this goal of returning to his native setting, dimension or world. Instead, his "home" becomes the mountain of K, which is both the Mountain of Kaf and Mount Kailasa, the "home" of Shiva. Kinsley notes that Shiva has no real home as such, although his consort Parvati urges him to stay in one place. On one occasion Shiva .describes his house as the universe "and argues that an ascetic understands the whole world to be his dwelling place." Philosophical arguments such as this "never satisfy Parvati, but she rarely, if ever, wins this argument and gains a house."[53]

In his novel *The Serpent and the Rope*, Raja Rao suggests that Shiva exists in the mystical conjunction of personal and cosmic space: "The Himalaya was like Lord Shiva himself, distant, inscrutable, and yet very intimate there where you do not exist. He was like space made articulate, not before you but behind you, behind what is behind that which is behind one; it led you back through abrupt silences to the recesses of your own familiar but unrecognized self."[54] Rushdie also links his mystical mountain to an "unrecognized" part of the self: "Calf Mountain: as alien to [Eagle] as it was to the world he had known; and yet there was a similarity: a likeness of self and mountain" (G 45). Shaivite symbology is especially applicable to the Sufi meanings in the text when one remembers that Qaf and God are at once impossibly far away and yet closer than the jugular vein.

There are other good reasons for associating Calf Mountain with Kailasa and Eagle with Shiva. The phallic "bone of K" Eagle uses to defeat the devotee of Axona may be the ithyphallic power of Shiva, and thus the power of the god's Kailasa as well as of Kaf and Kaos. The destructive element is crucial, and is underscored when Virgil tells Eagle that his name comes from the Amerindian symbol of "the Destroyer" and when Grimus tells him that his "Ionic Pattern ... is the strongest destructive pattern" he has ever seen (G 46, 234). Shiva is likewise most closely identified with destruction: he is "the embodiment of *tamas*, the centrifugal inertia, the tendency toward dispersion, toward disintegration and annihilation."[55] Eagle's mountain of K is both the Sufi mountain of Kaf, which "brings an end to all rhyme" (G 133), and the mountain of Kailasa, where Shiva's intercourse with Parvati is so intense that it threatens the foundations of the universe.

Crucial to the theme of multidimensionality is the link between Media and the many forms into which Eagle as Shiva pours his creative spirit. Eagle makes love with various women – ultimately represented by the multi-faceted Media – just as Shiva makes love with various women, who are "media" in that they are the matter and energy Shiva uses in his cosmic constructions. Shiva is the principle of spirit or *purusha* and his consorts embody the principle of nature (*prakriti*) and the related principle of energy (*shakti*).[56] Rushdie suggests the notion of femininity representing the combination of these principles when Elfrida and Irina "become one, joined by the intercession of his love" and when their names become fused into "Elfrina, Irida" (G 171–2). Media gives final expression to this theme of fusion by uniting many versions, styles or media in one person, and by having this person fuse with Eagle in a final union which is at once Shiva's destruction and Attar's annihilation.

Before recreation can occur, Eagle and Media enter into a destructive mode, one which constitutes the novel's sexual, eschatological and textual climax: "Deprived of its connection with all relative Dimensions, the world of Calf Mountain was slowly unmaking itself, its molecules and atoms breaking, dissolving, quietly vanishing into primal, unmade energy. The raw material of being was claiming its own. So that, as Eagle and Media writhed upon their bed, the Mountain of Grimus danced the Weakdance to the end" (G 253). While Shiva is often seen as the god of death and destruction, he is also "the reproductive power, perpetually creating again that which he destroys."[57] Because he exists at the juncture of being and non-being, and because he is "the link between the impersonal-substratum (*brahman*) and the causal-divinity (*ishvara*),"[58] he can reproduce himself and other forms of existence from his own death. He is, in this sense, Born-from-Dead, which is the name given to Eagle at birth. Eagle's other name, Joe-Sue, might be seen as an allusion to Shiva-Shakti or the Ardhanarisvara form, which is "half male, half female," also symbolized by the union of the *lingam* and the *yoni*.[59] The identification of Eagle with Shiva also makes sense in that it allows for the destruction of the mountain and it puts Eagle in a position where he can also fulfill his destiny as the traveller who is everything and nothing, who is "his own leftover" as in the epigraph from Hughes. This description, when taken to the cosmic level, is an excellent description of the Hindu god.

Conflating the annihilations on Kaf and Kailasa works on the level of character, yet not so much on the level of cosmology, given that Islamic and Hindu universes are not really compatible. Islam does not envisage a universe which is continually destroyed and created: "The idea of continuous emanation in contrast to the unique divine act of creation was considered, by both Muslim and Christian mystics, to be incompatible with the Biblico-Koranic idea of a *creatio ex nihilo*."[60] I would argue, however, that *Grimus* is a novel very much concerned with incompatibilities – especially with the paradoxes and conundrums of multidimensionality. Rushdie clearly believes in "change-by-fusion, change-by-conjoining," and he argues against "the apostles of purity, those who have claimed to possess a total explanation" (*IH* 394). While in *Grimus* Rushdie uses Attar's Islamic symbology and the Hindu god Shiva, his point is really that there are more philosophies and cosmologies than any one mind can dream of. Thus he follows Attar's schema throughout most of *Grimus*, yet he emphasizes Shiva toward the end in order to suggest that Eagle's journey has other possible directions. It is important that he does not insist on Shiva, but rather suggests the possibilities implied by this god.

The figure of Shiva also reintroduces the struggle between order and chaos which came up when Koax opened up an unregulated field of dimensions. By associating Eagle with Shiva, Rushdie aligns his protagonist with what O'Flaherty sees as a dominating oscillation in Hindu cosmology: "the tension between variety and pattern" and "the resolution of chaos into order, and its dissolution back into chaos." Against the Apollonian process transforming chaos into order, "there flows another, Dionysian, current in Indian thought, which views the act of creation as the transformation of order into chaos."[61] Like Koax, Rushdie is interested in extending the arenas in which the ordering and disordering game can be played. Shiva's infinite destructions and creations raise the possibility that there will be no final ordering and that there will be an eternal struggle between the forces of chaos and order.

By destroying the Rose and by having sex with Media, Eagle enters a nebulous sea of dimensions. The structures and paradigms which partially defined him are no longer definitive and even the paradigm of Shiva must be left behind. While the circularity of Hindu cosmology seems appropriate to Eagle's fate, it also has an aspect of closure, for it can be seen as "a closed system, a 'world-egg' with a rigid shell, so that nothing is ever 'created' *ex nihilo*; rather, things are constantly re-arranged."[62] If universes are eternally rearranged, if they are continually created and destroyed, where is the possibility of cessation? Such a possibility must be admitted if one is to entertain all possibilities. To insist on the eternity of Eagle's quest would be to fix him in an ever-changing pattern, an eternal series of scenarios which themselves become a fixed concept, albeit a very fluid one. Perhaps this is why Rushdie keeps Eagle's future vague. Rushdie suggests Shiva because Shaivite cosmology appears to open more possibilities than the relatively linear cosmologies of Christianity and Islam. Yet to insist on this Hindu element would be to go against the main thrust of the novel, which is to float the self in a stream of other worlds and to suggest that the ship of the soul may sail beyond that river and out into the ocean.

While I think *Grimus* is a successful exploration of multidimensionality, critics – with the exceptions of Parameswaran and perhaps Johansen – remain by and large unsatisfied. Ib Johansen calls the novel a "strange blend of mythical or allegorical narrative, fantasy, science fiction, and Menippean satire." He stresses its "heterogeneity, its refusal to adhere to any *one* particular semiotic code, any *one* narratological scheme." He argues convincingly that Rushdie's "predilection for code switching" fits with Menippean satire, which is typified by "its lack of homogeneity and its ability to incorporate and assimilate to its own purposes a number of *other* genres." Quoting Northrop Frye, he notes that the purpose of Menippean satire is not psychological realism, for it "deals less with people as such than with mental attitudes."[63] I think this goes a long way in explaining why Eagle is not an engaging character. While Johansen appreciates the natureless nature of the protagonist, he is less enthusiastic about the overall design. He argues that because Eagle's quest lacks a final destination it therefore parodies the journey in Dante's *Divine Comedy* and degrades the Simurg and Qaf in Attar's *Conference*. Perhaps because he ignores the figure of Shiva, he concludes that Rushdie parodies Dante and that "there is no successful search for an ultimate or divine truth."[64] Catherine Cundy makes a similar point when she says that the "confusion of genres and philosophies in *Grimus* means that the truth sought by Flapping Eagle is never clear, never entirely spiritual in a Sufi sense."[65] Yet Eagle's identification with Shiva allows him to enter a realm in which mystical truth – which need not be *clear* – can be explored in an elastic infinity of potential dimensions. Indeed, the notion of *clarity* itself clashes with the modes and ideals of mysticism, according to which the seeker is to transcend fixed epistemological frameworks and fixed concepts of the soul, God, or the journey of the spirit. Johansen contends that because Eagle does not implement Grimus's Sufi scheme, Rushdie's use of Attar constitutes "a degraded or down-graded or *ironic* version of the myth of the Simurg and the mountain of Kaf."[66] Yet Rushdie's lack of insistence on Attar's transcendent otherworldly mountain works *for* rather than *against* his narrative design: if he were to fix the mountain into one pattern he would be doing what Virgil and Eagle accuse Grimus of doing, that is, he would be denying the divine mountain its status as infinite, transcendent and "Impossible." Instead of parodying and downgrading the quests of Dante and Attar, Rushdie conflates them with a never-ending cycle of death and rebirth, of eschatology and cosmogony, suggested by noninsistent allusions to Shiva's cosmic dance and lovemaking.

Parameswaran differs from other critics in that she appreciates both the way Rushdie mixes genres and the way his use of Shiva makes sense of the novel's cosmology. She says that *Grimus* "combines imaginative flights of science fiction, extravagance of fantasy, and clever twists of sexual humour," and she argues that the various levels of the novel "are ingeniously interconnected through what the Gorfs in the novel call 'Ordering.'" She points out that "the narrative is reinforced at every step with a network of allusions" and that the plot suggests "there could be a space-time continuum parallel to our own, concurrent and conspatial but separated by the limitation of our senses."[67] I would expand on this and say that the plot to destroy Grimus' esoteric tyranny centres on the notion that there are an infinite number of parallel space-time continua, all of which might exist conspatially just as Sufi, Dantean, Shaivite and Germanic cosmographies are conflated to form the mountainous topography along which Eagle journeys.

Parameswaran also acknowledges the importance of Rushdie's allusions to Shiva, that is, to the "Hindu myths which are relevant to two main references in the novel – Dance and Dissolution – that come together in the final scene." Referring to the creation of Calf, to Eagle's destruction of Calf, and to Eagle's subsequent construction of a pristine otherworldly mountain, she explains that the universe comes into being when Shiva bangs his drum, after which "he dissolves the universe back into formless energy. Then another cycle begins."[68] I would add that Rushdie also alludes to Shiva's intercourse with Parvati on Mount Kailasa. Just as Shiva's union with Parvati "is so intense that it shakes the cosmos, and the gods become frightened,"[69] so Eagle's "Weakdance" with Media destroys the foundations of Calf, thus ending the cosmic superstructure maintained by Grimus, the self-styled god.

Although the "climax" of *Grimus* suggests heaven and bliss, the narrator very early on suggests that Eagle is not a liberated or happy man: "Bird-Dog had always been a free spirit. I say this with some envy, for I never was, nor am" (*G* 17). Various interpretations present themselves, none of which is conclusive, and all of which may be based on according too much importance to this early comment. Nevertheless, one might say that Eagle attains a moment of perfection with Media, a moment which can hardly be matched by subsequent experience. Thinking in terms of the *Divine Comedy,* one might see Eagle's fate as a return from the light-filled realms of Heaven to the obscure forest of this world. Keeping in mind Attar's Qaf, one might note that Attar's pilgrim returns to the mundane world after his union and annihilation. Given the Hindu references in the text, one might conclude that Eagle remains on the wheel of death and rebirth, and that after his heavenly experience with Media he will proceed to a less exalted state of being. This fits with the references to Germanic myth as well, for the afterlife in Gimle is not nearly as exciting as the heroic battles and the eschatological chaos which precede it. Referring to existence after Ragnarok, Puhvel notes that as "with the postconflict *Mahabharata,* life has gone out of the story, for paradises, posthumous or postcataclysmic, are almost by definition dull places of marginal mythic interest ... Norse cosmology begins with fire and ice ..., culminates with a bang in fire and water and ends as divine epigones whimper about the days that are no more."[70]

The ending of *Grimus* also makes a poetic kind of sense if we see it in terms of the upcoming start of *Midnight's Children.* For after this heavenward, unifying climax we arrive in the first chapter of Rushdie's next novel at the beginning of a new cosmological cycle, one starting with the fall of a man called Aadam.

4 *Midnight's Children:* The Road from Kashmir

The cycle which includes our coming and going
Has no discernible beginning nor end;
Nobody has got this matter straight –
Where we come from and where we go to.

Omar Khayyam, *Ruba'iyat*[1]

Midnight's Children is well known as a novel that breaks new ground with its magical visions and revisions of twentieth-century India. Yet it is more than a sensational romp across Indian time and space: it also careens across diverse otherworldly terrain, hurling its readers from an Edenic Kashmiri past into cities teeming with mystics and many-headed monsters. It steers with the wobbliest of rudders through a vast green Wall of Time into a surreal afterlife, and then crisscrosses back through a battlefield of mythic heroes and demons into a present trembling with possible futures.

While *Grimus* is structured along the epic and mystic paths of Dante and Attar, *Midnight's Children* is structured on history and on a mythic cycle, starting with a fall from a symbolic Garden of Eden and ending with a possible return to this Garden. And while *Grimus* is a philosophical exploration of multiple otherworldly dimensions, *Midnight's Children* uses other worlds to a more worldly end. Through his solipsistic narrator, Rushdie asks the same question he asks in his 1987 Channel Four documentary *The Riddle of Midnight*: will India survive? Will it be ravaged by the religious forces it brags of, or will it foster a sort of unity *à la* Attar, a happy ending *à la* Scheherazade? Rushdie makes it clear on the first page that he doubts a positive outcome: the bliss of Kashmir appears to be, like the glory of the Moghuls, a dream of faraway and long ago. For a deep fear of disintegration and fragmentation lies behind Saleem's writing at breakneck speed: "I must work fast, faster than Scheherazade, if I am to end up meaning – yes, meaning – something. I admit it: above all things, I fear absurdity" (MC 9). The metafiction here is not a mere postmodern game. Rather, it derives from the great hope of a nation finding its way toward harmony and tolerance, and from the great fear of it collapsing into chaos.

Rushdie starts his rambling, rambunctious account with the fall of Aadam Aziz, a feisty forebear whose name derives from Hebrew myth and from English literature in its Forsterian passage to the East. Also hidden behind the story of Aadam's fall is the story of his father, old Aziz sahib, who dies in a state of mystical bliss in the Eden in Kashmir. It is here that Aadam Aziz rebels against God and tumbles into the violent and divided subcontinent – the Fallen World. The lives of Saleem's father Ahmed (with his djinns, anger and lust) and Saleem (with his incestuous and gutter loves) are strong indicators of lives lived in the fallen world, lives which in the traditional scheme of things would lead to damnation and Hell. And indeed, both characters do seem to live in hells of sorts: Ahmed is tortured by the demon Ravana and by corrosive guilt, and Saleem is possessed by his two-headed demon and later enters a heart of darkness, a magic Hell in the jungle of the Sundarbans. Yet Rushdie does not leave Ahmed and Saleem in despair: the former is saved by the love of Amina, the latter by Mary and Padma – all flawed types of divine Grace. Finally, the cycle hints at completion when the Muslim Saleem and the Hindu Padma plan their honeymoon in Kashmir with their adopted son, whose name is – not surprisingly – Aadam.

The above suggests a mythic cycle, yet the novel can also be seen as two parallel lines of family and national history. The genealogical line is closest to the mythic curve, for along it Rushdie charts a line of inheritance from old Aziz sahib's thirty species of birds, to Aadam Aziz's involvement with the Hummingbird and his Free Islam Convocation, to Amina's valiant stand against the demons of communalism, to Jamila's nightingale voice, to Saleem's chairmanship of the Midnight Children's Conference (in which position he takes the guise of Attar's bird-guide, the Hoopoe). The national line is also strong in terms of myth, for the outcome of Indian history is influenced by figures with strong mythical associations. On the positive side of this influence we have the following: the life-sustaining figure of Padma, who is also the goddess of Fortune, Sri Lakshmi; Saleem in the multicoloured plumage of the Hoopoe and the yogic swan; Mary and Amina, as redemptive figures of forgiveness and love; Durga, as the great mother goddess, the powerful Mahadevi; and finally the new Aadam with the awesome powers of the god Abraxas. On the negative side we have Schaapsteker the mad snake man, Ravana the demon of communalism, General Shiva the gang leader and murderer of whores, the *apsaras* with their sexy evil, and the Widow as Kali with her bloodthirsty lust and her castrations of hope and democracy.

Whether the forces of peaceful unity or violent division will win is not clear, for Rushdie stresses that the future is like the empty thirty-first pickle jar that Saleem can never fill with his spicy stories. Despite the echoes of Attar's thirty birds in Saleem's age (30) and in his thirty chapters, and despite the echoes of Scheherazade's release in his "thirty jars and a jar (*MC* 461)," Saleem and the reader are too close to the present to see how it all turns out. In this sense there can be no final reckoning with this novel. Its last chapters point to the future of the subcontinent, and there can be no final reckoning with *that*.

THE LOSS OF EDEN

Rushdie kicks off Saleem's journey in Kashmir, which has strong links to Eden in both the Western and the Eastern imagination. It is here, in the first pages of the novel, that the "world was anew again" and that after a "winter's gestation in its eggshell of ice, the valley had beaked its way out into the open." It is here that we are given a Koranic version of cosmogony in which God "created Man from clots of blood," and it is here that Aadam tries to "recall his childhood springs in Paradise" (*MC* 10–11). While Aadam's recollection and his subsequent revolt weave the first engaging narrative thread, Aadam is not the first character in terms of mythic and genealogical time. This honour goes to the marginal figure of Aadam's father, an Aadam as he might have been had he stayed in India and had he not eaten so heartily from the forbidden fruit of knowledge, which he finds ripe hanging from the branches of Heidelberg.

Aadam's father, the gem-dealer old Aziz sahib, exists in a prior state, in a mystical and prehistoric unity with the serene and Edenic spirit of the archetypal Vale. Rushdie the iconoclast cannot refrain from at least partly debasing with humour this ideal geographic setup: it is not an overdose of spiritual energy but rather a stroke that drops a veil over the great-grandfather's brain. This stroke turns out to be a stroke of good fortune, for it animates the old man's inner world with a recognizable variant of Attar's thirty birds: "in a wooden chair, in a darkened room, he sat and made bird-noises. Thirty different species of birds visited him and sat on the sill outside his shuttered window conversing about this and that. He seemed happy enough" (*MC* 12). Rushdie further evokes a humorous combination of senility and Sufi annihilation when the old man sits "lost in bird tweets," is "deprived of his birds," and dies "in his sleep" (*MC* 14, 28). One may be tempted to argue that Rushdie's parody makes Attar's mysticism seem naive and ridiculous, that old Aziz sahib is guilty of what Rushdie in an attack on Orwell calls living *inside* the whale when the real world *outside* should occupy one's attention (*IH* 93–95). Yet old Aziz sahib's vision is germinal, taking dynamic form in the conferences of Aadam and Saleem. It reaches an intensely political pitch in the hum of the Hummingbird and in the songs of Saleem's sister Jamila.

Rushdie makes the link between old Aziz sahib and Jamila explicit on two occasions: Saleem tells us that his great-grandfather's "gift of conversing with birds" descended "through meandering bloodlines into the veins" of Jamila (*MC* 107) and he tells us that his sister "talked to birds (just as, long ago in a mountain valley, her great-grandfather used to do)" (*MC* 293). Saleem emphasizes the poetic and mystical associations of the *ghazals* she sings, and underscores the mix of divine and human love which characterizes this Persian and Urdu poetic form: "I listened to her faultless voice ... filled with the purity of wings and the pain of exile and the flying of eagles and the lovelessness of life and the melody of bulbuls and the glorious omnipresence of God" (*MC* 293–4). As I will make clear at the end of "Taking Wing" below, the greater the power of Jamila's mystical songs, the greater Rushdie's satire of the political machine that turns these songs into military propaganda.

Old Aziz sahib's conference is transmitted from generation to generation, beginning with the feisty Aadam Aziz. Aadam's surname links him to Forster's Indian protagonist in *A Passage to India*, who was last seen in a remote princely state (in the Merchant-Ivory film he reaches his beloved Kashmir). Forster's Aziz is also a doctor whose Western education alienates him from his Muslim roots. In this context, Rushdie's Aziz is much more alienated than Forster's, which makes sense in that the latter is personally betrayed by the English. While Aadam Aziz is strongly affected by the brutality at Amritsar, he is also frustrated by the stubborn piety of his wife and enraged at the ongoing religious indoctrination and communalism that is tearing his country apart. In many ways he longs, like Mirza in the *Verses* and Rai in *Ground*, for the secularism of the West.

Aadam's given name is even more significant, for it signals the first man of Middle Eastern fame. While Rushdie's Aadam has no Eve as such, he is seduced into marriage by visions of Naseem behind the perforated sheet, he does have his run-in with God, and he is chased by the Old Testament anger of Tai from the paradise of Kashmir. His fall, seen in terms of a "failure to believe or disbelieve in God" (*MC* 275), also derives from the traditional source: the forbidden pursuit of knowledge. Rushdie situates this source not only in the godless West so joked about in many of his novels, but also specifically in German lands, those of the great architects of uncertainty and revolt – Marx, Freud, Nietzsche, Einstein, and so forth. While Aadam's German friends mock "his prayer with their anti-ideologies," he does not capitulate to their Orientalism, in which India "had been discovered by the Europeans." Saleem comments that "what finally separated Aadam Aziz from his friends" was their belief "that he was somehow the invention of their ancestors" (MC 11).

Although I am concentrating on the otherworldly aspects of *Midnight's Children*, there remains much to be said about the novel's postcolonial strategy, part of which consists of marginalizing Europe from Saleem's account of Indian history, and of taking the occasional dig at Europe and its pretence of dispensing knowledge and light to the rest of the world. Apart from the raging Zagallo, whose Peruvian ancestry is dubious (MC 230), Methwold is the only representative of European imperialism we see in any detail, although what we see of him is ambiguous. What, for instance, is the meaning of his final, toupee-lifting wave? Goonetilleke writes, "When the sun finally set on Methwold's Estate, Methwold's head of hair with its centre-parting which had been a focus of attention, contributing to his impressiveness and being irresistible to women, is shown to be a hair piece, revealing him in a less attractive light and suggesting deception, the difference between the professions and practice of Empire."[2] Another of the very few Western characters, Schaapsteker, plays an ambiguous and largely occult role. He remains a peripheral figure, one who is assigned to an attic, yet he remains instrumental in Saleem's "diabolic" plan to bring down Lila Sabarmati. Like the German friends of Aadam Aziz, Schaapsteker remains a source of snaky Western knowledge.

Aadam's fall is expressed in general religious terms as well as in specific Islamic terms: his decision not to perform his morning prayers echoes what Milton calls "Man's First Disobedience," while his refusal to "kiss earth for any god or man" (MC 10) echoes Iblis's refusal to bow before Aadam, God's first human creation. At one point in the cosmic career of Iblis he is in the highest heaven and closer to God than any other angel. He resents God's interest in man, however, and he feels that his birth from fire makes him superior to this new creature made of clay. Iblis therefore refuses to bow before anyone but God. While Rushdie has a great deal of sympathy for Aadam, his secular hero, he also suggests that in refusing to bow, in revolting against God and Islam, Aadam loses something very precious. For when Aadam resolves never to "kiss earth for any god or man," rubies and diamonds drop miraculously from his nose and eyes (*MC* 10). Moreover, his rejection has the same consequence as that suffered by Iblis: a protracted, losing battle against God.

Aadam also loses his battle against religious extremists in Agra. The Free Islam Convocation which he supports against the Muslim League is not an entirely fictional concoction, as Parameswaran explains: "While the Muslim League was firmly established and intent upon the creation of Pakistan, Sheikh Abdullah, a Kashmir Muslim, founded the Muslim National Conference, which leaned towards Gandhi's undivided India and against the Muslim League. Sheikh Abdullah lived long after Independence, but Rushdie's Mian Abdullah [the "Hummingbird"], founder of Free Islam Convocation, is killed by six assassins, 'six crescent knives held by men dressed all in black,' but before he dies there is a supernatural aura given to him."[3] In *Shame* the death of the anticommunalist crusader Mahmoud is also accompanied by the supernatural, by "a sound like the beating wings of an angel" (*s* 62). The Hummingbird's fate is thus shared by the cinema owner who attempts the impossible task of uniting Hindus and Muslims in a double bill. Like Rushdie's other tolerant mystical figures – from Lifafa Das to Sufyan – the Hummingbird and Mahmoud are persecuted by those who want division rather than unity, by those who want strict definitions of culture rather than hybridity.

Curiously, the name of Sheik Abdullah's group was originally *Conference*, as in Attar, whereas Rushdie modifies it to *Convocation*, returning to *Conference* only with Saleem's Midnight Children's Conference. This may put some readers off the Attar trail, yet given the mention of old Aziz sahib's thirty species of birds, and given Saleem's yearning for unity and his fear of annihilation, it is not hard to see through this shift in names.

While the Free Islam Convocation may be based on reality, Rushdie associates it with all sorts of fanciful and literary elements, the most striking of which is a silver lapis-lazuli inlaid spittoon. This spittoon is linked to the common people (as opposed to the politicians), to the liberal joviality of the Hummingbird's group, and to the love between Nadir and Amina. In a lecture/interview Rushdie suggests that the silver and lapis-lazuli spittoon is one of the leitmotifs which helps hold his otherwise unwieldy novel together. He says that, along with the game of snakes and ladders and the pointing finger, the spittoon is one of the things "which in themselves have no meaning or no particular meaning but which form a kind of non-rational network of connections in the book."[4] Rushdie may be underselling himself here, for the game of snakes and ladders makes sense in light of Schaapsteker's snaky logic and Saleem's doomed attempt to ride the snake of evil to moral triumph. Likewise, the silver spittoon serves as a symbol, al-

most an objective correlative, of the ideal of peaceful coexistence.
Rushdie foreshadows its appearance when the betel-chewing old men
in Agra suspect that Aadam is being too optimistic about the future of
the country: "they had begun to talk about omens; calming themselves with their game of hit-the-spittoon, they speculated upon the
numberless nameless Godknowswhats that might now issue from the
fissuring earth" (MC 39). Through the fate of the humble, common
spittoon Rushdie indicts both the British and any of their Indian allies
for the coming plight of partitioned India: the army staff car with
Brigadier Dodson and Major Zulfikar inside it scatters the street ur-
chins and "knocks over the spittoon. A dark red fluid with clots in it
like blood congeals like a red hand in the dust of the street and points
accusingly at the retreating power of the Raj" (MC 44).

The "superb silver spittoon, inlaid with lapis lazuli" which Saleem
eventually inherits initially belongs to the Rani of Cooch Naheen, the
financial backer of the Free Islam Convocation. In sharing her spittoon, she desires to embellish the free speech and bonhomie that her
fellow members of the Convocation enjoy together: "Let the walls be
splashed with our inaccurate expectorating! They will be honest
stains, at least" (MC 45). Yet the Rani is right in ways she does not
mean, for the Convocation is "inaccurate" or out of step with the reality of political power, especially as this works through the separatist
aims of the Muslim League, the chief opponents of the Hummingbird
and the second conference which he plans to hold in Agra. The Rani's
full name, which translates as "the Queen of Some Nothing" is relevant here, since she dreams of and gives money (and a silver spittoon) to something that can never be: a good-hearted unity, an open
and loving conference between Hindus and Muslims. It is no surprise
therefore that the silver spittoon pops up again and again in the
novel, accompanying and comforting Saleem on his long and ardu-
ous journey through Indian history. It crops up most poignantly immediately after the defeat of the Convocation: we find it in the
basement of Aadam's house, a symbol of the Convocation's ideals
that are brushed under the carpet, and of the unconsummated love
between Amina and Nadir Khan.

It is of course Aadam who risks his life by backing the Free Islam
Conference and by harbouring the fugitive Nadir in his basement
(against the strong objections of his increasingly zealous wife). Aadam
is perhaps Rushdie's most feisty example of the secularist who is will-
ing to fight for his beliefs – or non beliefs. Intolerant of intolerance,
Aadam literally throws from his home the tutor who teaches his children "to hate Hindus and Buddhists and Jains and Sikhs and who
knows what other vegetarians" (MC 42–3). His antagonism to the

communalism which lies at the heart of India's major internal division reaches an extreme of its own when in "the iconoclasm of his dotage" he lashes out "at any worshipper or holy man within range" (MC 277). His final act is to steal the sacred lock of Muhammad's hair from the Hazratbal Mosque and bring it into the Hindu temple of Shankara Acharya (MC 277–8). This act can be seen as a desperate, symbolic attempt to bring Hinduism and Islam together under one roof, especially when one recalls that the temple of Shankara Acharya has both Muslim and Hindu history associated with it. In passing, one might note that this incident anticipates the communal conflict at Ayodhya (where Hindus won the Pyrrhic victory of tearing down a mosque to put up a temple) as well as Rushdie's denouncement of that conflict in the *Moor*.

The mythic cycle in *Midnight's Children* is depicted mostly in terms of patrilineage, yet Saleem's mother Amina also plays a major role. Just as Aadam fights Muslim separatism by supporting the Free Islam Convocation in Agra, so Amina stands up to Muslim zealots by defending the rights of a Hindu, Lifafa Das, who has the blind courage (or simply bad luck) to ply his trade in a Muslim part of town. Rushdie makes the link between father and daughter explicit: at the moment she turns against her neighbours in order to protect the harmless Hindu itinerant, "something hardened inside her, some realization that she was her father's daughter" (MC 77). Amina's refusal to demonize those who are culturally and religiously alien to her surfaces when, following Lifafa into the old city, she confronts her fear of the Others (Hindus, magicians, the poor) who live on "the wrong side of the General Post Office." These Others initially seem to comprise "some terrible monster, a creature with heads and heads and heads," yet Amina does not succumb to her fearful, demonizing imagination. Instead, she realizes that it is her fear that makes her see these people as monsters: "'I'm frightened,' my mother finds herself thinking" (MC 81). She learns very quickly to discard the "city eyes" which are blind to poverty, and to see that the powerless masses have little to do with the type of evil communalist monster that terrorizes her husband and threatened to kill Lifafa Das.

Rushdie skillfully contrives it so that the violent and fiery spirit of communalism is depicted in Lifafa's newspaper photo of "a fire at the industrial estate" (MC 76), that is, it is depicted within the very peepshow microcosm which remains antithetical to this intolerance. The fire is the work of the extortionist gang, Ravana, named after the most infamous of the Hindu demons or *rakshasas*. The "ten-headed Ravana, who ruled over Lanka and was the enemy of Rama, is the most celebrated king of the *rakshasas*," who "take any form they like," who "are children of darkness who wander at night" and whose "rule is unchallenged until midnight."[5] Saleem's Midnight Children are born *after* midnight and have little in common with the *rakshasa* demons except that they have special powers and some of them can change their forms. The darkness associated with the pre-midnight reign of the *rakshasas* seems concentrated in Shiva, who is born closest to midnight.

Lifafa's picture of the fire and Saleem's fabulous cloud in the shape of a pointing finger both serve to link the Muslim mob that threatens Lifafa in Amina's *muhalla* or neighborhood to the Ravana gang that sets fire to Ahmed's warehouse. The cloud forms as a result of the Ravana gang's burning of a Muslim industrial estate, and it hovers over Ahmed in the Red Fort. Floating "in the background of [his] own story," Saleem follows this cloud to the old city, where "the insanity of the cloud like a pointing finger and the whole disjointed unreality of the times seizes the muhalla" (*MC* 74, 76).

Given that Saleem titles his chapter "Many-headed Monsters," and that this chapter deals with the rages of the Hindu gang and the Muslim lynch mob, Rushdie may be implying that the mob is merely a less organized version of the gang. The tight intertwining of scenarios, the constant shifting from Amina's journey to Ahmed's Red Fort nightmare, underscores this parallel. Rushdie also makes another important point: members of both religions betray their own ideals by exploiting religious prejudice. In the Hindu epic *Ramayana* the monkey king Hanuman helps the hero Rama defeat the demon Ravana, who has abducted Sita, Rama's wife. By subjecting Muslims to extortion, Hindus create a twisted, nightmarish version of Hindu mythology, one in which the heroic monkey king Hanuman takes the form of mad monkeys who exacerbate rather than reverse the harm caused by the Ravana gang. Rushdie makes sure not to place all the blame on Hindus, however: the Muslims who persecute the defenceless Lifafa Das prove themselves to be anything but valiant soldiers for Allah. Amina shames her neighbours by crying out, "What heroes! Heroes, I swear, absolutely! Only fifty of you against this terrible monster of a fellow! Allah, you make my eyes shine with pride!" (*MC* 77). Instead of living up to their ideals of tolerance and heroism, Rushdie's Hindus and Muslims create a demon which, like Frankenstein's monster, turns upon those who are responsible for its creation.

Rushdie is fond of this type of dynamic in which worldly intolerance and coercion create a violent and scourging otherworldly force. He employs a variant of the many-headed monsters in the last book in *Midnight's Children*, where Saleem and his three comrades are punished by Hinduized figures after they scourge the land in the name of Allah. Also, in *Shame*, Raza is hounded by a Hinduized Satan after inflicting his version of Islamic Law on Pakistan.

Amina's stand against the demon of communalism provides a link between the generations of Aadam and Saleem, and between the historical locations of Kashmir and Agra (the mythic and Moghul past) and the contemporary location of Bombay. In between lies the Partition generation, those who were adults during the hideous massacres – represented succinctly by the phrase, "thousands killed in four days of screaming" – and by the single figure of the white beggar who thinks of her husband walking through the slaughter of nighttime Calcutta "with blood on his shirt, a white man deranged by the coming futility of his kind" (*MC* 82). Also, in between lies Delhi, the new nation's capital, which is also the home to the bright hopes of Nehru and the dark acts of Ravana and the lynch mob.

In terms of the mythic cycle which starts in Kashmir, Amina inherits Aadam's struggle against the violent, fractious forces in the fallen world while Ahmed inherits Aadam's rebellion against God and Islamic tradition. Ahmed compounds Aadam's refusal to follow Islamic tradition when he indulges in drinking alcohol, which Rushdie very appropriately refers to as the fiery spirits or "djinns" in his gin bottles. Djinns have a strong association with Iblis – who, as Al-Jahn, is father of the djinns – and in this sense Ahmed's worship of gin or "the djinns" reverberates with Aadam's refusal to worship. Djinns are also lustful, as can be seen from Ahmed's lechery: he makes sexual advances at his secretaries. His lasciviousness prefigures Saleem's search for impurity in Karachi, a search which leads him to the ancient crone Tai Bibi and to the realization that he is sexually attracted to his sister. Ahmed's possession by a fiery, djinn-like anger also has a devastating effect on the all-important mystical "Conference" in Saleem's head. When Saleem tells his father about the miraculous voices, Ahmed is contorted with a "wild anger," and he strikes a "mighty blow" that sends Saleem into "a green, glass-cloudy world filled with cutting edges," a "swirling universe in which [he] was doomed, until it was far too late, to be plagued by constant doubts about what [he] was *for*" (*MC* 165). Ahmed's violence exacerbates Saleem's fear of meaninglessness, and it turns Saleem's potentially coherent Conference into a confusing babble.

Ahmed's fallen nature can also be seen in his "dream" of rearranging the Koran (*MC* 82, 133). This dream is not shared by Muslims in general, many of whom "believe that the ordering of the chapters and verses was itself divinely inspired."[6] Ahmed's dream sets a precedent for Saleem, who claims to be "the first and only member of [his] family to flout the laws of halal" (*MC* 59). By "the laws of halal" Saleem means not so much the type of laws Gibreel breaks in the *Verses* when he gorges himself on pig meat (*SV* 30) as the treatment or "digestion" of forbidden topics. Among such topics is the notion that prophets in the days of Muhammad should not be considered "false simply because they are overtaken, and swallowed up, by history" (*MC* 305). Rushdie is treading on sacred ground here  – ground he stomps with much heavier boots in the *Verses*. He writes, however, with playful hyperbole when his Saleem claims that "future exegetes" will "inevitably come to this present work, this source-book, this Hadith or Purana or *Grundrisse*, for guidance and inspiration" (*MC* 295). By juxtaposing Karl Marx's materialist *Grundrisse* (his early groundplan of Marxism)[7] with the Hadith (sanctified religious accounts of Muhammad's life) and the Puranas (post-Vedic stories of the gods) Rushdie hints at Saleem's irreverent, comic mix of materialist and spiritual viewpoints.

Ahmed occupies the most debased position in family history and at the same time signals a turning point in the mythic cycle which starts with old Aziz sahib's annihilation. Interestingly, Amina plays a dual role here, for she carries on Aadam's battle against communalism and redeems her degenerate husband. Redirecting her illicit love from Nadir Khan to Ahmed (both men represent low points or *nadirs* in the prospects of Indian Muslims),[8] Amina replaces the anger of Ahmed's djinns with the laughter of her love: "under Amina's care, he returned not to the self which had practiced curses and wrestled djinns, but to the self he might always have been, filled with contrition and forgiveness and laughter and generosity and the finest miracle of all, which was love" (*MC* 297). Ahmed's redemption through love brings to mind the Sufi paradigm in which even the most frightening of djinns, Iblis, can be redeemed by the power of love. One might also say that Saleem's succour is anticipated by Ahmed's, in that Saleem falls into demonic and depraved states (he is possessed by his own two-headed demon and he dives into the gutters of Karachi) yet he eventually receives a redeeming (or at least regenerative) measure of love from Parvati, Padma and Mary.

Saleem of course occupies the prominent position in the mythic cycle. His Midnight Children's Conference is a curious version of Attar's Conference, for it merges magic with mysticism and it adds a pessimistic twist to Attar's notion of annihilation. The 1001 magical children come together in the Lok Sabha or Lower House of Saleem's mind only to squabble, and a diminished number of them (corresponding to the thirty who make it to Qaf) come together in the

Widow's Hostel only to be *sperectomized*, that is, only to have their hope and vitality drained from them. It is tempting to apply to *Midnight's Children* the moral Rushdie avows in *Ground*, that the real goal of myth is for it to die. His Rushdie-like narrator Rai argues that the real enlightenment of a civilization lies in its abandoning otherworldly ideas, in arriving at a place in time when the gods "move back, still leering, still priapic, still whimsical, from the realm of the actual to the land of so to speak – Olympus, Valhalla – leaving us free to do our best or worst without their autocratic meddling" (*GB* 575). This makes some sense in *Ground*, where the gods do retire, where the Cerebus so boldly emblazoned on the dustcover becomes a stray mutt. This is hardly the case in *Midnight's Children*, however, where the forces which work for and against the otherworldly ideal of conference maintain their momentum until the end of the novel, until the final clashes which I will look at in a later section of this chapter, "Battle of the Gods." Moreover, Saleem passes his preoccupation with Conference onto his son, who heralds at once a renewed sense of national identity and an awesome return of both magic and myth.

Aadam Sinai's regenerative power derives from the fact that he is the son of Shiva, from his status as "the new Aadam," and from his identification with the god Abraxas. The first word the new Aadam utters is not "abba" (father), but "cadabba," which makes Saleem think of abracadabra, the "cabbalistic formula derived from the name of the supreme god of the Basilidan gnostics, containing the number 365, the number of the days of the year, and of the heavens, and of the spirits emanating from the god Abraxas" (*MC* 459). Saleem suggests that the new Aadam inherits the urge to control the shifting tides of history, to encapsulate the world around him. Rushdie again mixes magic and myth, for abracadabra may signal a powerful Gnostic god, yet it also has strong popular links to magic and such phrases as "open sesame."

It is equally important that Aadam's powers are linked to Saleem's chances of survival, of finding his way back to Kashmir. After Padma proposes marriage, the "moths of excitement" stir in Saleem's stomach, and her words take on a magical power, "as if she had spoken some cabbalistic formula, some awesome abracadabra, and released [him] from [his] fate" (*MC* 444).

The new Aadam suggests the end of one cycle and the beginning of another. Convinced of his own "approaching demise," a worn-out Saleem sees post-Emergency India (symbolized by the new MCC, the Midnight-Confidential Club) as a dark "nightmare pit in which light was kept in shackles and bar-fetters." In this darkness Aadam's ears burn "with fascination; his eyes shone in the darkness as he listened, and memorized, and learned ... and then there was light" (MC 446, 454). In emphasizing this cosmogonic reference I do not mean to ignore Aadam Sinai's potential selfishness or his potential to fall; he is after all the son of the egocentric Shiva as well as the great-grandson of the Aadam Aziz who refused to bow to god or man. My point is that Rushdie suggests a movement from the darkness of non-existence (Saleem's death) to the light of existence (his son's life), and that this light is associated with a state of grace (like that of old Aziz sahib). This state of grace also carries with it the possibility of falling from grace (as does Aadam Aziz). If or when the new Aadam trips, his fall will be a hard one, for in identifying himself with the powerful Gnostic god Abraxas he expresses an even more exaggerated form of Saleem's "inflated macrocosmic activity" (MC 435).

Goonetilleke observes that the new Aadam's mix of working and middle class parentage "is desirable, and necessary, for India's welfare and progress," and that Aadam's surname *Sinai* has optimistic implications: "Moses saw the Promised Land from Mount *Sinai*, but Moses was told that *he* would never enter the Promised Land himself – only show the way. Saleem Sinai shows the way he himself cannot go – but his successor *may*." Goonetilleke implicitly links this Promised Land with Kashmir, a completion of the novel's "cycle," and a more positive ending than Rushdie and critics have in general given to the novel: "while on his way to Kashmir for a holiday with his newly wedded wife (the novel began in Kashmir and has now come full circle), Saleem disintegrates, not reaching his destination, literally and metaphorically, like the generation he represents. But the festive feeling of the atmosphere at this point in the narrative and his disintegration like a firework suggest a kind of apotheosis, something positive gained from the journey."[9] It may be that Goonetilleke is at once overly optimistic and pessimistic when he says that Saleem marries and disintegrates (these remain possibilities only), yet the note of optimism is worth emphasizing, for it responds to the optimism Rushdie builds into the novel at every stage. This optimism is conspicuous not so much because it is battered and beaten, but because it keeps resurfacing.

Having now finished my discussion of the mythic cycle in the novel, I must add that I am not really finished with it at all. For while I now move on to the dynamic between Schaapsteker the snake man and Padma the lotus goddess, it must still be kept in mind that Saleem's apprenticeship under Schaapsteker is a mini-fall as well as a product of the fallen, deceptive world into which he is born. And of course the optimism within the novel's mythic cycle relies in many ways on mythicized figures such as Padma, Durga, and Mary, who, together with Picture Singh, Saleem, and the new Aadam, constitute a sort of interreligious pantheon or conference which goes some way in countering the divisive violence of General Shiva and the Widow.

THE SNAKE MAN AND THE LOTUS GODDESS

In his long and at times frightening journey toward annihilation – be it peaceful or violent, enlightening or extinguishing – Saleem confronts a great number of dark and divisive forces. And as we found with Eagle in *Grimus*, some of the trickiest forces lie within him, in the underworld of the soul. In *Grimus* the trusty Virgil (Dante's guide, the Sufi's sheik, the Hindu's guru) helps both to unleash and to control the demons within the hero. Yet Saleem is not nearly so lucky. Instead, he falls prey to the anger of his father (who for all his liberality cannot appreciate the new angelic dimensions that open up inside his son) and to the necromantic powers of the snake man, Dr. Schaapsteker.

A "sibilant old man" who thinks of himself as "another father" to Saleem, Dr. Schaapsteker believes the "superstitions of the Institute orderlies, according to whom he was the last of a line which began when a king cobra mated with a woman" (*MC* 257–8). Saleem calls him "a mad-old man" and says that "the ancient insanities of India had pickled his brains," but Schaapsteker is no more a satiric caricature than the senile but mystically enlightened old Aziz sahib: the professor's occult medicine saves Saleem from typhoid, and the two-headed demon he conjures within Saleem is all too effective in exacting the revenge Saleem desires. Yet what Saleem desires serves only to ignite in him a self-destructive puritanical frenzy, which is at odds with his ideals of political and personal tolerance. Saleem's involvement with the snake-man thus reinforces, eventually, the traditional morality – the "twoness of things," the distinction between good and evil – that during his possession he attempts to subvert. Saleem's use of Schaapsteker's snaky logic also threatens indirectly his very existence, that is, his life with Padma in Mary's pickle factory.

Seduced by the logic of the snake-man, Saleem adopts a reasoning reminiscent of the serpent in the Garden of Eden: he challenges "the unchanging twoness of things, the duality of up against down, good against evil." He argues that the game of snakes and ladders lacks "one crucial dimension," that of the ambiguity which makes it "possible to slither down a ladder and climb to triumph on the venom of a snake" (*MC* 141). Saleem changes the rules of snakes and ladders to a point where he can no longer distinguish between good and evil, and this has disastrous consequences when he acts on the belief that he can use evil means for good ends. Lashing out at the adulteress Lila Sabarmati (and indirectly at his mother, who is having a rather chaste affair with Nadir Khan), he combines puritanism with violence. In so doing, he becomes more vicious than the woman who is the object of his vituperative frenzy: " 'Loose woman,' the demon within me whispered silently, 'Perpetrator of the worst of maternal perfidies! We shall turn you into an awful example; through you we shall demonstrate the fate which awaits the lascivious'" (*MC* 258). In a similar manner, Dawood in *Shame* and the Imam in the *Verses* combine religious zeal with diabolic violence. Yet unlike Dawood or the Imam Saleem eventually sees that his puritanical violence hurts himself as well as those he loves.

Saleem's *falling in* with the demonic snake leads indirectly to the death of his uncle Hanif, through the following convoluted, serpentine chain of events: Schaapsteker encourages Saleem to strike from cover (*MC* 258), which Saleem does by sending an anonymous letter (composed of newspaper clippings) to Commander Sabarmati, informing him of his wife's affair with Homi Catrack (*MC* 260); Sabarmati's consequent murder of Catrack deprives Hanif (whose wife was previously having an affair with Catrack) of his income (which Catrack gives him because he feels guilty for cheating with his wife); Hanif then kills himself by walking off his roof (*MC* 271). The death of Hanif is significant, not only because it underscores the traditional moral that the wages of sin are death, but also because Hanif's struggle to create a realistic "pickle epic" mirrors – in brilliant metafictional fashion – Saleem's own struggle to find meaning in Mary's pickle factory.

Remembering he is Aadam Aziz's son, Hanif fights "against everything which smacked of the unreal" and rails "against princes and demons, against gods and heroes, against, in fact, the entire iconography of the Bombay film." It is not coincidental that the realist "pickle epic" Hanif writes for the Bombay screen is the story of a pickle factory almost exactly like Mary's. In this case there is something very special about Mary indeed. For by indirectly destroying "the high priest of reality" who "espouse[s] the cause of truth and put[s] illusion to flight" Saleem unwittingly aligns himself with Homi Catrack, who does not take Hanif's "pickle epic" seriously (he is probably quite right that it would not be a box-office hit) (*MC* 243–4, 271). The snaky thread which connects Schaapsteker to Hanif is significant not only because it suggests that Saleem's involvement with evil leads to puritanical violence and death, but also because it suggests that this involvement leads to the death of the one man who insists on realism, and, in particular, the realism of Saleem's pickle factory scenario. Rushdie plays a convoluted game here, for Saleem almost destroys the theoretical ground on which he might stand, walk, marry Padma and lead a normal life.

Schaapsteker and Padma are antithetical both in their mythological associations and in the effect they have on Saleem's "existence" in the Bombay pickle factory. According to Saleem, Padma is named after the "Lotus Goddess" who "Possesses Dung" and who "grew out of Vishnu's navel." She is "the Source, the mother of Time" (MC 194–5). Parameswaran quite rightly calls Padma "the archetypal Earth-Mother put through the Rushdie anti-romance wringer."[10] Yet the critic takes exception to Rushdie's association of dung with the goddess: she says that dung has only "one meaning and that very definitely has nothing to do with the lotus or the goddess Lakshmi, one of whose names is Padma." She also notes that Saleem calls Padma a dung lotus "after a colloquial interpolation of a word that has beautiful connotations in Sanskrit," adding that "Rushdie is iconoclastic of both Hindu and Muslim beliefs."[11] While Rushdie may distort the attributes of the goddess, Padma's personality does not distort that of her namesake in the same drastic way that General Shiva's brutish and lascivious personality distorts the attributes of his namesake. Moreover, Saleem's momentary loss of Padma, resulting from his failure to perform as a lover and "to consider her feelings" (MC 121), echoes an episode in which Lakshmi disappears "from the three worlds" after Indra insults her: "In the absence of the goddess the worlds become dull and lustreless and begin to wither away. When she returns, the worlds again regain their vitality, and the society of humans and the order of the gods regain their sense of purpose and duty."[12] In the novel, Padma's absence makes Saleem confused and "afraid of being disbelieved." Without her, Saleem is reduced to statements such as, "if it hadn't happened it wouldn't have been credible," or, "Padma would believe it; Padma would know what I mean!" (MC 167, 140, 158). As in Hindu myth, Padma's return reinstates order, reestablishing the base from which Saleem can launch into his literary and philosophical flights: "once again Padma sits at my feet, urging me on. I am balanced once more – the base of my isosceles triangle is secure. I hover at the apex, above present and past, and feel fluency returning to my pen" (MC 194). While Padma does not succeed in reinvigorating Saleem's penis, she restores the power of his pen.

Padma's link to the Hindu goddess also crops up when, in her attempt to cure Saleem's impotence, she throws his "innards into that state of 'churning' from which, as all students of Hindu cosmology will know, Indra created matter, by stirring the primal soup in his own great milk-churn" (MC 193). Saleem refers here to myths in which "creation proceeds from an infinite body of primordial water"

and in which "the milk ocean when churned yields valuable es-
sences, among them, in most later versions of the myth, the goddess
Shri-Lakshmi."[13] Despite the fact that Saleem occasionally mocks
Padma's elevated mythic associations, Padma remains a "valuable
essence" to Saleem. Without her, he would topple into the mire of his
own incredulity or lose himself in his own tangents, circles and base-
less story lines. Padma at once feeds his imagination and supplies
him with a centripetal force which counteracts the centrifugal flights
of his imagination. Rushdie once observed that oral narrative in India
"frequently digresses off into something that the story-teller appears
just to have thought of, then it comes back to the main thrust of the
narrative."[14] With her "ineluctable Padma-pressures of what-hap-
pened-nextism," Padma forces Saleem back to the main thrust of his
story. This is comically evident when Saleem reads to Padma his rambling list of the many aspects of the feminine Divine, a list which
could easily include Padma's namesake. After reading the list,
Saleem receives the following rejoinder from his lotus goddess: " 'I
don't know about that,' Padma brings me down to earth, 'They are
just women, that's all' " (*MC* 39, 406).

In general, critics underestimate Padma's otherworldly qualities as
well as her insistence on taking other worlds seriously. I would argue
that she is perhaps Rushdie's finest – albeit comic – example of
Hindu belief, and that she rivals the curious figure of Srinivas in the
Verses. Indeed, in Padma Rushdie approaches R.K. Narayan's wonderful comic Hindu characters. I would also suggest that Padma puts
into practice what Rushdie preaches when he says that one ought to
"develop a form which doesn't prejudge whether your characters are
right or wrong," "a form in which the idea of the miraculous can coexist with observable, everyday reality."[15]

Timothy Brennan on the other hand sees Padma "as an image of
the Indian masses' gullibility."[16] I think this view undervalues the
"Indian masses" as well as Padma, who is a lively, provocative character, one who both brings Saleem down to earth and urges skeptical
readers to ponder other frameworks of reality. One could argue that
Rushdie makes fun of Padma and that therefore she cannot constitute
a serious audience, let alone a challenge to skepticism. Yet one would
have to ask, what character, including Saleem himself, remains un-
scathed in the novel? I would argue that Rushdie does his best to
make Padma, as much as any character, a realistic presence. More im-
portantly, by not dismissing Padma, readers may more readily contemplate the ramifications of seeing the world with her eyes. They
may entertain the significance of feelings and thoughts which allow
scope for such things as astrology, ghosts or telepathy. Such is the

case when, after claiming that Naseem could dream her daughters' dreams, Saleem watches Padma for her response: "Padma accepts this without blinking; but what others will swallow as effortlessly as a laddoo, Padma may just as easily reject. No audience is without its idiosyncrasies of belief" (*MC* 55). Rushdie here challenges his readers, for all of us have our "idiosyncrasies of belief." In addition, one ought to note that Padma's beliefs are not farfetched in the light of Hindu myths in which people can dream other people's dreams and in which a god can be "the place where we all meet in our dreams, the infinity where our parallel lives converge."[17] Padma reminds readers that the borders between reality and unreality, between truth and fantasy, are relative to cultural and personal interpretation. When the betel-chewers of Agra say that omens "matter," Saleem implies that this is not merely an exotic fiction, for to someone like Padma they do matter: "Padma is nodding her head in agreement." And after Saleem claims that Parvati has "the true gifts of sorcery" and that he disappeared in her magic basket, Padma is surprised, yet asks, "So, … she really-truly was a witch?" (*MC* 47, 378, 381). It is because of, rather than in spite of, Padma's extremely flexible beliefs that Rushdie provokes his otherwise skeptical readers into considering the possibility of such things as omens, dreaming other people's dreams, invisibility, sorcery, or mystical telepathy, which is the premise of the Midnight Children's Conference.

TAKING WING

In attempting to make his dream of a unified India come true Saleem identifies with two mystical birds: the Muslim Hoopoe and the Hindu *paramahamsa*. In the subcontinental context, this transreligious link is itself a statement, similar to the one Mahmoud makes in *Shame* when he screens his Muslim-Hindu double bill in religion-torn Delhi. And like Mahmoud's disastrous double bill, Saleem's mad bird-dreams lead to failure. Nevertheless, these ornithological versions of the "optimism disease" represent a very sane urge toward tolerance, democracy and unity. Rushdie also attacks Hindu-Muslim divisions indirectly and parodically by having Saleem identify with the moon god Sin and with the Buddha. These two figures represent detachment – in the case of Sin a positive detachment from communal conflicts, and in the case of the Buddha a negative detachment from, and a parodic compliance with, the religious indoctrination of the West Pakistani generals.

Modelled on Attar's *Conference*, Saleem's Conference aims at bringing a large and diverse number of souls together and directing them towards a common goal of freedom. Rushdie's use of Attar's bird-guide is subtle, as is his use of old Aziz Sahib's conversation with thirty species of birds and Jamila's birdlike voice. In this sense *Midnight's Children* differs from *Grimus*, in which Rushdie makes his use of Attar explicit. One of the reasons behind Saleem's muted style of leadership is that his announcement that he hears archangelic voices teaches him that speaking like a prophet can be dangerous. He learns that to keep secrets is "not always a bad thing" (*MC* 169). Saleem also learns that the Midnight Children are not destined for the type of unity and annihilation envisioned by Attar. Echoing his own fear of disintegrating into "six hundred and thirty million particles of anonymous, and necessarily oblivious dust" (*MC* 37), Saleem realizes that the Midnight Children are "as profane, and as multitudinous, as dust" (*MC* 168). Saleem's Conference is made up of imperfect individuals, most of whom will never reach the goal of which Attar's Hoopoe speaks. In Attar's *Conference*, "few perceive the throne" of God and "Among a hundred thousand there is one" who makes it to this throne. Saleem is among the many birds who struggle to find unity and who encounter pain and bewilderment along the way: "How many search for Him whose heads are sent / Like polo-balls in some great tournament / From side to giddy side – how many cries, / How many countless groans assail the skies!"[18]

Commenting on the imminent demise of the Midnight Children's Conference, Saleem gives a nihilistic twist to Attar's annihilation: "with the optimism of youth – which is a more virulent form of the same disease that once infected my grandfather Aadam Aziz – we refused to look on the dark side, and not a single one of us suggested that the purpose of Midnight's Children might be annihilation; that we would have no meaning until we were destroyed" (*MC* 229). Saleem entertains Attar's mystical paradox (that meaning can only be found once the self no longer exists) and gives it a tragic slant. This becomes clear when one compares the events in the chapter "Midnight" with the events at the end of *Grimus*: the Midnight Children are separated, tortured and sterilized in the Widow's dark Hostel whereas Eagle and Media unite, find bliss and create a new cosmos on the top of a newly liberated Qaf Mountain.

Saleem's adoption of the Muslim Hoopoe is complemented by his role as the Hindu mystical swan, "the hamsa or parahamsa, symbol of the ability to live in two worlds, the physical and the spiritual." He says he "shall take wing (like the parahamsa gander who can soar out of one element into another) and return, briefly, to the affairs of [his] inner world." He does not mention the *paramahamsa* again until 78 pages later, when, after his sinuses are drained, he writes that his "connection" to the Midnight Children has been "broken (for ever)" (*MC* 223, 226, 304). The *paramahamsa* is an appropriate figure given that it, like the Hoopoe, is an ornithological figure which represents mystical flight and unity. And like the Simurg figure to which the Hoopoe leads his flock, the *paramahamsa* contains within its name a mystical pun: "The goose or swan (*hamsa*) is the *vahana* or mount of Brahma. It swims on the surface of the water but is not bound by it. It is a homeless, free wanderer. It has a secret, for those who understand it, concealed in its name which in its inverted form, *sa-ham*, 'this-I' (i.e. 'this am I'), epitomizes the whole philosophy of the Upanishads. In *pranayama* or breath control, the inhalation is said to make the sound of *ham*, the exhalation, *sa*. *Hamsa* is thus the sound of the living *prana*. Hence the emancipated saint is given the title of *paramahamsa*, 'highest swan.'"[19] In having Saleem identify with both the *paramahamsa* and the Hoopoe, Rushdie may be entering into the spirit of the type of Hindu syncretism which allowed the image of the Simurg to be "assimilated" to the image of Vishnu's mount, Garuda: "By an interesting transference the old Persian Simurgh, a great mythical bird used as a Sufi symbol of the highest divinely spiritual element in man, became known in India with the coming of Islam. Sometime after 1600 it was assimilated to an older image of a great vulture-bird called Garuda, whose chief earlier role had been to symbolize the celestial air and light upon which the high god Vishnu was borne."[20] While Rushdie may or may not be aware of this use of the Simurg, he creates a Muslim-Hindu correspondence of his own when Saleem identifies with both the Hoopoe and the *paramahamsa*.

In identifying with the *paramahamsa* Saleem is not saying that he is God in the same way a Hindu mystic might say that his soul and God are one. Nevertheless, since the Hindu mystic identifies with a God who encompasses and exists in everything, and since Saleem wants to encompass India, it is natural for him to try on the garments of such a mystic. Saleem's identification with the *paramahamsa* also makes sense in light of his sinus condition, for the *paramahamsa* adept uses *pranayama* (control of the breath and the nasal cavities) to achieve personal liberation and mystical powers.[21] Rushdie makes use – and makes fun – of the practice of *pranayama* when Saleem first achieves his mystical powers: "snot rockets through a breached dam into dark new channels" and "within the darkened auditorium of [his] skull, [his] nose began to sing" (*MC* 162). Finally, Saleem's depraved state in Karachi may be a degenerative twist of the *paramahamsa* as "anti-Brahmanic ascetic tradition," one which foreshadows "certain 'extremist' yogico-tantric schools" and one which makes "no distinction between differing mundane values" or "opposing moral standards."[22] After his sinuses are drained Saleem becomes a *grounded parahamsa* (*MC* 304) and his high-flying search for unity takes on a lower, left-handed direction. He becomes "convinced of an ugly truth – namely that the sacred, or good, held little interest" for him. Instead, "the pungency of the gutter seemed to possess a fatally irresistible attraction" (*MC* 318).

Rushdie's use of the Hoopoe and the *paramahamsa* slyly links Hinduism and Islam, while his use of the Sumerian moon god Sin represents an attempt to rise above the two dominant subcontinental religious traditions. Saleem sees himself as Sin both when he is gripped by "the spirit of self-aggrandizement" and when he is in the grip of his own two-headed demon, his own "sin" (*MC* 175, 261). The "Sumerian god of earth and air," Sin is associated with Sinai (Saleem's family name) and with an all-encompassing yet distant control of events: "As 'lord of the calendar,' his cult exhibited monotheistic tendencies, since it was Sin 'who determined the destinies of distant days' and whose 'plans no god knows.' According to Genesis, Abraham hailed from Ur by way of Harran, both cities devoted to the moon god. In Arabia, Sin was also worshipped under various titles and it is likely that Mount Sinai, first mentioned in Hebrew texts about 1000 BC, was connected with moon-worship."[23] Saleem emulates Sin's inscrutability when he is gripped by his two-headed demon and secretly plots the downfall of Commander Sabarmati's wife. Saleem also attempts to determine "the destinies of distant days" by playing the role of "the ancient moon-god [who is] capable of acting-at-a-distance and shifting the tides of the world" (*MC* 175). Rushdie here uses the moon god to describe Saleem's active role in his story. Whereas before his birth Saleem imagines himself moving passively with the cloud that floats from the industrial estate to Amina's *muhalla*, after his birth he sees himself as a moon god actively overseeing events, actively controlling the "ebb and flow" of subcontinental history. The cloud and the mythological figure are both supraworldly entities, although the cloud points to the antagonism between Muslims and Hindus while Sin symbolizes a power which is above and beyond the Muslim-Hindu dichotomy. Rushdie makes it clear that Saleem is choosing a construction deriving neither from his own religious tradition nor from that of the Hindus who surround him: "I became Sin, the ancient moon-god (no, not Indian: I've imported him from Hadhramaut of old), capable of acting-at-a-distance and shifting the tides of the world" (*MC* 175).

Saleem's identification with Sin reflects his belief that he can influence the course of Indian history, yet with the benefit of hindsight he sees this "self-aggrandizement" as a self-protective delusion: "If I had not believed myself in control of the flooding multitudes, their massed identities would have annihilated mine." Two-thirds of the way into the novel, Shiva starts to usurp his control: the "modes of connection" which link Saleem to all Indians also enable Shiva "to affect the passage of the days" and to usher in his own selfish and violent brand of history-making (MC 175, 299). The turning point in Saleem's career as a unifier of his nation comes after his sinus operation, at which time he associates his last name, Sinai, with the barren dryness of the Sinai Desert. He no longer identifies with the distant control of the moon god Sin, with the loftiness of Mount Sinai, with the skill of Ibn Sina (the "master magician" and "Sufi adept")[24] or with the diabolical power of his two-headed demon or snake: "but when all that is said and done; when Ibn Sina is forgotten and the moon has set; when snakes lie hidden and revelations end, [Sinai] is the name of the desert – of barrenness, infertility, dust; the name of the end" (MC 304–5). The end of Saleem's mystical career comes in the Hostel where the Widow puts a permanent stop to the flow of his procreative power: she orders a "sperectomy" or excision of hope – the Latin infinitive for hope being *sperare* (MC 437).

After Saleem's high-flying ideals are brought crashing to earth, he sees himself as a failed Hoopoe, a grounded *paramahamsa* and a barren desert of Sinai. Yet the major indication of his defeat is his identification with a mindless amnesiac "Buddha." Clearly making fun of the Buddhist ideal of detached enlightenment, Rushdie expresses Saleem's amoral, doglike state of mind in terms of Buddha's *full void* or *no-mind*. Saleem says he uses the Urdu word for old man, *buddha*, to describe himself, yet he adds, "there is also Buddha, with soft-tongued Ds, meaning he-who-achieved-enlightenment-under-the-bodhi-tree." Rushdie parodies the state of *nirvana*, in which the self is "snuffed out" and merges with the Absolute, when Saleem's identity is snuffed out by the bombs that fall on his family's Rawalpindi bungalow and when he becomes "capable of not-living-in-the-world as well as living in it" (MC 349, 342–3, 349). The important distinctions between Buddha and Saleem lie in the qualities of their existence both *outside* and *inside* this world. Buddha's otherworldly state was one of detached awareness, while Saleem's is one of forgetful ignorance. And in worldly terms, Buddha fought a pacifist battle against ideas he felt impeded spiritual progress. Saleem, on the other hand, becomes the tool of a regime that uses religion to squelch freedom.

Saleem's parodic buddhahood helps Rushdie to express his view that Pakistani leaders crush the liberating, mystical aspects of religion. Saleem asserts that Pakistan is less real than India because in "the Land of the Pure" the magic of religion is replaced by an unsavoury mix of dogma, propaganda and blind allegiance. He takes the fact that "Islam" literally means "Submission" (to God's will) and twists it to mean that the "submission" of Muslims in Pakistan boils down to acquiescence and conformity. Also, he takes the fact that "Pak" means "Pure" and then complains that in Pakistan he is "surrounded by the somehow barren certitudes of the land of the pure." He suggests that he becomes "the buddha" not so much because of the explosion that knocks him senseless, but because he starts to think in what he considers a Pakistani mode: "emptied of history, the buddha learned the arts of submission, and did only what was required of him. To sum up: I became a citizen of Pakistan" (*MC* 308, 316, 350).

Saleem also accuses the Pakistani military of exploiting and degrading the heavenly voice of his sister. Instead of following the example of Aunt Alia, who speaks "out vociferously against government-by-military-say-so," Jamila becomes a tool of the dictatorship and its bizarre mix of religion and violence. The Brass Monkey who was "once so rebellious and wild" falls "under the insidious spell of that God-ridden country" and adopts "expressions of demureness and submission." She sings "patriotic songs" which raise her into a "cloud" – not the "rosy cloud" of Hashmat Bibi's mysticism in *Shame,* but a "cloud" which Saleem likens to the closed minds of Pakistani students (*MC* 330, 292, *S* 34, *MC* 315). The degree to which the Pakistani leaders mix religion with their own militaristic agenda becomes evident in Ayub Khan's praise of Jamila, and in Saleem's sarcastic comments on this praise: " 'Jamila daughter,' we heard, 'your voice will be a sword for purity; it will be a weapon with which we shall cleanse men's souls.' President Ayub was, by his own admission, a simple soldier; he instilled in my sister the simple, soldierly virtues of faith-in-leaders and trust-in-God" (*MC* 315). Saleem also mocks the government's use of phrases such as "Holy war," "the evildoers of the earth" and "soldiers-for-Allah" (*MC* 339, 353, 357). His mockery is aimed at the abuse of religion rather than at religion *per se,* for Rushdie changes his tone – from satiric to sympathetic – when Saleem carries the bisected Shaheed to the height of a minaret and then accidentally turns on the loudspeaker. Saleem tells us that the "people would never forget how a mosque screamed out the terrible agony of war" (*MC* 377). Although Islam may be used by generals as an excuse for killing, the mosque cries out against the suffering caused by this abuse of religion.

THE MAGIC JUNGLE

In the later stretches of his journey across subcontinental time and space Saleem enters a variety of magical, surreal worlds, the two most striking being the Rann of Kutch and the Sundarbans Jungle. Both settings comment negatively on the militarism of the West Pakistani generals, yet they are worlds apart in the sense that the Rann is basically of this world while the Sundarbans is a world unlike any other. In his depiction of "the phantasmagoric Rann," Rushdie exposes what he sees as the lies and deceptions of Pakistani leaders: the Rann is "phantasmagoric" not just because it changes rapidly, but also because the layers of propaganda, which surround events which take place in it, are so thick that these events become unreal. Saleem does not even bother to relate the official version of events in the Rann. Instead, he relates a story "which is substantially that told by [his] cousin Zafar" and which is "as likely to be true as anything; as anything, that is to say, except what we were officially told" (MC 335). To illustrate his satiric point, he makes his story as outrageous as possible: he repeats "legends" of "an amphibious zone, of demonic sea-beasts with glowing eyes," fish-women who tempt "the unwary into fatal sexual acts," a sorcerer's world in which "each side thought it saw apparitions of devils fighting alongside its foes," "great blubbery things which slithered around the border posts at night," and a ghost-army and "spectres bearing moss-covered chests and strange shrouded litters piled high with unseen things" (MC 335–6). Saleem's treatment of the Rann's "sorcery" is similar to that of Ramram's "levitation" in Old Delhi: both seem miraculous until Saleem uncovers the illusion behind the apparent magic.

While the ghost-world of the Rann is a figment of frightened minds, the Jungle of the Sundarbans is "an other world" which operates according to its own otherworldly logic yet also manages to fly in the face of the propaganda of the West Pakistani generals. While the generals promise their soldiers a Heaven replete with vitality-replenishing young girls, the Magic Jungle is in fact a Hell or Purgatory complete with soul-draining nymphs. The Jungle also contains something that the generals could not even imagine: a magic tidal wave which washes Saleem and his crew back into the currents of Indian history.

Except for Kanaganayakam, critics say little about the episode in the Sundarbans. In his interview with Rushdie, Haffenden remarks that the episode "seems to be an eternity of disintegration and mania."[25] Harrison notes that it is a "strangely ecumenical episode" in which four Muslims spend many nights in a Kali temple and "emerge in some sense cleansed."[26] Swann compares Saleem's flight into "the magical night-forest" with "Simplicissimus's descent to the bottom of the lake" and he stresses the importance of the journey "back from the jungle of forgetfulness."[27] Durix comments that su-

[handwritten margin note: Jungle is outside time + reason (10)]

perfluity of dreams leads to "the gradual disappearance of all social identity and existence," and that the "journey to the end of dreams opens out onto the void."[28] Kanaganayakam puts greater emphasis on this bizarre journey within a journey, arguing that it "can only be understood in relation to myth." He notes the strangeness of the *houris* appearing in the Kali temple and he suggests that "Saleem's sojourn in the jungle is not unlike the period of exile imposed on the Pandavas in the *Mahabharata*." He adds that "Shiva's presence in Bangladesh and his failure to spot Saleem are not very different from the attempts made to spot the Pandavas before the allotted time and consign them to a further period of exile. Subsequently, Saleem returns to India and is called upon to confront Shiva. Saleem, instead of vindicating the cause of justice by destroying Shiva, runs in abject terror and is all but killed by the latter." This mythic inversion happens during the turmoil of the Emergency, thus reemphasizing "the dichotomy between the harmony of the past and the chaos of the present."[29]

Rushdie also directs the reader's attention to the mythic element in what he says were his "favourite ten or twelve pages to write": "It seemed to me that if you are going to write an epic, even a comic epic, you need a descent into hell. That chapter is the Inferno chapter, so it was written to be different in texture from what was around it."[30] While the chapter remains apart in many ways – it comes very close to depicting an other world which detaches itself entirely from twentieth century chronology – it nevertheless remains integral both to Rushdie's political attack on the generals and to Saleem's potential regeneration. As a result of the mystic workings of the Jungle, Saleem goes from *rejecting* to *accepting* his life, from being an empty-headed dog of war to becoming a socially aware citizen. The episode in the Sundarbans also fits curiously into Rushdie's oeuvre: the motif of the journey, with its requisite trip to hell, has a prominent place in *Grimus* (Eagle enters his own Inferno), *Shame* (Omar finds his own ancestral hell inside his family's mansion, Nishapur), the *Verses* (Chamcha is plunged into the satanic narrator's contemporized hell), the *Moor* (the protagonist finds hell in prison and in his father's gangster underworld) and *Ground* (Ormus descends into his own drug-induced hell in search of Vina, his Eurydice). *Shame* may be Rushdie's darkest work in this respect, for it is the only novel in which a protagonist gets a one-way ticket to the underworld. Saleem, on the other hand, gets a round-trip, swooping down into the mire of his own credulity and violence and then swooping up again, as if on the magical wings of the birds that sing high in the treetops.

Rushdie configures his Magic Jungle as a world apart: "Strange alien birds" hover in the sky above it; the trees are so tall "that the birds at the top must have been able to sing to God"; the edge of the Jungle is "an impossible endless huge green wall, stretching right and left to the ends of the earth!" (*MC* 359–1). Before Saleem and his unit enter the Sundarbans, an enraged peasant attacks Saleem with a scythe, apparently as a result of something (perhaps rape) that the mindless Saleem has done to his wife. The scythe-wielding farmer takes on the allegorical status of Father Time, and when Ayooba shoots him, "Time lies dead in a rice-paddy" (*MC* 359). These two events imply the rape of Bengal and the violent suppression of Bengali indignation, yet also mark the barrier between a worldly realm in which one finds time and violence, and an otherworldly realm in which one finds timelessness and the result of violence: death.

In the phantasmagoric Rann propaganda distorts the contours of geography and history, yet in the Sundarbans the weird logic of an other world erases these contours altogether. Space and time become as impossible as the "impossible endless huge green wall" that reaches to the end of the world, a verdant wall "so thick that history has hardly ever found the way in" (*MC* 359). What lies beyond the known world is a realm where myth becomes reality and the fabric of the self wears thinner than gauze.

The Magic Jungle operates with an otherworldly logic according to which the afterlife promised by the Pakistani generals is, like their official account of war, the opposite of what it purports to be. The generals tell their soldiers that they are "Martyrs," "Heroes, bound for the perfumed garden" where they will "be given four beauteous houris, untouched by man or djinn" (*MC* 340), yet the "afterlife" in East Bengal resembles Hell rather than Heaven.

The notion of a celestial reward for fighting does not come only from politicians, but also from the poor, who need promises of heaven to make their lives bearable: Rushdie waxes pathetic (and of course political) when Shaheed's father weeps all over his son, and expresses the hope that he will "perhaps become the first of their family members to enter the perfumed garden, leaving behind this pitiful world in which a father could not hope to pay his debts and also feed his nineteen children" (*MC* 352).

Rushdie takes this promise of perfumed gardens and beautiful virgins and turns it on its head: he makes the Jungle's temple a place of "double-edged luxury," a realm which is initially seductive yet subsequently horrific. For when the four "daughters of the forest" have sex with the soldiers, the girls appear to fulfill the soldiers' innermost desires as well as the promises of the generals (*MC* 363, 366). In Islamic terms, these girls first appear to be *houris* or "female companions, perpetual virgins, of the saved in paradise." They are the "symbols of spiritual states of rapture" found in Qur'an 2:23, 3:14 and 4:60.[31] Their "heavenly nature" takes on a suspicious aspect, however, for they live in a Kali temple, and Kali's polytheistic femininity ill suits the monotheistic patriarchy of Islam. Rushdie works subtly towards his point, for under their saris the daughters "wore nothing at all." Their saris "were torn and stained by the jungle," their caresses "felt real enough," and their scratches "left marks." In the end the Muslim Heaven becomes a Hindu Hell and the four girls do not resemble *houris* so much as *apsaras*, the Hindu nymphs whose "amours on earth have been numerous" and who, by "their languid postures and sweet words rob those who see them of their wisdom and their intellect."[32] Appropriately, the "daughters of the forest" leave Saleem and his unit "without a single thought in their heads." There is a humorous edge here, for this is both a trick of the *apsaras* and what naturally happens to men after good sex.

Saleem and his comrades come to understand that by giving in to their own desires the Jungle "was fooling them into using up their dreams, so that as their dream-life seeped out of them they became as hollow and translucent as glass" (*MC* 366–7). While it may seem that Rushdie's aim is to parody a mystical state of oblivion (the Buddhist state of *samadhi* or *nirvana* or the Hindu *moksha*), his deeper aim is to attack the type of empty-headed, uncritical thinking into which Saleem and his fellow Pakistanis have allowed themselves to fall. Their spiritual death with its hollowness and translucence has little to do with the full void, the inner light or the annihilation of mysticism. Rather, it has everything to do with performing the dirty work of undemocratic leaders and with believing that as a reward for this they will be flown first-class, direct to heavenly oblivion.

Here the distinction between the mysticism of *Grimus* and that of *Midnight's Children* becomes clear. Eagle can reach a mystical paradise with Media because he defeats Grimus's tyranny. In *Midnight's Children* no one reaches a meaningful annihilation, since no one defeats tyranny – especially not Saleem, who excludes Shiva from his conference, helps his militarist Pakistani uncle strategize a coup, and sniffs out the democratically elected members of the Awami League, whom the Pakistani military call "subversive elements" and "enemies of national unity" (*MC* 357).

The Sundarbans holds a final surprise: in the same swampy abyss in which worms drain colour from the blood and nymphs drain life from the soul lies an inexplicable regenerative force, one which turns Saleem's violent trajectory toward oblivion into a boomerang ride back into this world of time and space, history and geography. In coming to terms with this nebulous force, one might recall that in the upper reaches of the Jungle the birds "must have been able to sing to God" and that the word "impossible" (which Rushdie consistently associates with Attar's mysticism) is used twice on the page which introduces the Jungle (*MC* 361, 359). The notes of the Jungle's birds thus echo the chirpings of old Aziz sahib's thirty species of birds, the supernatural hum of the Hummingbird, and the ethereal bulbul-like songs of Jamila Singer, Saleem's deepest, most forbidden love. The exact nature of the Jungle's regenerative power must needs remain enigmatic in order to work its otherworldly magic. Despite its vague nature, the Magic Jungle is distinct in its effect: from deep within it comes a tidal wave which interrupts Saleem's atemporal oblivion with a single, powerful stroke of temporal linearity. The Jungle's wave washes Saleem back into the flow of history and back into the violent world he has helped militarists to create.

Saleem's experience in the otherworldly Jungle corresponds to one of the darkest moments in subcontinental history – the brutal months during which the subcontinent's East and West wings are violently torn asunder. I borrow this metaphor from *Shame*, in which the narrator says that pre-1971 Pakistan is a "fantastic bird of a place, two Wings without a body, sundered by the land-mass of its greatest foe, joined by nothing but God" (*s* 178). This metaphor is especially appropriate to *Midnight's Children*, in which Rushdie takes a closer look at the West-East split than he does in *Shame*, and in which Saleem sees the unity of the subcontinent and India in terms of the bird-figures of the Hummingbird, the *paramahamsa* and the Hoopoe.

Rushdie gives this violent moment in history a human dimension when Deshmukh, the "vendor of notions," is reduced to scavenging gold fillings from dead corpses on a killing field on the outskirts of Dacca. The understated but powerful pathos of this scene reminds one of the moment when Aadam Aziz returns from the corpse-spattered compound of Jallianwallah Baag and tells his wife that he has been "Nowhere on earth" (*MC* 36). The scenario near Dacca is perhaps even more powerful in light of the atrocities Saleem has witnessed and abetted. And even after all the senseless slaughter – the dirty self-serving politics, and the ruthless attacks on the "enemies of national unity" – one of Saleem's fellow soldiers suspects him of being an Indian spy and turns on him. Just when nothing at all seems to have been learned in this war, just as Shaheed springs on Saleem with "an irrational energy" and pushes him to the ground, Deshmukh cries out, "Ho sirs! Enough fighting has been already. Be normal now, my sirs. I beg. Ho God" (*MC* 373).

Deshmukh is a moving, down-to-earth character who brings the emotional content of Saleem's narrative back into the contours of space and time, back into this world of geography and history, location and memory. In this sense, he closes the door of an other world which is beyond logic, and ushers the reader back into a world which at least has the potential to make sense.

BATTLE OF THE GODS

Yet Rushdie does not let his reader off easily: the world to which Saleem returns may have a resemblance to the world we know, yet it also carries with it something of the monstrous and satanic, something from the earlier Ravana-haunted streets of Delhi. From the moment Saleem is washed back into India, he is stalked by two Hindu figures who are bent on destroying his vision of a tolerant, peaceful, democratic nation. While these monsters succeed in dismembering his Conference, the ideals of conference linger on, just as they did after the members of the Free Islam Convocation were murdered and cowed into submission. For in opposition to the dark and terrifying figures of Shiva and the Widow stand the ultrapowerful Durga, the life-nourishing Padma/Sri Lakshmi, the merciful Mary, the New Aadam, Picture Singh, and, of course, Saleem himself.

The figures bent on destroying Saleem and his pan-Indian vision act in concert, and borrow their nefarious power from the darker fringes of Hindu myth. First and foremost among these is Shiva, who is aligned with a decadent occult Benares against a progressive secular Bombay. Curiously, this same Benares-Bombay polarity crops up in another novel published in the same year as *Midnight's Children*. In Arun Joshi's *The Last Labyrinth*, Bombay is a haven of skyscrapers and businessmen, while Benares is a cluttered, dangerous, labyrinthine world of winding streets and mystical conundrums. Joshi also makes spectacular use of Hindu gods – in this case a redemptive Krishna rather than a ruinous Shiva. *The Last Labyrinth* also contains an intricate and somewhat mysterious use of Islamic mysticism, Aftab's threatening yet ultimately benevolent conundrums running in some ways parallel with Rushdie's crushed yet stubborn Sufi ideals.

In Rushdie's novel ancient Hindu practice is clearly at odds with Bombay modernity when worshippers use Narlikar's wave-breaking tetrapods as lingams of worship, a comic incident given the gynecologist's obsession with science and birth control (*MC* 176–7). While Shiva is here associated with an ancient mix of religion and fertility, in Benares he is associated with fertility and forced sterilizations, a duality which is perhaps meant to illustrate both his creative and his destructive aspects. Rushdie is making use of already established links between Shiva and Benares (the city Daniélou calls "the resplendent city of Shiva")[33] and when he reminds us that it is in Benares that the "goddess Ganga streamed down to earth through Shiva's hair" (MC 432). Yet little of Ganga's beneficence streams into the city as Saleem experiences it. Benares may be "the shrine to Shiva-the-god" and the "City of Divine Light, home of the Prophetic Book, the horoscope of horoscopes, in which every life, past present future, is already recorded" (MC 432), yet what occurs in the city's Hostel is anything but enlightening: General Shiva helps the Widow to pervert the sacred notions of Mother India and OM, and, together, they drain all hope from the magical children.

Rushdie emphasizes the dark powers which crush Saleem and his multivocal Conference by associating the Widow with the frightening figure of Kali. The Widow aspires "to be Devi, the Mother-goddess in her most terrible aspect, possessor of the shakti of the gods" (MC 438). Kinsley notes that several Tantra texts "proclaim Kali the greatest of the vidyas (the manifestations of the Mahadevi, the 'great goddess') or divinity itself; indeed, they declare her to be the essence or own form (svarupa) of the Mahadevi."[34] In his short work on The Wizard of Oz (1992) Rushdie notes that in Saleem's portrait of the Widow "the nightmare of Indira Gandhi is fused with the equally nightmarish figure" of the Wicked Witch of the West.[35] The depiction of the Widow in Saleem's dream also strongly suggests the more contextually relevant figure of Kali, who "is always black," who "has long, disheveled hair" and "clawlike hands," and who "gets drunk on the hot blood of her victims."[36] In his nightmare, Saleem sees that the hair of the Widow is "black as black," her "arm is long as death," her skin is green, and her "fingernails are long and sharp and black." She rips children in two, rolls them into "little balls" and eats them, leaving only "splashing stains of black" (MC 207-208). Seeing the Widow as Kali also makes sense in that mythologically Kali is Shiva's "consort, wife or associate" and she excites him "to take part in dangerous, destructive behavior that threatens the stability of the cosmos."[37] Shiva's status as "midnight's darkest child" and his subsequent "love of violence" (MC 441, 430) make him a fitting conspirator with the Widow as Kali, the black deity associated with dissolution into "shapelessness in the all-pervading darkness of the eternal night."[38] While together these two dark figures succeed in crushing the Midnight Children, a note of optimism creeps in when the Widow allows Shiva to escape vasectomy. She thus unwittingly makes it possible for him to give rise to the hopes of a new generation – symbolized by one of Shiva's sons, the tough and unblinking Aadam Sinai.

While Saleem invokes the Hoopoe and the *paramahamsa* to unify Indians, the Widow invokes the Hindu notion of OM to divide and conquer her nation. Her servants "sperectomize" the Midnight Children in the name of OM, that is, in the name of the syllable which expresses a sacred unity and which serves as a link between the world of humans and the other worlds of the gods. This syllable is extremely important in Hinduism; among other things it can be seen "as the first thought-form from which the universe develops."[39] The Widow's helper mocks this sacred paradigm when she tells Saleem, "You are Muslim: you know what is OM? Very well. For the masses, our Lady is a manifestation of the OM" (*MC* 438). The Widow thus anticipates the Imam in the *Verses*, who uses Islamic ideals to stop the flow of history and to fix reality into one pattern. Joseph Swann puts it concisely when he says that the Widow "would stop the flow of history, fixing the 'OM' (which cannot be fixed) in the narrow limits of her own being."[40]

The Widow is countered by a number of forces and figures, first among these being the mythicized figure of Durga. This formidable washerwoman may be a "monster" who forgets "each day the moment it ended," yet she also wet-nurses Aadam "through his sickness, giving him the benefit of her colossal breasts" (*MC* 445). In case the point is lost that what Durga does for Aadam, she also does for Saleem, the father and son both nurse themselves at her breasts. This first and second infancy is not just playful titillation, for it signals the life-giving, story-rendering power that Durga contains within her. Saleem tells us that she is rumoured to have two wombs and that she represents "novelty, beginnings, the advent of new stories events complexities" (*MC* 445). Durga is thus important to Saleem in his *Arabian Nights* role of Scheherazade, for he must come up with more stories in order for him and his nation to survive and prosper. Durga's narrative fecundity also helps to defeat the effects of the Widow, who would stop people from telling their stories in the speaking place or *parle*-ment of the nation. One might remember that Durga does not stick clothes in a machine, but rather beats them clean. Her mythic credentials are even more powerful: Kinsley notes that in mythology Durga displays a combination of "world-supportive qualities and liminal characteristics that associate her with the periphery of civilized order." As a fierce warrior who resembles Kali in her liminal aspects, and who can create goddesses (such as Kali) from herself, Durga is a formidable opponent.[41] Rushdie's description of Durga suggests that while the Widow may have done her worst to his generation, there is a fierce spirit in the land which rises in response to her tyranny.

Picture Singh is attracted to the down-to-earth *dhoban* or washer-woman in a far different way: " 'That Durga, captain,' the old snake-charmer said, his voice betraying the fact that, in his old age, he had fallen victim to the dhoban's charms, 'What a woman!' " (*MC* 445). The possibility of romance at so late a stage in the novel and at so late a stage in Picture Singh's life parallels the possibility of romance be-tween Padma and Saleem in the last pages of Saleem's account. Equally important is that Picture Singh provides a crucial link be-tween what seems to have been crushed (Attar's pre-Partition and pre-Emergency ideal of conference, seen in the Free Islam Convoca-tion and the Midnight Children's Conference) and what may yet live on in the late 1970s and in the future, seen, albeit problematically, in the Midnight-Confidential Club. Living with the magicians in Delhi, Saleem remarks that during "the early months of the Emergency, Picture Singh remained in the clutches of a gloomy silence." While Saleem wishes his Rajasthani charmer would speak out as he once did for the repressed and the dispossessed, it is because of, rather than despite, this mimicry of the effect of the Widow's clamp-down, that Picture Singh more closely conforms to, and more meaningfully fights against, the repressions of the Widow. There's *something* – and note Saleem's own vague words – about Picture Singh that makes Saleem feel that "*one day*, one millennial dawn at midnight's end, *somehow*, at the head of a great jooloos or procession of the dispos-sessed, *perhaps* playing his flute and wreathed in deadly snakes, it *would be* Picture Singh who led us toward the light" (*MC* 426, italics mine). Suggestions of snake-charming, the Pied Piper, and Krishna with his famous flute, all combine here, to work their magic against the infernal snakes of Schaapsteker, the wayward parents of the na-tion (whom Saleem clearly implicates in the bad behaviour of the magic children, for "children are the vessels into which adults pour their poison" – *MC* 256), and the twisted violence of the mythicized figures of General Shiva and the Widow as Kali. Picture Singh also more specifically counters the harm that was done to the Humming-bird and his ideals at a time when Muslims had a chance of constitut-ing an integral part of a greater non-partitioned India. Despite Picture Singh's denials that he has no lofty politico-mystical aims (a denial which only raises his mystical currency) Saleem tells him, "There is a precedent – there was Mian Abdullah, the Hummingbird ..." Saleem raises the tenor of his invocation when he writes that his "last father, tall gaunt bearded, his hair swept back into a knot behind his neck, seemed the very avatar of Mian Abdullah" (*MC* 426).

Saleem remains pessimistic about the chances of a vibrant future for India or himself, and Picture Singh falls exhausted to the floor after coming to Bombay, where he fights his final snake-charming match against the Maharaja of Cooch Naheen. Yet the appearance of this King of Some Nothing refigures and reverses, at least poetically, the defeat of the long-forgotten Queen of Some Nothing, the silver-spittoon-supplying Rani of Cooch Naheen. It is in this allusive and impossibly idealistic sense that Picture Singh plays Krishna's redemptive role and counters the darkness of the millennial midnight. Flute to mouth, Picture Singh steps out of the darkness into the "single shaft of light" that "spilled into a pool on the floor of the Midnight-Confidential Club." At the end of his brilliant performance, he knots "a king cobra around the Maharaja's neck" (*MC* 454–5).

Goonetilleke notes that because magicians can influence crowds, change the world and perform illusions they "can be taken on a metaphorical level as a representation of politicians." He notes that Rushdie's Delhi magicians are communists and that Picture Singh as leader of these magicians is "an inspirational figure." I would add that this puts Picture Singh and Saleem on the same ground, given that Saleem influences crowds (sometimes unintentionally) and tries to change the world by leading his magic children. Goonetilleke would seem to concur with me in general: while Picture Singh's victory in Bombay leaves him feeling exhausted, "as in the case of the Rani of Cooch Naheen, Mian Abdullah and Nadir Khan, his positive worth is not negated."[42] The link between Picture Singh and these older social leaders might also be seen in terms of magic, given that the optimism disease turns out to be a sort of illusion, and given that the Rani's name also suggests creating something out of nothing. The sad part about all this is of course that Rushdie is suggesting that such magical otherworldly ideals simply cannot exist in the real world. This is, I think, why he works the ideals in sideways, esoterically, hinting at the continuation of the Hummingbird in Picture Singh and at the magic of Saleem's 1001 children in the new Aadam's abracadabra.

Saleem's son Aadam is another largely optimistic figure who dominates the sometimes pessimistic final two chapters, "Midnight" and "Abracadabra." Kanaganayakam contends that Aadam's birth, modelled as it is on the birth of Ganesh, the son of Shiva and Parvati, "brings in a ray of hope." He adds that there is "the suggestion that good is born out of evil and that the present collapse might lead to a future unity."[43] I agree with this, yet would add that Rushdie also suggests that the new cycle started by Saleem's son will run its course and that this cycle will repeat itself *ad infinitum.* For "until the thousand and first generation, until a thousand and one midnights have bestowed their terrible gifts and a thousand and one children have died," Indians will continue to be "sucked into the annihilating whirlpool of the multitudes, and to be unable to live or die in peace" (*MC* 463).

Like his ancestors and India's future generations, Saleem is on a giant wheel, one which may turn towards an optimistic future or towards the Hindu Dark Age, Kali Yug, which Saleem glosses as "the worst of everything." Saleem claims that it is due to Kali Yug that his beloved Midnight Children are "always confused about being good" (*MC* 194, 200). If readers focus on the notion of Kali Yug, which Saleem correctly informs us began in 3102 B.C. and lasts 432,000 years (*MC* 194), then there appears to be no relief in sight from the violence and division that has characterized recent subcontinental history (it is hard to derive much comfort from the notion that the other three happier Yugs last for 1,728,000, 1,296,000 and 834,000 years respectively).[44] If, on the other hand, readers focus on other aspects of Hindu myth (the figures of Parvati or Durga, for example) or if they follow Rushdie's early cue and emphasize the Middle Eastern paradigm of the fall, then brighter prospects present themselves: the notion of destruction is countered by creation, fall by redemption.

A CONCLUSION IN WHICH NOTHING IS CONCLUDED

Rushdie offers the possibility that Saleem will return to Kashmir with Padma and Aadam, as well as the opposite possibility that Saleem's involvement with the demon snake and the Pakistani generals may combine with other dark forces in the subcontinent to abort any meaningful future. He leaves open the question of whether or not Saleem and his nation will find the road back to the mythical Paradise of old Aziz sahib and his thirty species of birds. He indicates that while we can, to some degree, see where we have come from, we cannot see where we are, or where we are going – a fact he illustrates with an analogy from the movie halls so sacred to both Rushdie and his Saleem. At a distance from the screen, which corresponds to a temporal distance from the present, we can see what is taking place on the screen. Yet when we move closer, closer to the present, the picture starts to break up and we see only "dancing grain" and "tiny details" (*MC* 165–6). Rushdie is refreshingly honest, for in writing a novel which ends in the present, he places his narrator-protagonist, himself, and his readers with their noses up against that screen.

Both *Grimus* and *Midnight's Children* force their readers to think about what might come next. But where *Grimus* strongly hints at a unifying, syncretic mysticism, *Midnight's Children* overwhelms the reader with its multiplicity of motifs and possibilities. In *Grimus* Eagle's quest leads him – almost as if he were being drawn by a magnet – to annihilation on the peak of Qaf/Kailasa. In contrast, Saleem's crisscrossing of the subcontinent resembles the flight of a confused and increasingly tired bird around a mountain that hosts a bewildering mix of good and evil beings. Saleem's flight might be seen as taking place on the Hindu Mount Meru, the "meeting place and pleasure ground of the gods," a place which "overshadows the worlds above and below and across" and on whose slopes hosts of "gods, celestial musicians (*gandharva*), genii (*asura*), and demons (*rakshasa*) play with heavenly nymphs (*apsaras*)."[45] Rushdie himself compares *Midnight's Children* to "the spire of the Hindu temple," which is "a representation of the world mountain" and which is "crowded [and] swarms with life, all forms of life."[46] While Rushdie supplies *Grimus* with a sense of completion and closure when Eagle unites with Media in a cosmic dance strongly reminiscent of Shiva's union with Parvati on Mount Kailasa, in *Midnight's Children* no such sense of completion can be found: Saleem remains unable to make love with his wife Parvati and he is left a widower after she is killed in the slum-clearings which accompany the 1975–1977 Emergency. Rushdie does, however, return to the possibility of a Muslim-Hindu alliance on the personal level when Saleem contemplates marriage with Padma, his Hindu lover.

While Saleem forges strong ties with Parvati and Padma, he often reflects his Muslim upbringing by seeing harmony in Muslim terms and discord and confusion in Hindu terms. He tells his readers that he is born and raised in "the Muslim tradition" but that he finds himself "overwhelmed all of a sudden by an older learning," one which throws everything into confusion with its notion that reality is nothing but an illusion, a "dream-web of Maya." He uses this notion of cosmic illusion to his advantage when he argues with those who think he is crazy: "If I say that certain things took place which you, lost in Brahma's dream, find hard to believe, then which of us is right?" (*MC* 194, 211). Saleem uses Hinduism to express his dismay at the confusing, violent currents of history that are whirling around him. He emphasizes the destructive aspects of Shiva and Kali, and he measures his narrative against the tales of Mary Pereira (*MC* 79), his ayah and patron, who repeats ancient stories about the "supernatural invasion" of ghosts and *rakshasas*, and who finds "the old-time war of the Kurus and Pandavas happening right outside." Saleem calls these stories "rumours and tittle-tattle," yet he adds, "I remain, today, half-convinced that in that time of accelerated events and diseased hours the past of India rose up to confound her present" (*MC* 245). Mary's

reality as an illusion (13)

notion of a Hindu "invasion" and Saleem's notion that the Hindu past "rose up to confound" suggest that, being Christian and Muslim, they do not feel entirely at home or comfortable with the Hindu world around them.

Islam and Hinduism are not the only religions that Rushdie uses and abuses in his bizarre version of the twentieth-century subcontinent. I have already mentioned how Saleem's empty-headed "buddhahood" is used to satirize submission to authority in Pakistan. Even more bizarre is the transmogrification Zoroastrianism undergoes in Saleem's description of a cult which mixes Hinduism, Zoroastrianism and anti-Jewish propaganda (MC 267–9). This cult results from the early illumination of Saleem's friend Cyrus or "Fair Khusrovand," and it parodies cults, hyperbolic religious language and the use of science to promote religion. Khusrovand's cult may also parody the Iranian Sohrawardi's mysticism of Light. Quoting Corbin's *Histoire de la philosophie islamique*, Mircea Eliade observes that Sohrawardi's vast oeuvre "arises from a personal experience, a 'conversion which came upon him in his youth.' In an ecstatic vision, he discovered a multitude of the 'beings of light whom Hermes and Plato contemplated, and the heavenly radiation, sources of the *Light of Glory* and the *Kingdom of Light* (*Ray wa Khorreh*) which Zarathustra proclaimed, toward which a spiritual rapture lifted the most faithful king, the blessed Kay Khosraw'."[47] Saleem's cult of Cyrus may parody Sohrawardi's Khosraw or it may be yet another of Rushdie's bizarre conflations that cannot be tied down to a single source or meaning.

Christianity is also transmogrified – this time into a rather worldly or non-committal faith: Saleem refers to Tai's "bald gluttonous Christ," to "the Christians' considerately optional God," and to his sister's "flirtation with Christianity" (MC 16, 230, 253). These references fit with the stereotypical polarity Rushdie sets up between the mysticism and magic of India and the worldliness of Europe. After returning from Germany, Aadam Aziz rejects "the hegemony of superstition, mumbo-jumbo, and all things magical [that] would never be broken in India"; Dr. Narlikar feels that Shiva-lingam worshippers represent "all the old dark priapic forces of ancient, procreative India"; Saleem says that Schaapsteker's brains are pickled by the "ancient insanities of India" (MC 67, 176, 257). The anti-religious bent initiated by Aadam crops up later in Rushdie's oeuvre in the Mirza Saeed of the *Verses*, another Indian who cannot help expressing his "imported European atheism," who makes statements such as "trust in Western technology," and who rails against the "mumbo-jumbo" of the "God-bothered type from ancient history" (SV 485, 232, 238). In addition, Mirza's Mercedes Benz is seen by the orthodox as a sign of his impure Western materialism, as is Aadam Aziz's pigskin medical bag from Germany.

Saleem's allusions to Christianity are sometimes implied – as in Mary's grace at the end of the novel – and are sometimes puzzling or confusing, as when he alludes to Jamila and "the hidden order of Santa Ignacia" and to "the dreadful logic of Alpha and Omega" (*MC* 316, 123). This latter reference is to both Saleem's blood-type (which confirms that he is not genetically part of the Sinai family) and to Saleem's fear of death at the hands of the Black Angel. Other references to Christianity include those to Mary's "good Christian folk," who ought to remain apart from communalist fighting because the communalists are "Hindu and Muslim people only," to a Jesus who takes on the blue colouring of Krishna so that he will be more comprehensible in the land of the blue god, to Saleem's questioning of Christ's resurrection, and to Mary's fear of the notion (accepted by Ahmadiyya Muslims) that "the tomb of Lord Jesus" lies in Kashmir (*MC* 105, 103, 136, 211, 245).

Given the plethora of worldly and otherworldly references in the novel, it is not surprising that Rushdie employs narrative strategies and motifs which help to hold it together as a work of literature. Apart from the use of a mythic cycle, and apart from the more obvious use of historical chronology and autobiography, Rushdie employs a literary style deriving from Hindu oral tradition to unify his unwieldy tale. One must remember that Saleem is reading his story to Padma, an important fact for at least two reasons: this reading links the reader to a Hindu audience (as I argued in "The Snake Man and the Lotus Goddess") and it links his literary style with oral tradition.

In an October 1983 interview Rushdie gives a lively account of a reading he went to see in Baroda, a city of half a million north of Bombay. To him this reading shows that "the idea of literature as performance in the same way as the idea of music as performance is absolutely central to Indian culture." He says that there were 600,000 people at this reading, and if "ever there was a way of making a novelist feel humble, that was it." Much of what Rushdie heard that weekend can easily apply to the great epics *Mahabharata* and *Ramayana* as well as *Midnight's Children*: "Listening to this man reminded me of the shape of the oral narrative. It's not linear. An oral narrative does not go from the beginning to the middle to the end of the story. It goes in great swoops, it goes in spirals or in loops, it every so often reiterates something that happened earlier to remind you, and then takes you off again, sometimes summarizes itself, it frequently digresses off into something that the story-teller appears just to have thought of, then it comes back to the main thrust of the narrative. Sometimes it steps sideways and tells you about another, related story which is like the story that he's been telling you, and then it goes back to the main story. Sometimes there are Chinese boxes where there is a story inside a story inside a story inside a story, then they all come back, you see. So it's a very bizarre and pyrotechnical shape. ... It seemed to me ... this shape conformed very exactly to the shape in which people liked to listen, that in fact the first and only rule of the story-teller is to hold his audience."[48] Saleem's story also loops, zigs and zags, and includes a diversity and spontaneity which link it to the oral tale.

A precursor to the fluid, rambling, myth-laden orality of *Midnight's Children* might be found in Raja Rao's famous 1938 novel *Kanthapura*, a village-eye view of Indian history in the days of Gandhi's campaign to free India from the British. The narration of Rao's elderly widow applies in many ways to the tales of Mary and Saleem, for the widow's speech "is characteristically Indian, feminine with a spontaneity that is coupled with swiftness, vivid with a raciness suffused with native vigour, and exciting with a rich sense of drama shot through and through with humour and lyricism. The villager in India is an inveterate myth-maker, and he has not lost his links with the gods of tradition: the heroes and heroines of epics jostle with historic personalities, and time past and time present are both projected into time future."[49] Rushdie has done a brilliant job in connecting Saleem to the masses and to families with their eccentric characters and their hidden secrets. And unlike the urbane, detached and largely rational narration of *Shame*, Saleem's account is spontaneous, mixes time frames, and jostles gods, heroes and historic personalities.

Midnight's Children also owes some of its narrative unity to *The Arabian Nights*, a collection of Indian and Arabian stories from the turn of the first millennium, which is alternatively titled *The Thousand and One Nights*. Following Scheherazade, Saleem fights his demise (which he sees as a physical and metaphorical "cracking up") by telling a long rambling story in which there are many interconnected smaller stories. Whereas Scheherazade is successful, Saleem's success appears to be a matter of debate. His imagined dissolution remains at odds with the equally convincing (or equally unconvincing) fiction in which he lives in Mary's pickle factory and in which he may return to the Kashmir of old Aziz sahib and Aadam Aziz. While Rushdie himself imagines Saleem dying at the end of the novel, he writes the ending in an ambiguous manner. Rushdie comments that the story "is on Saleem's part a sort of heroic attempt to reconstruct his picture of the world. He's writing when he knows the end, and he's trying to say 'this is how I thought it was' and at the end of the book he again has to say 'it wasn't like that' and then he dies. I mean, it's not overt in the book in any way but that's how I thought about it."[50] Rushdie misses a chance here to enhance the ambiguity he has built into his ending. Saleem realizes that it is an illusion to think that "it is possible to create past events simply by saying they occurred," and this realization renders suspect his later resolve "to write the future as [he has] written the past, to set it down with the absolute certainty of a prophet" (*MC* 384, 443, 462). Saleem's "certainty" about his demise remains as hypothetical as any other thirty-first chapter scenario – for instance, one beginning with, "No, that won't do. In fact, I saw neither the dark god Shiva nor the Black Angel ..." In depicting Saleem's open-ended fate, Rushdie creates a variant of the *"line of flux"* in *Grimus;* he likewise anticipates the "parallel universe of history" in *Shame* and the "parallel universes of quantum theory" in the *Verses* (*G* 235, *S* 64, *SV* 523).

Rushdie further complicates Saleem's fate – and any conclusive interpretation of his story – by combining hints of Scheherazade's release with hints of Attar's mystical annihilation. Saleem's speculation that "the purpose of Midnight's Children might be annihilation" (*MC* 229) gains mystical significance when one remembers that Saleem at the end of the novel is thirty years old, that he writes thirty chapters or "pickle jars," and that he leaves readers with the image of an empty or "annihilated" thirty-first pickle jar. Just as Scheherazade is set free by the magical logic of her 1001 nights, so Saleem may be set free by the magical logic of his "thirty jars and a jar."

5 *Shame:* An Other World Strikes Back

The bodies that occupy the celestial vault,
These give rise to wise men's uncertainties;
Take care not to lose your grip on the thread of wisdom,
Since the Powers That Be themselves are in a spin.

Omar Khayyam, Ruba'iyat[1]

In *Midnight's Children* Rushdie throws a spinning cosmos at his readers. Yet he manages to give this cosmos hidden meanings: he supplies sparkling impossible ideals which transcend, at least in part, the meaningless violence of figures such as the Widow with her scalpel or General Shiva with his crushing knees. In *Shame* Rushdie also throws a cosmos at his readers, yet it is neither so complex nor so studded with hidden meaning. For while at the end of *Midnight's Children* Saleem still has hopes of a meaningful future, at the end of *Shame* Omar is confirmed in his fears that the universe is controlled by malevolent forces beyond his control.

Shame takes to a more dire level the same dynamic found in the Sundarbans chapter of *Midnight's Children*. In the Sundarbans Saleem is punished by otherworldly forces (*apsaras* and the purgatorial Jungle itself) for blindly following the orders of a zealous military. Likewise, in *Shame* Omar and Raza are punished by mythic figures (the Beast and Kali) for following and for giving similar orders.

Rushdie prepares the ground for the rise of the Beast and Kali by suggesting that both the polyvocality of democracy and the polytheism of Hinduism have been repressed by Islamic militarism. The mix of repression and religion creates an invisible, underground realm, a bizarre collective unconscious seething with frustration and anger. A demonic monster then rises from this subterranean world to wreak havoc and to scourge the militarism and puritanism which created it. It is important to note that Rushdie is not here championing the demonic against the Godly or the polytheistic against the monotheistic

– as his narrator does in the *Verses*. Rather, he is suggesting that repression creates a horrid backlash. And, not surprisingly, religious repression creates a religious or otherworldly backlash.

Throughout the novel Rushdie takes aim at Iskander Harappa and Raza Hyder, fictional versions of the late Pakistani authoritarians, Zulfikar Ali Bhutto (1928–79) and Zia ul-Haq (1924–88). Rushdie's main point is that Iskander sets up a secular regime which leads to Raza's religious dictatorship. Iskander's culpability is dramatically depicted by his wife Rani in her fourteenth shawl, titled "Iskander the assassin of possibility." Rani shows Iskander throttling the nation's potential, seen "as a young girl, small, physically frail, internally damaged: she had taken for her model her memory of an idiot, and consequently innocent, child, Sufiya Zinobia Hyder" (s 194). Rushdie suggests another link between the repressions of Iskander and Raza when, in his death cell, Iskander wonders if "someone is dreaming him" and he asks if this someone is God. He then answers his own question: "No, not God," but Raza, the "General of whom this cell is one small aspect, who is general, omnipresent, omnivorous." Iskander expresses an ironic view of his place in history when he adds the following exaggerated cosmogonic observation: "Death and the General: Iskander sees no difference between the terms. *From darkness into light, from nothingness into somethingness. I made him*" (s 230).

In imagining that he "made" Raza Iskander admits to himself that he fostered the conditions which allowed Raza to rise to power unchecked by any firm democratic process that he might have put into practice. In this Rushdie seems fairly accurate, for while Bhutto's Pakistan People's Party started off well, it effectively banned opposition from 1974–7, its reelection in 1977 was suspicious and much contested, and it followed the familiar authoritarian course with its "imposition of martial law in order to save the country from 'chaos and disintegration'."[2] In a 1985 interview Rushdie highlights the irony of Bhutto's choice of Zia: Bhutto "chose Zia because he wanted a weak command. He didn't want the army to be strong so he picked the stupidest man he could find, absolutely explicitly, he used to say so ... He made him out of nothing on the grounds of his stupidity. Then you get this bizarre relationship where the protege becomes the executioner."[3]

Iskander thus sets the stage for Raza'a tyranny, and together they represent the opposing forces of "the epicure against the puritan." But Rushdie cannot of course leave matters there. Instead, he raises the stakes of this conflict to cosmic proportions: "Virtue versus vice, ascetic versus bawd, God against the Devil: that's the game.

Messieurs, mesdames: faites vos jeux" (*s* 240). Neither Raza the God nor Isky the Devil fares well in this game: as a libertine Devil, Iskander creates the conditions for his own fall and thus for the rise of a God-centred tyranny; as a puritanical God, Raza exacerbates the devilish Iskander's throttling of the nation's potential and thus gives rise to the Beast.

Shame's peripheral, shabby hero, Omar Khayyam Shakil, is only partly, only peripherally, to blame for the rise of the Beast. Rushdie's overweight and cowardly version of the great Persian poet shamelessly complies with the dictates of Iskander and Raza, and abandons all professional morality when he mesmerizes his female patients so that the can have some "highly charged sex" with them (*s* 128). He also jumps at the first chance to indulge his Lolita complex by marrying Raza's mentally deficient young daughter. Although Omar appears to love his child-wife Sufiya, his attempt to keep her alive through sedation suggests the repression of the nation's anger – not to mention that of women in general. His death in the maw of the Beast, "the most powerful mesmerist on earth" (*s* 236), thus takes on a type of poetic justice. While Omar is in many ways peripheral to the strictly political context of the novel (and I am not talking about gender politics here, for Omar is crucial to that), he's central to its otherworldly theme, as he is the first to spy the dark forces which will eventually surface to destroy both him and Raza. Omar's importance will thus become increasingly pronounced throughout this chapter.

RAZA'S STATE

Rushdie's fierce antagonism to Zia's dictatorial Islamic regime of the early 1980s led him to take great liberties in depicting his life. In reality Zia never disguised himself as a woman, never fled for his life to the home of three witch-like mothers, and certainly never suffered a gruesome death in the jaws of a satanic Beast. In fact, all of these bizarre Rushdean fantasies were written while the Pakistani dictator still held power. Much of the novel does, however, follow historical accounts. For instance, Zia mounted "Operation Fair Play" in 1978, an operation which led to the incarceration and eventual hanging of Ali Bhutto in April 1979. In a 1995 interview, Rushdie says that the public incident which triggered *Shame* was "the execution of Mr. Bhutto." He adds that this incident was not simply a case of a tyrant executing a democrat: "the Bhutto government in its time of office had been at least as oppressive and corrupt as the military dictatorship that followed it."[4] In the novel Rushdie spends more of his rhetorical force against Zia than Bhutto, and this is almost certainly because Raza's dictatorship displays the type of religious rhetoric Rushdie despises. While Rushdie argues against any type of dictatorship, he betrays his secular bias when he says in a 1995 interview that even though the Bhutto regime "was a military dictatorship it didn't have anything like the degree of what's called Islamization that it now suffers from."[5]

At the time Rushdie was writing *Shame* it was impossible to say if or how Zia's dictatorship might be toppled (in fact, Zia lifted martial law in 1985 and died in 1988). It is perhaps for this reason that opposition to Raza takes a mythic rather than a political or military form. In one of his many metafictional comments, the narrator defends his use of a mythicized agent of revolt: "My dictator will be toppled by goblinish, faery means. 'Makes it pretty easy for you,' is the obvious criticism; and I agree, I agree. But add, even if it does sound a little peevish: '*You* try and get rid of a dictator some time'" (*s* 257). Rushdie's use of "goblinish" and "faery" belies the more serious and terrifying aspects of the Beast which possesses Sufiya and which stalks Raza, following him all the way to Nishapur. Elsewhere, Rushdie admits that he was frightened by Sufiya, and he claims that the "dark area at the centre of her" is what the "book is about."[6] He also admits that what happens in the novel is "very alarming" and that it is certainly "the most savage writing" he has ever done.[7] He even had a nightmare about Sufiya as Beast: "I woke up and realized that I had been scared out of my mind by somebody I'd made up." Rushdie's discovery that Zia had "a mentally retarded daughter" – a discovery made after he had already written Sufiya into the plot – also gave him "a really eerie feeling."[8]

Before proceeding to a more in-depth look at the novel, I should note that just as Zia and Bhutto are fictionalized as "Isky" and "Raza," so Rushdie is fictionalized as the cosmopolitan narrator. Both Rushdie and his narrator are Londoners with strong personal ties to Pakistan, and both betray a fascination with the tangled web of Pakistani politics, culture and religion. In an interview Rushdie says that he *is* the narrator in *Shame*. He adds, however, that "novelists, being sneaky people, will fictionalize even the bit that looks like autobiography."[9] Unlike the narrators in *Midnight's Children* or the *Verses*, the narrator in *Shame* does not complicate or obscure the main points of the novel. Whereas in my chapter on *Midnight's Children* I make a point of maintaining the distinction between author and narrator, in this chapter an insistent distinction between the two seems awkward and unnecessary.

In seeking for the reason why Rushdie creates a demonic figure to punish Raza and his Islamic State, one must first understand the author's uncompromising secularism. Regardless of the manner in which a political leader might implement Islamic Law, Rushdie remains antagonistic to the very idea of such implementation. Rushdie fervently resists any political philosophy whereby "Law" deriving from an other world of angels, demons and gods can become paramount in this world of citizens, dissidents and presidents. He believes that all law must be flexible enough to accommodate cultural and historical change. In promoting this secular view Rushdie mocks the notion that a text can ever be infallible, and he paints unsavoury portraits of those who support fundamentalism or Islamization – chiefly Raza Hyder and his zealous advisor Maulana Dawood. He also devises ingenious punishments for these two characters: Dawood enters a senility in which he degrades the Islamic sanctities he tries to promote; Raza falls into a schizophrenic state of mind in which he is harassed by an angel and a demon, and eventually hounded (literally to death) by the Beast. Rushdie is here of course peddling his own brand of poetic justice, for all these avengers – angel, demon and Beast – are mythological figures drawn from the very cosmology Raza has projected into the relatively secular arena of Pakistani politics. Raza thus eventually enters a *state* of mind in which he is terrorized by the offspring of his Islamic *State*.

All of this does not necessarily mean that Rushdie is against Islam or Islamic values, or that he cannot see any way to accommodate Islamic values under the rubric of a secular society. In his essay "Zia ul-Haq. 17 August 1988," written immediately after Zia's death, he praises the tolerant spirit of subcontinental Islam and he argues that Zia's version of Islamic Law violated this spirit: "It needs to be said repeatedly in the West that Islam is no more monolithically cruel, no more an 'evil empire,' than Christianity, capitalism or communism. The medieval, misogynistic, stultifying ideology which Zia imposed on Pakistan in his 'Islamization' programme was the ugliest possible face of the faith, and one by which most Pakistani Muslims were, I believe, disturbed and frightened. To be a believer is not by any means to be a zealot. Islam in the Indo-Pakistani subcontinent has developed historically along moderate lines, with a strong strain of pluralistic Sufi philosophy; Zia was this Islam's enemy" (*IH* 54). In the novel itself Rushdie attacks and satirizes a zealous, fundamentalist Islam, arguing that Islam "might well have proved an effective unifying force in post-Bangladesh Pakistan, if people hadn't tried to make it into such an almighty big deal" (*s* 251). He also suggests that if honest and sincere Islamic sentiments were heard, Pakistanis would be better able to fight authoritarianism. Unfortunately, these voices are silenced before they have a chance to change things for the better:

"there were a few voices saying, if this is the country we dedicated to our God, what kind of God is it that permits – but these voices were silenced before they had finished their questions, kicked on the shins under tables, for their own sakes, because there are things that cannot be said. No, it's more than that: there are things that cannot be permitted to be true" (*s* 82). At the core of Rushdie's attack lies his view that Pakistani leaders impose fundamentalism "from above" (*s* 251), that is, without allowing for free and open debate, without attempting to convene the type of Conference Saleem promotes in *Midnight's Children*. In Rushdie's Pakistan, those with opposing views are "kicked on the shins under tables."

Rather than creating an open forum in which everyone can be heard, Raza imposes his suspiciously convenient understanding of religion "from above." And by using a religious language which Pakistanis are "reluctant to oppose" (*s* 251) he infuses authority into his political decisions. While Rushdie argues against these decisions, he is even more concerned with breaking the spell of religious language, both because it can be abused for political ends, and because he fears the hold it can have over people's minds in the first place. He therefore implies that all language is a fallible human construction, however divine the original inspiration or source. To illustrate his point, he mocks the manner in which the story of Bilquis's flight from her father's burning cinema takes on the rigidity of a sacred text: her "story altered, at first, in the retellings, but finally it settled down, and after that nobody, neither teller nor listener, would tolerate any deviation from the hallowed, sacred text." He further mocks this sanctification when he says that the account of Bilquis's life in Delhi becomes inscribed in "formulaic words which it would be a gross sacrilege to alter" (*s* 76, 78).

This is not the first or last time that Rushdie mimics and questions the notion of an infallible sacred text. In *Grimus* both Liv's "recitation" of Virgil's diary and Virgil's exhortation to believe what he has written mimic the Quran. Surah 96 begins with "Recite," many verses begin with "Say," and the Koran is constantly reminding its readers not to doubt its contents (for instance, the first surah begins, "ALIF *lam mim*. This book is not to be doubted"). Virgil's diary also contains a thinly disguised cosmic history, complete with the fall of the Devil (Deggle) from God's grace (communion with the Rose). In *Midnight's Children*, Ahmed dreams of rearranging the Koran, and Saleem thinks of his autobiography as a Hadith or Purana. Saleem observes that "Memory's truth ... selects, eliminates, alters, exaggerates, minimizes, glorifies, and vilifies," and he claims that "no sane human being ever trusts someone else's version more than his own" (*MC* 211).

Saleem also draws his reader's attention to the spaces that are outside a given picture frame (*MC* 122–3), thus emphasizing the selective nature of any depiction or version of reality. Likewise, *Shame*'s narrator observes that "snapshots conceal as much as they make plain" (*s* 116). Rushdie's antagonism to "formulaic words which it would be a gross sacrilege to alter" also surfaces in the *Verses* and *Haroun*: the clock-smashing Imam believes that history ought to stop because the words of the Koran are the final Truth, and Khattam-Shud wants to stop the endless permutation of stories and to replace this creative flow with his idol Bezaban or "Without-a-Tongue."

In *Shame* Rushdie's opposition to making revelation a fixed, normative standard ranges from light-hearted humour to harsh satire. He writes playfully when he has Bariamma insist that sex cannot be "like sitting on a rocket that sends you to the moon" because "the faith clearly stated that lunar expeditions were impossible" (*s* 146). He hits a more serious note when the "organizers of the war" in Kashmir give their soldiers promises of an afterlife in a blissful other world: "Those who fell in battle were flown directly, first-class, to the perfumed gardens of Paradise, to be waited on for all eternity by four gorgeous Houris, untouched by man or djinn. 'Which of your Lord's blessings,' the Quran inquires, 'would you deny?'" (*s* 77). In *Midnight's Children* the Pakistani State similarly urges Saleem and his fellow soldiers into battle with cries of Holy War and with promises of perfumed gardens and *houri* girls. In *Shame* the backlash against using religious propaganda for military purposes is not as immediate as in *Midnight's Children*, in which Saleem and his troop proceed directly into a hellish "afterlife." In Rushdie's fictional Pakistan, anger first goes underground and then surfaces in the forms of the Beast and Kali.

Rushdie does, however, make his antagonism to Raza's Islamization clear from its inception. After his coup, Raza appears on national television, "kneeling on a prayer-mat, holding his ears and reciting Quranic verses." Rushdie forces his readers to wonder what is in Raza's hand while he is telling the nation that in putting Iskander under house arrest he simply wants to be an honest broker, an "honest ref or ump" to the nation: "What, leatherbound and wrapped in silk, lent credibility to his oath that all political parties, including the Popular Front of 'that pluckiest fighter and great politician' Iskander Harappa, would be allowed to contest the rerun poll?" Rushdie delivers his answer in studied fashion: "The television camera travelled down from his *gatta*-bruised face, down along his right arm, until the nation saw where his right hand rested: on the Holy Book" (*s* 223). Rushdie emphasizes the word "right" partly because the left hand is considered less pure, yet mostly because Raza justifies his elimination of the Opposition by declaring that Iskander's leftist politics are incompatible with Islamic rule: "He announced that God and socialism were incompatible, so that the doctrine of Islamic Socialism on which the Popular Front had based its appeal was the worst kind of blasphemy imaginable" (*s* 247).

The word "right" also brings to mind Raza's right-hand man, Dawood, who reviles socialism, secularism and everything he considers impure or "un-Islamic." Prior to the Imam of the *Verses*, Maulana Dawood remains Rushdie's most caustic portrait of "the violent Muslim fundamentalist." Dawood tells Raza that the reason the Army "must not stop at stamping out tribal wild men" (by which he means the separatist Baluchis in Needle Valley) is that violence can be elevated to a religious plane: "Prayer is the sword of the faith. By the same token, is not the faithful sword, wielded for God, a form of holy prayer?" (*s* 99). Rushdie combines the type of puritanical violence Saleem directs at Lila Sabarmati – "we shall demonstrate the fate which awaits the lascivious" (*MC* 258) – with the ruthlessness of Saleem's Pakistani leaders when he has the ghost of Dawood scream into Raza's right ear that he should punish women who speak out against Islamic Law: Dawood counsels Raza to "strip the whores naked and hang them from all available trees." Responding to Dawood's suggestion that he kill the leader of these "whores," Raza feels "reluctant to ask God to make the bitch disappear, because you can't ask the Almighty to do everything, after all" (*s* 249).

Dawood appears to be a caricature of Abu'l Ala al-Maududi, who "feared that Pakistan (which means 'Land of the Pure') would become na-Pakistan ('Land of the Impure') in the hands of Muslims of doubtful faith." Politically, al-Maududi "was never much of a force until the time when the free-living, modern-thinking Zulfikar Ali Bhutto was ousted from power by General Ziaul Haq. [Zia] was basically a military dictator, not answerable to the people; his support of the Jama'at [Maududi's religious organization], therefore, had no popular approval. He was not a fundamentalist, but in order to give legitimacy to his seizure of power, he made use of the Jama'at."[10] Dawood's name also suggests two possible origins. First, "Maulana" may be an ironic allusion to the commonly used name of the Persian poet Jalalud-Din Rumi. Dawood's violent politics and intolerance are antithetical to Rumi's mystical love and tolerance. "Dawood" could also allude to N.J. Dawood, who first translated the Koran into contemporary English (1956) and whose translation of *Tales from the Thousand and One Nights* was published (as Penguin No. 1001) in 1954. N.J. Dawood's translation of the "pure Arabic" of the Quran could be seen as a blasphemous act in itself, as could the fictional senile Dawood's unwitting adulteration of the Koran "with other, coarser dialects" (s 205).

Rushdie escalates his attack on the political abuse of religion when he has his dictator identify himself with God. After rounding up Talvar and two other highly placed officers, Raza says to their executioners, "Well, well, now it is all in the lap of God." Rushdie underscores Raza's presumption of otherworldly authority when he recounts the Baluchi "joke" about God being gulled into helping successive dictators destroy their opposition, and when he deliberately confuses God with Raza: "God was in charge, and just in case anybody doubted it He gave little demonstrations of His power: he made various anti-faith elements vanish like slum children" (s 250, 112, 248). One might note in passing that in the *Verses* Rushdie also satirizes those who, he feels, usurp God's position in the otherworldly chain of command: the Imam "summons, conjures up, the archangel, Gibreel" and commands him, *"you must fly me to Jerusalem"*; also, Mahound "just laid down the law and the angel would confirm it afterwards" (sv 211–12, 365). Rushdie likewise does his best to underscore the arbitrary nature of Raza's rule of Law: Raza replaces the legal system with "religious courts presided over by divines whom Raza appointed on the sentimental grounds that their beards reminded him of [Dawood,] his deceased advisor" (s 248).

Rushdie emphasizes his main point – that religious tyranny creates a devilish backlash – when he has the Beast appear dramatically just at the moment Raza becomes comfortable in his exercise of a God-like power. Raza exclaims that the Russian invasion of Afghanistan is "the final step in God's strategy," immediately after which he is confronted by the devastating effects of his tyranny: the Beast. Omar tells him that Sufiya is on the loose, and the ghost of Iskander whispers in his left ear that Sufiya resembles "Fortune" and "an impetuous river" that destroys everything in its path. Sufiya takes on mythic dimensions when she becomes a "white panther" and when it is rumoured that this magic animal "could fly, or dematerialize, or grow until it was bigger than a tree" (s 254–6). She also anticipates the Beast's final disappearance (s 286) when she becomes "a demon" that can vanish into thin air (s 254). This demon panther circles its prey, "moving slowly inwards, spiralling inexorably in to the centre, to the very room in which [Raza] paced." It is at this point that Raza fully realizes that he is no longer in God's position of omnipotence. Instead, he feels he "had been left to his fate by God" (s 258).

Rushdie likewise punishes the violent fundamentalism of his Dawood by subjecting him to senility and to hallucinations which mock elements of the very religion he tries to enforce. Rushdie has his

Dawood make a fool of himself by walking through Islamabad "with his hands opened before him like a book, intoning verses from the Quran in an Arabic which the loss of his reason led him to adulterate with other, coarser dialects" (s 205). Dawood also prostrates himself "outside fish-shops as if they were the holy places of Mecca," abuses the citizens of Islamabad "for their irreligious blasphemies," and mistakes an activated sludge tank for Mecca's holy Kaaba (s 205–6). Rushdie emphasizes Dawood's "vision" of the Kaaba – which in Islam is "a sanctuary consecrated to God since time immemorial ... a spiritual centre, a support for the concentration of consciousness upon the Divine Presence"[11] – by having this "vision" occur at the moment of Dawood's death, a moment in which one is supposed to "see" into the upcoming spiritual world (as Mirza appears to do in the *Verses*). In thus depicting Dawood's senility and death, Rushdie takes a dangerous step beyond his previous depictions of religiously obsessed senility, in which old Aziz sahib loses himself in his mysticism and Aadam Aziz brings a lock of the Prophet's hair into a Hindu temple. While Attar's symbology supplies meaning to old Aziz sahib's senility, and while Aadam's disgust with communalism makes some sense of his crazed act, Dawood's vision only points to his utter senility, only underscores Rushdie's intense antagonism to this specimen of "the violent zealot."

Dawood and Iskander both play punitive posthumous roles: Dawood the "angel" and Iskander the "devil" sit on Raza's shoulders and talk into his right and left ear respectively, driving him to distraction. As always, Rushdie betrays his anti-clerical bias: Iskander's voice is rich, modulated, often ironic and self-deprecating; Dawood's on the other hand (or in the other ear!) is an apocalypse without redemption, a torrent of abuse. Rushdie has no friendly nickname for Dawood, yet he uses "Isky" almost endearingly, as when Raza ignores his predecessor, "even though Isky kept trying to make his points" (s 246). Dawood's voice never borders on the humorous; it remains pious yet furious, always the utterance of the stern schoolmaster who is losing his mind. Curiously, these voices travel all the way to Nishapur, where the three sisters cut Raza to pieces in their elevator of many blades. At this point Omar's hallucinating mind hears the dichotomous voices that once tortured Raza. This unsettling switch may suggests that Omar and Raza deserve a similar fate, one that cannot be avoided by closing one's eyes or ears.

A chilling point might also be made about the *absence* of Dawood's voice (s 258), for it appears to result from Raza's refusal to follow Dawood's advice, which is to kill his child (the increasingly dangerous Sufiya) in a sacrifice modelled on that of Abraham.

If we enter into the novel's cause and effect logic of repression and retribution, we might surmise that such a sacrifice would only further repress the forces that will eventually rise against Raza. Even if Raza killed his possessed daughter, the Beast could easily possess another body, given that it "has many faces" and "takes any shape it chooses" (s 279).

In an unnerving mix of the apocalyptic and the surreal, Rushdie has Iskander "the monkey" make his final point: Omar "shut his eyes, but eyelids were no defence any more, they were just doors into other places, and there was Raza Hyder in uniform with a monkey on each shoulder. The monkey on the right had the face of Maulana Dawood and its hands were clasped over its mouth; on the left shoulder sat Iskander Harappa scratching his langoor's armpit. Hyder's hands went to his ears, Isky's, after scratching, covered his eyes, but he was peeping through the fingers. 'Stories end, worlds end', Isky the monkey said, 'and then it's judgment day.' Fire, and the dead, rising up, dancing in the flames" (s 276). Omar's hallucination anticipates those of Gibreel in the *Verses*, for Gibreel sees demons "with open eyes" and also with closed eyes, just as the monk Richalmus "would shut his eyes and instantly see clouds of minuscule demons surrounding every man and woman on earth" (sv 321). Raza's "monkeys" also anticipate the "demons of jealousy" that sit on Gibreel's shoulders (sv 442). Yet there is a big difference between the hallucinations of Gibreel and Raza: Gibreel's irreligion opens the door to uncontrollable visions whereas Raza's politicized religiosity opens this door.

Omar's hallucination also echoes the earlier horrific image of Sufiya's body being engulfed by the fire of the Beast: "the fire pulls the nerve-strings of the corpse, which becomes the fire's puppet, conveying a ghastly illusion of life amidst the flames" (s 243). This image of dancing in flames resurfaces in Iskander's apocalyptic words about "judgement day," and both of these can be associated with the Beast as Antichrist scourging the world on Judgment Day, as well as to the Hindu goddess Kali, who dances in the chaos wrought by her own cleansing destruction – a blood bath if ever there was one! Daniélou notes that it is "under her fierce aspect as the Power-of-Time" or "the power of disintegration closely connected to the power of liberation, that the consort of Shiva [i.e. Kali] is mainly worshipped. She is then shown under a fearful form. She is a fierce-looking goddess, fond of intoxicants, of lust, of bloody sacrifices. Cruel and orgiastic rituals are performed in her honor by the followers of the Tantra cult."[12] These associations help to provide a subtle, poetic infrastructure for Rushdie's main point: by imposing a violent and puritanical form of Islam upon his people,

Raza precipitates the coming of the Beast in the forms of the Antichrist and the scourging goddess.

THE LAYERS BENEATH

The cause-and-effect relation of Raza's repression to the Beast's vengeance remains fairly subtle, yet not as subtle as the way Rushdie builds up to it by laying an underground foundation from which the Beast erupts. The surname "Harappa" and the estate names "Mohenjo" and "Daro" are telling here, for, apart from acknowledging Bhutto's family lands,[13] they signal the ancient layer in time when the Harappan culture flourished in the Indus Valley. Iskander's first name refers to President Major-General Iskander Mirza (1956–58) as well as to the famous Greek general Alexander, and thus also casts a hint backward in time. The tectonics of the novel depend partly on the fact that Islam is not the indigenous religion or sensibility; before it were the Harappans, and for many centuries the polytheism of Vedic and other gods held sway. Deep beneath the present geopolitical configuration of desert, plain and mountain we find a mixture of pagan and other repressed forces: sexual and democratic impulses denied by puritanism and Islamic Law; the anger of marginalized women (Rani banished to Mohenjo, Bilquis banished to Daro, and Sufiya chained *à la* Jean Rhys's madwoman in Raza's attic); Hinduism and its powerful gods and goddesses; Baluchistan's subterranean angels brutally kept down by Raza's centralized State; and a host of underground and peripheral forces feared by Omar. The undercurrents and pressures in this realm accumulate throughout the novel and find their outlet in the marginalized, pagan, polytheistic, female, demonized figure of the possessed Sufiya.

Rushdie's use of "shame's avatar" and "disorder's avatar" to describe the possessed Sufiya is important, for the term *avatar* derives from Hinduism, which of course originates in the remote past. But in the minds of the novel's Pakistanis Hinduism is seen as a recent threat and is associated with the Indian immigrant, seen in terms of the *"mohajir* ancestry" (S 254) held against Raza. (The problems of the *mohajir* date largely from Partition, when Pakistan gained 7.2 million refugees from India, most of whom settled in and dominated the cities and towns of the south.[14]) Retaining vestigial notions from his homeland, Raza hopes to father a "reincarnation" or "avatar" of his first still-born son. It may be important to note that an *avatar* refers to the freely willed descent of a deity into human or animal form, whereas reincarnation or *samsara* means the rebirth of a soul from one body to the next. Rushdie uses *avatar* rather loosely, perhaps in order to suggest that his Muslims do not grasp the distinction between it and *samsara*, or perhaps in order to accommodate the "descent" of the deity Kali into Sufiya. Another possible explanation may be that Raza invents such a spectacular fictional life for his still-born son (S 83) that this son's spirit might be seen as godlike, descending into Sufiya's body. In any case, when Bilquis has a second child the "shame" of giving birth to a dead baby is replaced by the "shame" of giving birth to a female baby. Thus Sufiya is at once an "avatar" of the still-born child and of the "shame" associated with the female replacement.

One might find some degree of irony in the fact that it is the same Raza who once believed in the Hindu notion of avatars who imposes Islamic dogma onto Pakistani life. Raza thus exacerbates the Pakistani tendency to deny "that Indian centuries lay just beneath the surface" of Pakistan (s 87). In depicting a revolt – or striking back – against such denial, and against the repression of polyvocality in religious, cultural and political forms, Rushdie constructs the composite figure of the Beast/Kali. This figure takes on satanic and Hindu associations, which is understandable, given that it revolts against a centralized, monotheistic, patriarchal power that is at once Mosque and State. One might also see the Beast/Kali as an avatar in that the spirit of Sufiya (and the innocence and sympathy she represents) is repressed, dies and then comes back from the dead in a destructive form which avenges those who kept her spirit down and snuffed it out.

While Rushdie initially lends a degree of humour to the insults Pakistanis direct at Hindus and the *mohajir*, he eventually makes it clear that the violence behind these insults is anything but funny. Highlighting the ludicrous degree to which religion divides the citizens of pre-Partition Delhi, he remarks that "going to the pictures had become a political act. The one-godly went to these cinemas and the washers of stone gods to those; movie-fans had been partitioned already." Bilquis's father, Mahmoud, revolts against this division by playing a Hindu-Muslim double bill, that is, by playing a film in which cows are set free along with another film in which cows are eaten (the "non-vegetarian Westerns"). Aadam Aziz's "optimism disease," which in *Midnight's Children* amounted to the belief in a tolerant, united subcontinent, here takes the form of Mahmoud's "mad logic of romanticism" and of a "fatal personality flaw, namely tolerance" (s 62). Aadam's heroic status in Amritsar and Agra also anticipates Mahmoud's celestial status. When Mahmoud's theatre explodes in a "hot firewind of apocalypse," Bilquis hears "a sound like the beating wings of an angel" (s 62-3). Rushdie's imagery suggests that Mahmoud's death is not merely a worldly event, but partakes in the divinity associated with angels. In giving the name

Mahmoud to his anti communalist crusader, Rushdie may also be borrowing from the Sufi depiction of Mahmud of Ghazni, whose love of his slave Ayez represents a love so great that it crosses the otherwise impenetrable boundaries of status and rank (and perhaps heterosexual mores). In the novel Mahmoud crosses the all too fortified boundary between Muslims and Hindus, and he thus attains a sort of angelic status.[15]

The zealotry which results in the double bill of Mahmoud's destruction resurfaces when Bariamma assails Raza and Bilquis for importing the notion of reincarnation into her Muslim country. The matriarch learns that they think God has "consented to send them a free substitute for the damaged goods" – a new child for their stillborn child: "Bariamma, who found out everything, clicked her tongue noisily over this reincarnation nonsense, aware that it was something they had imported, like a germ, from that land of idolaters they had left." Iskander also uses Raza's Indian background against him when he reminds people (during Iskander's trial) that the pro-Islamic Raza once believed in *avatars.* Iskander's supporters then mutter that there is "evidence of a Hindu great-grandmother on Raza's father's side," and that "those ungodly philosophies had long ago infected his blood." While these comments are somewhat humorous because they are ridiculous in the extreme, the humour evaporates when Bariamma calls Bilquis "a fugitive from that godless country over there" and when she yells at Raza's wife, "Come on, *mohajir!* Immigrant! Pack up double-quick and be off to what gutter you choose" (*s* 83–5).

In *Shame* the association between the Other and the demonic pertains mostly to Muslim demonization of Hindus, yet Rushdie's Pakistanis demonize Westerners and Christians as well. Given Rushdie's love of rock and roll and his far from puritan morality, one can imagine the delight he takes in parodying the view that there is a "demonic quality" in "Western-style dance music" (*s* 16) and that products from the West are "Foreign devilments," "Devil things from abroad" and "items from hell" (*s* 99). He also has fun describing the "wild lovers" copulating "in the aisle of the vegetation-covered house of the Christian God" (*s* 55) and the international hotels "where the naked white women go" (*s* 97). Rushdie's account of bias against Westerners is of course as damning to Pakistanis as to Christians, especially when his Pakistanis relish thinking about the shameful acts they attribute to Christians. For instance, speculating on the relationship between the Christian Rodrigues and his Parsi student Farah ("Disaster Zoroaster") the "good people of Q. hit upon the most shameful, scandalous explanation of all" (*s* 48).

Rushdie contends that to build Pakistan "it was necessary to cover up Indian history, to deny that Indian centuries lay just beneath the surface." He sees "the subsequent history of Pakistan as a duel between two layers of time" (s 87), and he quite decidedly champions the Indian layer. He invests this hidden layer with a variety of cosmic forces, and creates an effective dichotomy between those forces which are marginalized and rebellious and those which are centralized and conservative. This he does by having Omar's younger brother Babar join the subterranean angels of the Baluchis (an ethnic group marginalized and repressed by the central government) and by having Omar, who keeps close to the centre of power, fear the type of rebellious mythic force suggested by these underground angels. While Rushdie does not make it clear that the Beast (as fallen angel) rallies the subterranean angels, he clearly uses Omar's fears of peripheral and underground forces to create a foreboding backdrop for the Beast/Kali, who surfaces right in front of Omar's terrified eyes.

Whereas Omar moves from "Q" (Quetta, near the border with Afghanistan) to Karachi, Babar drifts from Q to the furthest hinterland of the country, that is, to the camps of the Baluchi rebels in the mountains surrounding Q. Babar's move to the hinterland is initially an "act of separatism" against his three mothers and their idealization of Omar (s 131), yet his subsequent revolt is against the central government and the control it exerts through its military strongman Raza.[16] The suppression of the Baluchis has a long history in the subcontinent, for the five million Baluchis in Pakistan speak an Indo-Iranian language and they have never been well integrated with "British India" or the rest of Pakistan. After attempting to subdue them, the British "accorded" them an autonomous region in 1876. "On the partition of India [in] 1947 the khan of Khalat [the large central region south of the regional capital, Quetta] declared Baluchistan independent; the insurrection was crushed by the new Pakistani army after eight months."[17] Early in the Bhutto era opposition governments "in Baluchistan and the Northwest Frontier [home to the Pathans] suffered open discrimination; their leaders were frequently criticized for being unpatriotic. Finally, on February 12, 1974, the Baluchistan government was dismissed on the charge of inciting the people of that province to rebel against the central authorities."[18] Since the creation of Pakistan, there have been three rebellions, the last being from 1973 to 1977 (roughly corresponding to the Bhutto era), when 3,300 Pakistani soldiers and some 6,000 Baluchis were killed.[19]

Babar writes in his notebook that Baluchi separatists believe their desire for freedom is supported by "golden angels" who are trapped beneath the surface of the earth (presumably by an unjust "God" or by such a God's stand-in, a despot such as Raza): "their belief that the golden angels were on their side gave the guerrillas an unshakable certainty of the justice of their cause, and made it easy for them to die for it. 'Separatism,' Babar wrote, 'is the belief that you are good enough to escape from the clutches of hell' " (s 130). When Babar dies for this cause he finds Heaven *below* rather than *above* the earth: he soars "lucent and winged into the eternity of the mountains" and he is "received into the elysian bosom of the earth" (s 132).

Given that this account is imagined by the three mothers, one cannot ascribe it a straightforward meaning. While the three sisters first idolize Omar and then Babar, their initial idolization and their subsequent hatred of Omar is not inconsistent. Omar is initially a product and symbol of their revolt against marriage (they conceive and raise him out of wedlock), yet he eventually leaves the three mothers and befriends Raza, who not only kills their only other son, but also promotes the patriarchal religious standards they vehemently reject. One could also argue that their idolization of Omar serves to torture Babar, who, once dead, is in turn idolized (or "angelized") so as to make Omar feel guilty. Whatever the case, the story of the three mothers suggests that when forces of resistance are defeated they join other forces of resistance, other angels trapped beneath the earth. The rise of Sufiya *as Beast* makes sense in this context, for the Devil is a fallen and, to some degree, a trapped angel who would find it in his interest to rally all rebellious powers.

Omar aligns himself with the central powers in the land (Iskander and then Raza) and he fears the peripheral, repressed, destabilizing powers joined by Babar. Omar's friendship with Iskander gives him momentary relief from his recurrent psychological and spiritual fear of the periphery, a fear which makes him dream that he's "falling off the world's end"; "It should be said that his professional success, and his friendship with Iskander Harappa, have had the effect of reducing the frequency of these giddy spells, of keeping our hero's feet a little more firmly on the ground. But still the dizziness comes, now and then, to remind him how close he is, will always be, to the edge" (s 127). Whereas Babar gains glory when he joins the periphery and is defeated by the centre, Omar loses both body and soul when he is devoured by the force which stalks the central powers in the land. The punishment of Omar may seem harsh, yet one should remember three points. First, Omar is punished by the Beast and the three mothers. One cannot expect lenient or gentle justice from such vindictive and evil figures, despite the fact that they act as the necessary scourge of Raza's tyranny. One cannot expect even-handed justice from

Madame Guillotine or Kali, both of whom are used to describe the possessed Sufiya. Second, Omar is punished largely for the company he keeps, for his friendship and compliance with the autocratic Iskander and Raza. Third, Omar is not merely an innocent bystander. As the "top man" in Karachi's leading hospital, he hypnotizes women so that he and Iskander can have "some highly charged sex," after which he rationalizes his abuse of power by saying that it is impossible "to persuade a subject to do anything she is unwilling to do" – a rationalization he also used after hypnotizing and impregnating the very young Farah Zoroaster (s 128, 52). Omar's sexual abuses and shamelessness, combined with the many other instances where women are marginalized and repressed in the novel, make it easy to see why the agent of revolt and retribution takes a female body, and why this agent bears a striking resemblance to the goddess Kali and to "old Madame Guillotine with her basket of heads" (s 240).

Rushdie skillfully conflates cosmology and psychology when he combines Omar's escalating fear of the dark forces lurking in the depths of outer space with images of the mountains of Baluchistan and the subterranean "mountains" of Nishapur. He sees the mountains surrounding Quetta as the last barrier between humanity and a fearsome, meaningless cosmos inhabited by "silicon creatures or gas monsters" (s 23): "the child Omar Khayyam surveyed the emptiness of the landscape around Q., which convinced him that he must be near the very Rim of Things, and that beyond the Impossible Mountains on the horizon must lie the great nothing into which, in his nightmares, he had begun to tumble with monotonous regularity" (s 22). Omar's fear of unseen cosmic forces multiplies when he explores the depths of Nishapur, where a terrifying abyss yawns beneath: "he discovered ruined staircases made impassable by *longago* earthquakes which had caused them to heave up into tooth-sharp mountains and also to fall away to reveal dark abysses of fear ... in the silence of the night and the first sounds of dawn he explored beyond history into what seemed the positively archaeological antiquity of 'Nishapur'" (s 31). This passage differs tellingly from an earlier description of the Impossible Mountains, in which readers find the image of "crumpled ochre slopes," as well as a skillfully placed ellipsis between "stonemasonry" and "divine dream-temples" (s 23). In place of such imagery, readers now find "tooth-sharp mountains," as well as an ellipsis between "dark abysses of fear" and "silence of the night." Omar appears to see the "mountains" beneath Nishapur in terms of a tradition not emphasized by Attar, one in which "the chief abode of the Jinn is in the mountains of Qaf, which are supposed to encompass the whole of our earth."[20] This possibility is enhanced when the three mothers appear to fly to these

Impossible Mountains at the end of the novel. Such a flight suggests that they are returning to their homeland of mischievous spirits.

The imagery of "stonemasonry" and "divine dream-temples" is given its most harrowing and its most overtly psychological twist when Omar returns to Nishapur at the end of the novel. Here he hallucinates that the destabilizing forces under the mountains, the angelic pressures which make the dream-temples rise and fall (*s* 23), have descended upon the rest of the country: "The world was an earthquake, abysses yawned, dream-temples rose and fell, the logic of the Impossible Mountains had come down to infect the plains. In his delirium, however, in the burning clutches of the sickness and the foetid atmosphere of the house, only endings seemed possible. He could feel things caving in within him, landslips, heaves, the patter of crumbling masonry in his chest, cog-wheels breaking, a false note in the engine's hum" (*s* 274). Rushdie combines earlier images of tectonic shifting with Omar's mental and anatomical breakdown. He gives all of these a cosmic and apocalyptic tone, suggesting that Omar's universe turns out to be as dark and destructive as the portentous nightmares of his childhood.

Much of Omar's terror can be attributed to the influence of his three witchlike mothers, who actively discourage their son from exploring the consolations of science, philosophy and mysticism. When Omar sets out "the most elegant proofs of Euclidian theorems" and "expatiate[s] eloquently on the Platonic image of the Cave," Munnee responds, "Who is to understand the brains of those crazy types? ... They read books from left to right" (s 36). The three sisters quickly reject Greek ideas, which can be associated with the poet Omar Khayyam.[21] They also reject the mystical symbolism developed by that other famous twelfth-century resident of Nishapur, Farid ud-Din Attar: "And one day the three mothers sent a servant into the study to remove from their lives an exquisitely carved walnut screen on which was portrayed the mythical circular mountain of Qaf, complete with the thirty birds playing God thereupon" (*s* 33). While Omar goes on to study the "arcane science" of hypnotism and the medical science of immunology, he does not pursue the mystical ideas suggested by the screen or by its curious association with Hashmat Bibi's mystical death. After the three sisters' removal of the screen, after the "flight of the bird-parliament," Omar uses hypnotism to give Hashmat Bibi "glimpses of non-being." Hashmat Bibi then "apparently will[s] herself into death" (*s* 33–4). Whereas Omar's grandfather old Mr Shakil dies cursing himself and other people to Hell (*s* 12, 14), Hashmat Bibi dies with whispers of Heaven and God on her lips: "at the very end she had been heard muttering,

'... deeper and deeper into the heart of the rosy cloud'" (s 34). Her somewhat comic "mystical death" (her name suggests a flight into oblivion on a carpet or *mat* of *hash*ish) echoes that of old Aziz sahib in *Midnight's Children*. Yet in *Shame* Attar's notion of mystical annihilation does not recur as it does in *Midnight's Children* to suggest ideals of conference, unity, divine song or a meaning which transcends death. Rather, the three sisters seem to have succeeded in expunging Attar and his mystical flight from the mansion and the metaphoric city of Omar's birth.

The three mothers' dismissal of science and mysticism make Nishapur a "third world that was neither material nor spiritual, but a sort of concentrated decrepitude made up of the decomposing remnants of those two more familiar types of cosmos" (s 30). Instead of encouraging the best of twelfth-century Nishapur, the three mothers have the effect of the Mongol hordes who sacked the city in 1221. Most disturbing is the notion that one's own parents can be evil, can play the part of Khayyam's malicious wheel of heaven or Attar's "hundred monsters loosed from hell."[22] Rushdie's Omar finds what the author of the *Ruba'iyat* finds: a cosmos in which humans exist "beneath unscrupulous stars" and in which the wheel of heaven "is a thousand times more helpless than you."[23]

Rushdie's use here of Khayyam and Attar reflects two sides of his sensibility: the hedonist and the mystic. The dichotomy may not be an unbridgeable one given the dual nature of Khayyam's *Ruba'iyat*, for some people feel that it can be read both as a literal text in which the love of wine and women signifies a love of physical pleasure and as an allegorical text in which drunkenness stands for the intoxication of divine ecstasy and sexual union signifies the bliss of union with God (the Beloved, the Friend). One must also remember that Attar condemned Khayyam for his hedonism. A curious parallel exists between the way Khayyam was rejected by Attar and the way Rushdie has been rejected by many Muslims. In his Introduction to Khayyam's *Ruba'iyat,* Peter Avery notes that Attar imagines an afterlife for Khayyam in which the latter is "ashamed and confused on being rejected at God's threshold." Avery adds that Khayyam thus "stood condemned alike by the spiritually and intellectually tolerant Sufi poet, from whom, exceptionally, he received no compassion because he was so heinously a materialist, and by the Sufi schoolman, who abhorred him as a spurner of religion, lacking the grace to attain the Sufi's gnostic beatitude."[24] Like Khayyam, Rushdie employs metaphors drawn from Sufism, and, like Khayyam, he has not been embraced by those who use such metaphors within a more orthodox framework of belief – for instance, one Ayatollah Khomeini, author of the Sufi poem which starts, "I've become possessed by the beauty spot above your lip, oh friend," and ends, "I was awakened by the hand of the idol of the wine house."[25]

While the three science-hating, religion-hating sisters might initially seem heroic, even feminist, they are, as Haffenden observes, an "enjoyable but ultimately sinister complex."[26] From the start, Rushdie associates them with the Satan who plots the downfall of Adam and Eve, for they sleep in "a huge mahogany four-poster [bed] around whose columns carved serpents coiled upwards to the brocade Eden of the canopy" (s 21). They reject religious customs by refusing to circumcise, shave or whisper to their newborn son, and by living apart from the Ummah or community which gives meaning to the social ideals of Islam. Their rejection of men and patriarchal authority is also suggested in their status as the three weird or lesbian sisters, for rumour had it that they "would indolently explore each other's bodies during the languorous drowsiness of the afternoons, and, at night, would weave occult spells to hasten the moment of their father's demise" (s 13). Their inseparability mocks the "three-in-oneness" of the Trinity (s 35), and their communal pregnancy, during which no one can identify the father or the mother, mocks the immaculate conception of Christ. Later they say, perhaps merely to spite Omar, that Babar's father was an angel while Omar's was a devil, and this suggestion of a satanic conception is not, given the satanic rape of Sufiya, out of the question. Rushdie suggests the three sisters' antagonism to God and mysticism in a variety of ways, explicitly in Munnee's assertion that "there is no God" (s 281) and more subtly when they discard the walnut screen of Qaf.

Further evidence of the demonic nature of the three sisters can be found in the way their traits and actions complement those of the Beast. Three of the main forms of the possessed Sufiya – the Beast, Kali and Madame Guillotine – can be associated with the three Shakil sisters: the Beast can be seen in the triune mothers' antagonism to God, in their vicious acts and in their refusal to perform Islamic rites; Madame Guillotine can be seen in their violent rejection of traditional hierarchy and in their body-shredding contraption which dispatches the tyrant Raza; Kali can be seen in their female revolt against the patriarchal and monotheistic power structure central to Islamic cosmology. Rushdie strengthens the link between the Beast and the three sisters when they all join forces in Nishapur, killing Raza and Omar and lifting themselves above the final gruesome scene: the Beast leaves Sufiya's body and hovers ambiguously over Nishapur; the three sisters crumble, "perhaps, into powder under the rays of the sun," or they grow wings and fly off "into the Impossible Mountains in the west" (s 285). In his interview with *Scripsi*, Rushdie says that he "was very pleased" with the way "the text sets up the expectation that The Beast, this nemesis figure, is coming to get the general and then she doesn't. Somebody else gets the general." This "somebody else" is the three sisters, who Rushdie calls the "sort of Macbeth-like witches [who] become the avengers at the end."[27] On the level of plot, Rushdie makes a good point about the upsetting of expectations. Yet the final actions of the three weird sisters also fulfill literary expectations about the way these *Macbeth*-like witches work behind the scenes with the Devil to bring about the fall of those in power.

The fear of metaphysical evil instilled in Omar during his childhood in the home of the three mothers gives him a sharp and intuitive awareness of the evil lurking in the universe. Observing the sulphurous "pricks of yellow light" in Sufiya's eyes, Omar admits to himself that there are more things in the universe than can be explained by a scientific philosophy: "From the flickering points of light he began to learn that science was not enough, that even though he rejected possession-by-devils as a way of denying human responsibility for human actions, even though God had never meant much to him, still his reason could not erase the evidence of those eyes, could not blind him to that unearthly glow, the smouldering fire of the Beast" (s 235). Having demonstrated considerable skill as a mesmerist, Omar is well qualified to recognize the "eyes of Hell ... the golden eyes of the most powerful mesmerist on earth" (s 236). Terrified, he turns instinctively to the only cosmic force able to counter the Beast: "'God help us,' said Omar Khayyam, in spite of his uncircumcised, unshaven, unwhispered-to beginnings. It was as though he had divined that it was time for the Almighty to step forward and take charge of events" (s 239).

Omar's experience with the strange forces of the universe and the subconscious combine with his attraction to the young Sufiya to make him the ideal observer of the transformation of Sufiya into the Beast. Omar's dreams about the pedophile Rodrigues were "prescient warnings against the dangers of falling in love with under-age females and then following them to the ends of the earth." For once one is at the edge of the world (presumably near "the Rim of Things") the young girls "inevitably cast you aside" and "the blast of their rejection picks you up and hurls you out into the great starry nothingness beyond gravity and sense" (s 141). With his overactive imagination that fills the depths of space with "silicon creatures or gas monsters" (s 23), and his understanding that young females can cast older men into the void, Omar provides the reader with a unique vantage point from which to watch the rise of the Beast in Sufiya – a point Rushdie stresses by having the possessed Sufiya escape through a brick wall and by having Omar stare for "hours on end" at the "fantastic outline" of "his departed wife." Rushdie also signals Sufiya's larger metaphysical dimensions when Omar's "eyes, roving outwards through the attic window, seemed to be following someone, although there was nobody there" (*s* 243). Omar's life has come full circle, since he is once again terrified by the haunted spaces of his childhood. This time, however, the cosmic force which haunts him does not lurk beneath the precipices of mountainous staircases or hide in the depths of outer space. Rather, it appears right in front of his very eyes. Even more frightening, it disappears, and then tracks him all the way back to Nishapur.

A NECKLACE OF SKULLS

Rushdie himself was unnerved by the extremely dark undercurrents let loose in Sufiya. In an interview he says that she "is the most disturbing thing in the book, and she was very disturbing to write because she more or less made herself up [... She] did frighten me. I think it's unusual to be frightened by one's own creations, but she did make me worried about her. I worried about what she meant ... Yes, I know where she comes from and the process of making her, but she seems to transcend her source material. There is a dark area at the centre of her, and the book is about that dark area."[28] Rushdie's narrator tells us that in creating Sufiya he borrows from three different media accounts, the first two pointing to the way shame is inflicted by sexist puritanism. In London "a Pakistani father murdered his only child, a daughter, because by making love to a white boy she had brought such dishonour upon her family that only her blood could wash away the stain." Again in London, a teenaged "Asian" girl is beaten by white boys, after which she feels shame rather than anger (*s* 115, 117). The first instance illustrates the imposition of shame, the second the internalization of shame. In the main story Sufiya is subject to both. The third media account supplies a hint of the metaphysical mechanics which lie behind Sufiya's transformation: a boy "had simply ignited of his own accord, without dousing himself in petrol or applying any external flame. We are energy; we are fire; we are light. Finding the key, stepping through into that truth, a boy began to burn" (*s* 117). Sufiya blushes so hotly that her skin burns whoever touches it, yet she does not step into any liberating truth. While Sufiya as cultural metaphor may derive from the above sources, the deepest, darkest, scariest part of her derives from the mythology surrounding Satan and demonic possession – the latter supplying an inversion of mysticism if ever there was one! Disturbingly, Rushdie combines horrific images of satanic possession with those of rape, all the time making the parallel between the Beast's rise in Sufiya and the rebellion of underground forces – the fallen angels, Baluchi rebels, frustrated and abused women, and so forth.

Just as Rushdie constructs an underground realm for the nation, so he constructs an underwater realm for Sufiya. The young girl unwittingly becomes a "sponge" which soaks up invisible shame and shamelessness; she becomes a janitor "of the unseen," mopping up the "dirty waters" so that Pakistan can live up to its name, "Land of the Pure" (s 120, 122). Sufiya is empathetic and compassionate to those around her, yet she unknowingly pollutes her own soul, imbibing the dirty water of military, political, ethnic, sexual and religious repression. These waters constitute the ocean from which the satanic Leviathan rises.

The most horrifying aspect of Sufiya's possession is satanic rape. Rushdie establishes the depth of the sea as a metaphor for sexuality when Bilquìs tells Good News to think of male penetration as "having a fish up your fundament" and when, on the eve of Sufiya's wedding, Shahbanou tells her to think of herself as the ocean and the man as a "sea creature." Shahbanou tells her, "that is what men are like, to live they must drown in you, in the tides of your secret flesh." Sufiya replies "obstinately in her voice of a seven-year-old girl, which was also the eerily disguised voice of the latent monster: 'I hate fish'" (s 146, 199). Rushdie suggests that Sufiya's childlike mind is not ready for sex, although her body may be. The monster takes advantage of this situation by harnessing and magnifying her body's sexual energy. And Shahbanou does not help matters: by denying Sufiya any release of the accumulating sexual energies in her body she only gives the monster more scope. Because of Shahbanou's overprotective or selfish actions (she sleeps with Omar in Sufiya's place), the monster usurps Sufiya's subconscious "sea" and then stalks the land in its seven-league boots. Given the link between phallus and fish, one could say that Rushdie's writing takes on a shocking quality when the Beast stirs in Sufiya's "ocean": "There is no ocean but there is a feeling of sinking. It makes her sick. There is an ocean. She feels its tide. And, somewhere in its depths, a Beast, stirring" (s 215).

This description evokes a great deal of pathos in itself, especially since it comes immediately after a moving account of Sufiya taking images and "people" in and out of her head (s 213–5), an account which shows that while she has sympathy for the world around her, her mental retardation does not allow her to construct any form of meaningful understanding. Even worse, while she "packs her head full of good things so that there won't be room for the other things, the things she hates," these other, foreign things "that don't seem to be from anywhere" invade her mind: "They come most often during the sleepless nights, shapes that make her feel like crying, or places with people hanging upside-down from the roof." These invasions confuse Sufiya as to whether she is good or evil: "If she were good the bad things would go elsewhere, so that means she is not good. Why is she so bad? What makes her rotten, evil? She tosses in her bed. And pouring out from inside the fearsome alien shapes" (*s* 214). It is not only the world which is against her: the otherworldly satanic force which preys on the blindness and cruelty of this world also steals her body and terrifies her fragile consciousness.

Rushdie hits a similar horrifying psychological note in the *Verses* when Chamcha sees Pamela's face as "a saintly mask behind which who knows what worms feasted on rotting meat (he was alarmed by the hostile violence of the images arising from his unconscious)" (*sv* 402), and when Chamcha asks himself, "What evil had he done – what vile thing could he, would he do? For what was he – he couldn't avoid the notion – being punished? And, come to that, *by whom*? (I held my tongue.)" (*sv* 256). One of the main differences in the possessions of Sufiya and Chamcha is that while both have a strong societal cause, Sufiya's is explicitly the work of the Beast whereas Chamcha's is implicit (the Devil holds his tongue). Also, Chamcha is to some degree aware of, and responsible for, his actions. Sufiya, on the other hand, remains completely ignorant of what is really going on in her mind and body.

Sufiya cannot understand her world, and Rushdie's Pakistanis refuse to understand theirs. Much of what Rushdie says about Pakistani culture in *Midnight's Children* may apply here, although the brunt of his criticism seems aimed at Raza's militarism and his sexist betrayal of his own daughter and wife. Yet Rushdie's critique funnels out into a wider national arena on numerous occasions, and also becomes a generalized principle when he says that it is in the nature of humans to "pretend the menace is not loping towards them in seven-league boots" (*s* 199). They do not examine the monster they create, for to do so would mean to question their most basic beliefs: to "comprehend Sufiya Zinobia would be to shatter, as if it were a crystal, these people's sense of themselves" (*s* 200). Rushdie underscores society's ignorance when he has its bewildered members concoct myths to explain the invisible "demon" and the "white panther" (*s* 254) and when Sufiya indiscriminately tears the heads off youths and no one knows where these heads have landed.

These severed heads suggest Kali for a number of reasons. First, the Hindu goddess would naturally remain incomprehensible to those who are immersed in an Islamic version of reality, to those who have forgotten that Indian centuries lie beneath them. Second, Kali's status as a female, polytheistic deity makes her a fitting figure of opposition to Raza and his male-dominated, monotheistic State. Sufiya's initial confinement in the attic indicates repression in general and the oppression of women in particular. (Her location in the attic suggests the plight of the "madwoman" in Brontë's *Jane Eyre* and Rhys' *The Wide Sargasso Sea*.) That the "darkened room" is "an echo of other death-cells" (*s* 237) suggests Iskander's prison cell and anticipates the elevator in which Raza dies. Not surprisingly, the anger which springs from Sufiya's chained state has as its primary target a man who epitomizes patriarchal culture and religion. Peter Van der Veer emphasizes the link between sexual oppression, which Rushdie calls "the intolerable burdens of honour and propriety" (*s* 173), and a Hinduized backlash against this repression: "The more [Sufiya's] father restrains women and female sexuality through his Islamic laws, the more frightening becomes his daughter, who ends as a monster wandering through Pakistan beheading men and drawing out their entrails like a Muslim version of the Hindu goddess, Kali."[29] O.P. Mathur comments that Sufiya suggests Beauty and the Beast, Medusa, Kali, and Yeats's "terrible beauty" of revolution.[30] M.D. Fletcher also observes that the "details of the victims being beheaded and having their entrails eaten link the beast's *modus operandi* to that of the goddess Kali ... despite the beast's whiteness in contrast to Kali's blackness the nudeness, matted hair, terrifying eyes, 'blood-curdling howls,' nauseating stench of death, and ability to be everywhere at once also fit."[31] While Sufiya stands for many things – repressed sexuality, marginalized women, the guillotine which avenges despotism, brutalized innocence, and so forth – the Kali associations are strong, particularly given Sufiya's "*mohajir* ancestry" and her ominous names, "disorder's avatar" and "shame's avatar." Rushdie also alludes to Kali when Sufiya finds "four youths," kills them by yanking off their heads, and then hurls these heads "into the scattered clouds." Rushdie emphasizes the point that the "heads were never found" and that "nobody saw them fall" (*s* 216, 219). The heads are missing, presumably, because the Kali in Sufiya has taken them with her and has strung them around her neck – thus adding more skulls to her necklace.

Just as one must follow associative links to see Sufiya as a sea-monster rising from the nation's oceanic subconscious, so one must follow links to see how necklaces and nooses punish the chief culprits in the novel: Dawood, Iskander, Raza and Omar. The first of such necklaces of vengeance is a "garland of shoes" which Bilal accidentally throws around Dawood's neck, thus humiliating the man who tries to whip up a pious fervor against the three sisters (s 43). In the next instance, Iskander sees the instrument of his death (a hanging rope) in terms of the umbilical cord that strangled Raza's son in Bilquis's womb. Iskander also sees his prison cell as "an inverse womb, dark mirror of a birthplace" and he feels that "its purpose is to suck him in, to draw him back and down through time, until he hangs foetal in his own waters" (s 231). His final thought, *"I am being unmade,"* suggests that while he "made" Raza (he fostered the conditions under which Raza rose to power), he is now being "unmade" by his own creation. As with Rani's shawl implicating Iskander in the throttling of Sufiya, the umbilical cord links the tyrannies of Iskander and Raza. This link is strengthened when, in Nishapur, Raza recovers from his illness to find himself immersed in excrement, making him feel "as if a hangman's knot had smashed him in the back of the neck" (s 280). Events have come full circle, for Raza's blatant sexism inculcates the shame which becomes associated with the umbilical cord, which is in turn associated (via Iskander's umbilical noose) with the punishing "hangman's knot." Raza's fate is sealed when, after Munnee tells the promoter of Islamic Law "there is no God," the three mothers push him into the small room of the elevator (reminiscent of Iskander's cell) and pull the lever which sends knives through his body (s 281–2). That one of these knives emerges through his Adam's apple suggests the action of "old Madame Guillotine" (s 240), whose mode of execution also involves a metal blade slicing the neck.

Omar is likewise visited by a necklace of vengeance when his three mothers place Dawood's garland of shoes around their son's neck: "Behind his eyelids Omar Khayyam saw his mothers placing, around his neck, the garland of their hatred. This time there was no mistake; his sweat-drenched beard rubbed against the frayed laces, the tattered leathery tongues, the laughing mouths of the necklace of discarded shoes. The Beast has many faces. It takes any shape it chooses. He felt it crawl into his belly and begin to feed" (s 279). By transforming Dawood's garland into a sinister leather being, and by claiming that the Beast "has many faces," Rushdie underscores both the magic which allows invisible forces to take a form or a face, and the idea that cosmic vengeance can take many forms – here those of an innocent girl, a white panther, Kali and Madame Guillotine. Sufiya's final action is to tear Omar's head off, and her final form is that of a cloud in the shape of a "giant, gray and headless man," both of which further link her to Kali with her necklace of skulls and to "old Madame Guillotine with her basket of heads" (s 286, 240).

A curious similarity exists between Sufiya and the composite monster depicted in Rushdie's short story, "Yorick." The story begins with metafictional gamesmanship reminiscent of *Tristram Shandy*, and it includes a banquet at which a table is loaded with "boars' heads, sheep's eyes, parson's noses, goose-breasts, calves' livers, tripes, venison haunches" and "pig's trotters" (*EW* 72). The narrator refers to "the anatomy of the table," and speculates that "were its several dishes assembled into a single edible beast, a stranger monster would lie there than any hippogriff or ichthyocentaur!" This edible beast prefigures the possessed Sufiya in that both are explicitly fabricated from disparate animal and demonic elements. The narrator of "Yorick" asks, "is it not conceivable that [Fortinbras], seeing upon the laden board the dismembered limbs of this fearsomely diverse and most occult of creatures, and constructing in his mind's eye a behemoth with antlers on his giant turkey's head and hooves set weirdly down beneath his scaly lower half, might lose all appetite for the fray"? (*EW* 73). Sufiya is similarly a "fearsomely diverse and most occult of creatures" who takes an active role by severing the heads of turkeys and humans, and who takes the form of a white panther stalking its prey. Sufiya is also "diverse" in that she incarnates various repressed aspects of society, she expresses a positive scourging side as well as a demonic side, and she combines aspects of Leviathan, the Beast, Kali and Madame Guillotine. Another link between "Yorick" and *Shame* might be found when the narrator of "Yorick" exclaims that Ophelia's breath resembles a witch's brew, "a tepid stench of rats' livers, toads' piss, high game-birds, rotting teeth, gangrene, skewered corpses, burning witchflesh, sewers, politicians' consciences, skunk-holes, sepulchres, and all the Beelzebubbling picklevats of Hell!" (*EW* 66). *Shame* itself might be seen as a hellish vat in which Rushdie boils the consciences of his four main male characters.

Whether one associates "shame's avatar" with a noose, a necklace of shoes, Madame Guillotine or Kali, this otherworldly force operates by violently severing the head from the body – a poetically just mode of operation in that the main reason shame and violence accumulate is that the head (of the State or the anatomy) refuses to listen to the body. Sufiya is the victim of this accumulation since she is close to the dictatorship of Raza and since society's puritanical rules (which Shahbanou enforces and Omar agrees to) make it impossible for her to fulfill her body's needs. Her dual status as innocent victim and agent of violence is reflected in one of Omar's final hallucinations in Nishapur: he sees her on the day of their wedding with "a noose around her neck" (*S* 275). This rope links her to Dawood's ignominy, the strangulation of Raza's son, the hanging of Iskander, and Omar's gruesome death. The rope around her neck also suggests that while the Beast and Kali punish the four male culprits in the novel, the most pathetic victim is Sufiya herself.

The vengeance of the Beast, and of the three Shakil sisters who act in concert with it, marks the end of the story, although Rushdie provides a hint that just as the Beast took the form of Sufiya, so it will take other forms if required. In his malarial delirium, Omar imagines "visions of the future, of what would happen after the end": "And at last Arjumand and Haroun [are] set free, reborn into power, the virgin Ironpants and her only love taking charge. The fall of God and in his place the myth of the Martyr Iskander. And after that arrests, retribution, trials, hangings, blood, a new cycle of shamelessness and shame" (s 276–7). Rushdie here predicts the rise of the more democratic and secular leader Benazir Bhutto, and he suggests that even such a turn of events will not put an end to the vicious cycle which he sees as inherent in Pakistan's mix of religion, culture and politics. In this sense he ends the novel much as he ends *Midnight's Children*, that is, with the notion that generation upon generation will make the same mistake before they will be able to live or die in peace.

6 The *Satanic Verses:* Dreamscapes of a Green-Eyed Monster

Iago. Work on,
> My medicine, work: thus credulous fools are caught,
> And many worthy and chaste dames, even thus
> All guiltless, meet reproach.

Othello IV.I.44–7

In *Othello* Iago brings the great war hero to his knees, foaming like a dog and ready to kill his only love. Iago manages to do this through insinuation and deception, but why he does it is anyone's guess (it is hard to believe the reasons he gives). In the *Verses* the narrator suggests that he knows the cause of Iago's malice, yet he does not tell us what it is. Instead, he points to the animosity Chamcha feels toward Gibreel. The point becomes slightly clearer when we think in terms of myth, in terms of what might lie behind the deep-seated jealous grudge that Chamcha, who once had horns and a tail but is now a hoofless demi-devil, holds against Gibreel, the great star who never seems to have fallen from public grace or from his heavenly bliss with Alleluia. Shakespeare's play thus hints at a satanic element that remains obscure even after the closing act.

Othello's villain also helps us to get at the insidious game in which a Devil narrator refuses to be straight with us, and instead works out an ancient grudge on a contemporary stage. Yet this is just the tip of the iceberg in a novel which has jeopardized for over ten years now the existence as well as the good name of its author. This is also a novel which is enormous and complex, one which shifts from Bombay to Tehran in the blink of a schizophrenic's insomniac eye; one in which immigrants grow horns and tails in London, and hot icebergs float up the Thames. And to cap it all, steering at the helm is an Iago-like captain, a super-subtle man of wealth and taste, injecting his crude oily voice in our left ear, and laughing as credulous fools fall into his crooked trap.

The Satanic Verses presents one of literature's most difficult, dangerous, and one might even say reckless experiments. And it is not as if
Rushdie did not know what he was doing. Having taken his MA in
Islamic history at Cambridge, he must have known that one of the
things most likely to incite heated controversy was a reworking of the
"satanic verses incident," an episode in the life of Muhammad which
to Muslims demonstrates the scrupulousness of the prophet but
which Western scholars have often used to suggest the fallibility of
both Muhammad and the Koran. Referred to by Muslims as "the *gha-
raniq*" or "birds" incident, it refers to the trick played on Muhammad
by Iblis, the Muslim Satan. Reprising his Edenic role as the great be-
guiler, Iblis tricks Muhammad into thinking that God has permitted
goddesses (the "three high-flying birds") to act as intercessors between Himself and humans. Muhammad initially accepts the goddesses, then rejects them when he realizes that the idea came from
Satan rather than Gabriel, that is, when he realizes they are satanic
rather than angelic verses.

While this conflict between angelic and diabolic forces gives the
novel its title, and while the cosmic power struggle behind the incident works its way into every layer of the narrative, critics have focused on the worldly politics surrounding the Rushdie Affair rather
than on the otherworldly politics in the text itself. They have by and
large glossed over what in a work such as *Faust* or *Paradise Lost* they
would make a concerted effort to explain: the power struggles which
pit angel against angel, Deity against Devil, man against God. As a
result, few readers are encouraged by them to examine the intricacies
of not only who does what to whom, but also who controls the account of manipulations this way and that. And herein lies the rub, for
without a close look at these otherworldly politics one can easily
overlook Rushdie's most disturbing construction: a narrator who
swoops in and out of the text like an evil wind.[1] Like a mad captain,
this sinister guide steers the massive structure of the novel straight
into an icy wall.

This insidious narrator is not obvious, yet upon close scrutiny,
and with help from sources as diverse as Shakespeare, Attar and
Bulgakov, one can see that he invades the text sporadically, sometimes to comment on morality and politics, and sometimes to influence events so that evil prevails over good. He is by and large a
traditionally evil Satan, and as such he uses his puppet, Chamcha,
to play out his antagonism to God (his cosmic enemy), salvation
and mysticism (represented by Alleluia), and Gabriel (his archangelic rival, of whom Gibreel is a parody). I should note that in order to avoid confusion between Rushdie's character and the

Archangel, I refer to God's archangel by the European name Gabriel, rather than by the Muslim name Gibreel.

Throughout the novel, Rushdie conflates the satanic verses incident and *Othello,* keeping in the background all the time the story of Adam and Eve and the paradigm of Attar's Qaf. In Rushdie's reworking of Shakespeare's play, Gibreel plays the part of the bright but falling star Othello, Allie plays the innocent and forgiving Desdemona, and Chamcha the deceptive Iago. Rushdie inserts key elements of the satanic verses incident into this Shakespearean drama when the possessed Chamcha whispers doggerel satanic verses over the telephone, thus driving Gibreel into a monstrous green-eyed jealousy. Chamcha succeeds in turning Gibreel's Edenic garden of love into a hellish labyrinth of jealousy, thus bringing to *fruition* – and I use this word in its full mythic sense – the revenge of that ancient, apple-offering, heel-biting serpent. Like *Othello,* the novel ends bleakly, and there is only an echo left of the spiritual freedom represented by the murdered Alleluia, whose unwavering devotion to her Impossible Mountain of Everest gives us yet one more version of Attar's Qaf.

At this point an important distinction between the *Verses* and *Othello* presents itself: Gibreel does not attain Othello's self-knowledge, nor does he praise the virtues of the woman he has murdered. Instead of delivering an impassioned eulogy before killing himself, he stutters that Allie was a "whore" and a "bitch" but that he loved her anyway. Instead of falling on his dagger in heroic style, he puts a gun in his mouth and pulls the trigger (*sv* 544–5). The anticlimax comes when Chamcha, conveniently purged of his evil by a heart bypass, reconciles with his Bombay love-interest and with his Indian self. While on the worldly level this reconciliation suggests optimism, on the otherworldly level it contains what Aravamudan calls "the slyly ironical last laugh of the devil, who has conquered by fading away into innocuous moral virtue."[2]

The sly diabolical plan is not the only reason why readers have difficulty figuring out what game Rushdie is playing. Another reason is that the novel is written in a slippery postmodern way. Srinivas Aravamudan comments on this serpentine strategy in "Being God's Postman is No Fun, Yaar," an article which employs deconstructive theory and relates elusiveness of meaning to Satan's vagrancy. One should remember that Rushdie starts the *Verses* with Satan's indefinite travels, and borrows from Daniel Defoe's *Political History of the Devil* (1726) in his epigraph: "Satan, being thus confined to a vagabond, wandering, unsettled condition, is without any certain abode; for though he has, in consequence of his angelic nature, a kind of empire in the liquid waste or air, yet this is certainly part of his punishment, that he is ... without any fixed place, or space, allowed him to rest his foot upon." Aravamudan argues that "the slipperiness of the devil is that of the signifier itself; it is the very indeterminacy of the devil's actions that make him truly diabolical. The *desinterrance* of his vagrancy, his lack of address which summarizes his delinquency, his nomadic refusal to recognize the law of settlement, is an eternal escape from the transcendental signified – God."[3] This indeterminacy might also apply to the satanic narrator's mode of operating, for he moves in and out of the text in order to insinuate that there is no such thing as a single, transcendental Meaning and Unity, no Ideal toward which all beings can aspire.

Returning to terms used in chapter 2, *When Worlds Collide*, I would say that by casting doubt on sacred orientation, Eliade's *hierophany*, Rushdie seems to be offering us an and/or proposition that is not very comforting: continual doubt and/or a choice of deities, both of which seem to exist in a universe in which no irruption of the sacred can truly orient the self. One might also say that in partly replacing the God-like author with a satanic narrator, Rushdie drifts in the "rising tide of occultism," the darker side of Kliever's "polysymbolic polysymbolism." Yet even here, in the most blasphemous of his writings, he manages to suggest Qaf, that transcendental signified which can neither be defined nor discarded, and which might in some desperate manner serve as an invisible nemesis to the insidious indeterminacy of the Devil.

While the Devil slides unseen through the novel, creating a meaningless and hellish world for Chamcha and Gibreel, Rushdie also suggests that Satan's elusiveness differs in kind from the mysticism, love and ineffability represented by Allie and her Everest/Qaf. In her spiritual intoxication Allie enters a blissful realm of angels and Deity, against which the satanic narrator sets all his powers of rhetoric. Not only does he try to convince the reader that this realm is ruled over by a tyrannical God, but he also manipulates events so that Allie cannot find a meaningful annihilation in this realm. He appears to stop her from remaining at the peak of Everest by firing a gun (which echoes the initial explosion of the plane Bostan and anticipates Gibreel's final gunfire), and he manipulates events so that she eventually falls from the roof of Everest Vilas. The satanic narrator's antagonism to God, Allie and Everest underscores the fundamental cosmic division which he does his best to disguise when he argues that good and evil are interpenetrable, that God is mainly evil and that Satan is also good.

Thus the *Verses* contains hidden within it the same ideal one finds most clearly expressed in *Grimus* and *Haroun*, and which one finds in tragic, marginalized forms in *Midnight's Children* and *Shame*. Everest stands for a meaning which lies beyond the arguments and manipulations of the satanic narrator, just as the Qaf of Virgil and Eagle lies beyond both the twisted mysticism of Grimus and the diabolic manipulation of Deggle. Grimus fashions himself into his vision of the Simurg, yet because he does not control the narrative he cannot perpetuate his vision. Nor does Deggle appear to be much more successful: the peak toward which he journeys dissolves before he can gain any power. The entire narrative is shaped in favour of Virgil, who wants to free the inhabitants of Calf and who has no interest in gaining cosmic power (at the end of the novel he walks down to the beach while Deggle heads for the mountain's peak). This narrative set up is very different from that in the *Verses*, which is shaped in favour of the devil figure. Moreover, this Devil can insert himself into the narrative at key moments so as to destroy Gibreel's heavenly union with Alleluia, and to stop her from ascending the peak a second time. This does not, however, mean that the ideals represented by Allie are demolished. As with Desdemona in *Othello*, on the worldly level a character may be defeated, yet on the otherworldly level the spirit and the ideals of this character may live on in an annihilated, impossible form.

In terms of structure, the *Verses* is also a confusing and problematic text, its various settings and themes tenuously linked by the oneiric, surreal imagination of Gibreel. The kaleidoscopic dreams into which he slips and slides appear to have their genesis in the tales of his childhood, stories about "the avatars of Jupiter," "the incident of the Satanic verses," "the politics of Muhammad's harem," and newspaper accounts "in which butterflies could fly into young girls' mouths, asking to be consumed" (*sv* 23–4). These stories make sense of the chaotic jumps from setting to setting, for these locations can be seen as psychological manifestations of ideas and scenes which had formative influences on his mind. Also, the "inaccurate" stories about the Prophet told by his adoptive mother (*sv* 22) help to link the novel's title to the diverse settings in which the satanic verses incident is reworked: to the Arabian peninsula, where Iblis tempts Mahound to compromise his monotheism by allowing the intercession of the three goddesses; to rural India, where Mirza tempts Ayesha the butterfly girl to compromise her faith by accepting his help; and to London, where Chamcha whispers his satanic verses to Gibreel and where Rekha tempts Gibreel to say "just three-little-words" (*sv* 334). These three words may be *I love you*, yet they also imply the three short names of the goddesses of the satanic verses incident (Lat,

Manat and Uzza), and hence they imply a compromise in what Gibreel mistakenly sees as his archangelic mission.

Another origin for Gibreel's hellish novel-structuring visions lies in the sunken world he finds in his youth. For sometimes, "when he looked around him, especially in the afternoon heat when the air turned glutinous, the visible world, its features and inhabitants and things, seemed to be sticking up through the atmosphere like a profusion of hot icebergs, and he had the idea that everything continued down below the surface of the soupy air: people, motor-cars, dogs, movie billboards, trees, nine-tenths of their reality concealed from his eyes" (*sv* 21). In constructing Gibreel's sunken world, Rushdie might have been influenced by the notion of the *alam al-malakut*, the "subtle or immaterial – or subtly material – world ... into which the material and physical world is plunged, as if into a liquid." Glassé explains that "the physical world is a 'crystallization,' or projection, out of the subtle world, the 'ether'; the 'ether' is a projection out of the surrounding formless, or Angelic world; and the Angelic world is projected out of Being."[4] The schema might be simplified thus: Being) -> angels) -> ether) -> our world. Even if Rushdie did not have this schema in mind, it still aids in understanding Gibreel's perception. For anyone in our world would be two removes from the angelic world. And for a schizophrenic, the subtle or ethereal world would act as a murky, distorting lens, which would make it difficult to see what lies two (or three) worlds away. A schizophrenic could mistake fallen angels for good angels, even the Devil for God. One might also speculate that Gibreel's world is but a projection of the fallen angel – a possibility enhanced by the notion that the *alam al-malakut* contains ambiguous figures as well as those that are purely good: that Gibreel's visionary world contains "God, angels, demons [and] afreets" makes sense in this context, for afreets are one of the five types of djinn, all of whom live in the *alam al-malakut.*[5] Although I don't want to put too fine a point on this speculative analogy, I would add that Iblis, as Al-Jahn, is the leader of the djinns.

Also important, given that the novel is structured by Gibreel's dreams and hallucinations, is Iblis's renown for manipulating the dreaming mind. In his very helpful study, *Satan's Tragedy and Redemption: Iblis in Sufi Psychology,* Peter Awn notes that "Man's confrontation with Satan's disguised form attains its fullest intensity not in man's everyday conscious life, but in the semiconscious realm of dream and sleep. The power of the spirit world is felt with far greater force there than in the waking state because Satan can avail himself of the most frightening of nightmarish forms."[6] Satan's power in the dreamworld was considered to be so great that it "even seemed conceivable that

Satan might appear as the Prophet of God himself," although Muhammad is reputed to have said that this cannot happen.[7] In the *Verses* Satan does not appear in Gibreel's waking dreams as Muhammad, although he does appear disguised as God. In addition, a strong case can be made for asserting that Satan disguises himself as Gabriel in the dreams which rework the satanic verses incident.

In depicting Gibreel's novel-structuring visions, Rushdie conflates cosmology, mythology and psychology much as he does in *Shame*, where powerful and terrifying figures emerge from the depths of outer space, earth, ocean and mind. Likewise in the *Verses* the Devil slides out of the distant or submerged world and plants himself, as he does in Sufiya, in Chamcha. He then works more obscurely and indirectly – mostly through Chamcha – on Gibreel. Both characters have inklings of the evil operating in and on them, yet they never fully grasp what is going on. In this sense they lie between Sufiya, who does not have a clue about what is happening to her, and Omar, who sees all too clearly that he is running headlong into the maw of the Beast.

The chaotic, oneiric structure of the *Verses* makes it a challenging novel to read, yet even more perplexing is the way Rushdie fuses the narrator's account of Gibreel's dreamworld with the demonic scheming and innuendo of his satanic narrator. While it is something of a simplification to say that the text has *only two* narrative voices, I would argue that it has a conventional, omniscient narrator as well as an otherworldly satanic narrator. These two narrators are not clearly distinguishable, except when the satanic narrator tells readers he is Satan, when he expresses a personal antagonism to God and to the angels who did not rebel against God, and when he specifically plays the role of Iblis in distorting revelation. The satanic narrator exerts a surreptitious influence over the conventional narrator's text in much the same way as he exerts influence over Gibreel's mind: just as Gibreel loses awareness at important moments of satanic intervention, and just as Gibreel's mind is increasingly thrown into a hellish chaos, so the text is taken over by the satanic narrator at key moments and is often slanted toward violent and chaotic scenarios: the riots and racial hatred in London, the genocide in the Imam's homeland, the mining disaster and the drownings in India, the surreal multiple deaths of Gibreel in Rosa's Argentina, the execution of Baal, the bombing of the Shaandaar Café, the murder of Sisodia and Alleluia, the black water of violent thoughts inundating Chamcha's mind, and the suicide of Gibreel. While it is tempting to suggest that the conventional narrator is at times possessed, this is not indicated, at least not in any substantial way. Likewise, there is no indication that Gibreel is possessed in the traditional sense, that is, in the way Saleem is temporarily possessed by his two-headed demon or Sufiya is inundated by the oceanic Beast. The exact relation between the conventional narrator and the satanic narrator remains problematic. Readers are alerted about the possibility of demonic narrative incursions, yet they cannot expect everything to have demonic significance. Unlike readers of C.S. Lewis's *The Screwtape Letters*, they cannot simply invert each immoral point into its moral opposite. Not surprisingly, this type of postmodern experiment has little to recommend it to the religiously orthodox.

One of the most confusing yet crucial moments of satanic narration occurs in Allie's bedroom, where the satanic narrator disguises himself as a bumbling God, an Oopervala or "Fellow [from] Upstairs" whose appearance resembles that of Rushdie himself (*sv* 318). Readers are initially led to see Oopervala as an anthropomorphic Deity who is archaic, obsolete, a ridiculous "Thing." God is made to look old and myopic, an inversion of the conventional God who sees all, or a parodic take on the conventional narrator who operates on the God-like, third-person premise of omniscience. Thus God becomes a stereotype to be manipulated, just as Chamcha conveniently becomes a heroic rebel angel and Gibreel conveniently becomes an angel without a will of his own. Yet there is far more to this bedroom scene. We do not discover the real identity of Oopervala until ninety pages later: echoing the devilish Iago, who says, "Demand me nothing, what you know, you know, / From this time forth I never will speak word,"[8] the satanic narrator says, "I'm saying nothing," yet then tells readers that it was he rather than God who "sat on Alleluia Cone's bed and spoke to the superstar" (*sv* 408–9). Oopervala plays both the role of Shakespeare's Iago and that of Milton's infernal Serpent: his obscurantism has the effect of confusing Gibreel and of turning him away from Allie, who is the one person who might be able to restore his sanity and lead him to a state of grace. For after giving up his appeal to God in his sickness, and after gorging himself on forbidden pork, Gibreel concludes that not being struck by a "thunderbolt" proves his point, that is, proves the "the non-existence of God"; Allie then tells him that his appeal to God and his subsequent survival is "the point" (*sv* 30).

Immediately following the satanic narrator's admission that it was he who spoke to the superstar, Rushdie gives a strong indication that his satanic narrator is in the process of dipping in and out of his text: the satanic narrator states matter-of-factly, "I'm leaving now," after which the narrative of Rushdie's conventional narrator takes over (*sv* 409). This is one of the few instances where the satanic narrator's presence is clearly indicated. In most cases, one can be sure neither of his presence nor of his absence.

Rushdie plays a subtle and dangerous game here, one far surpassing that of the unreliable narrator in *Midnight's Children*. While Saleem's story contains elements of chaos, uncertainty and mythic evil, Rushdie highlights Saleem's desire for a mystical, democratic "conference" and he shows that imitating the actions of the snake (implementing Schaapsteker's strategy of striking from cover) leads to death and meaninglessness. The *Verses* contains even greater elements of chaos, uncertainty and mythic evil, yet these are not given moral disapproval, either directly or indirectly. Moreover, the *Verse's* narrative structure is not held together by the hopeful dreams of an idealist like Saleem; it is instead torn apart by the inescapable nightmares of a schizophrenic. Gibreel calls his increasingly fragmented life a "bloody dream" and wonders if he and everyone around him are merely cogs in the greater archangelic machinery of Gabriel. When he wails, "Then what the hell ... is going on in my head?" (*sv* 83), readers might answer that the "bloody dream" which ends in murder and suicide is not that of the loyal archangel Gabriel, but, rather, that of the fallen archangel Satan.

THE SATANIC NARRATOR

Most critics do not discuss the idea of a satanic narrator, and those who do vary widely in their views. Harrison sees it as a vestigial notion while Knönagel sees it as central to the ideology of the text.[9] Yet Knönagel's article is at once too brief and too wide-ranging to do what I hope to do, that is, make an in-depth argument about the way the satanic narrator fits into the text's sliding fabric of worlds. I should add that I hope this chapter will work in reverse, that is, that my premise of a satanic narrator will become clearer the more I show the way this figure rewrites his own disastrous fall from Heaven, possesses Chamcha, manipulates his Iago-puppet to torture and destroy his Othello-puppet, argues that it is better to reign in Hell than serve in Heaven, and, finally, crushes and marginalizes the mystical aspirations of Alleluia and Sufyan.

Only two critics, Alex Knönagel and James Harrison, directly confront the question of satanic narration. In "*The Satanic Verses*: Narrative Structure and Islamic Doctrine" (1991), Knönagel argues for a "'satanic' point of view as the novel's ideological centre."[10] He admits that this narrator is not easy to identify, yet he maintains that "the text contains some hints that the novel's narrator ... is the inversion of 'the Cherisher and Sustainer of the Worlds' (Qur'an, 1: 2)."[11] My position is slightly different, for I would not say that *the* narrator is Satan, but that Satan is *one* of the narrators. Knönagel also notes that the "Guy Upstairs" who looks like a stereotype of God (*sv* 318) is in fact Satan parodying God, and that "His" appearance in Alleluia's bedroom can be linked to the satanic verses incident in which Satan impersonates Gibreel. He argues that the incident in the bedroom, and the narrator's comments about it, identify "the devil not only as the narrator of the whole novel but also as the origin of the mysterious revelations in the Mahound dreams."[12] Yet Rushdie plays an intentionally tricky game: "Initially, Mahound correctly identified the source of the confusion, but the narrative attempts to dispel this knowledge, and the narrator uses numerous tactics to confuse the reader's insights into the novel's structure, but a careful reader with a background in Islamic cosmology is nevertheless provided with sufficient information to recognize the novel's narrative situation."[13] While Knönagel goes into little detail, he makes two other quick points which support the notion of a satanic narrator: because the worldview presented in the *Verses* is antithetical to that of the Koran, "the whole novel can be read as an inversion of the qur'anic text"; the narrator insinuates that because God has very little power one may as well start worshipping "other deities as well," including (one would assume) Satan.[14]

In his book *Salman Rushdie* (1992) James Harrison makes a specific argument against the idea of sustained satanic narration, which he says is a bright idea Rushdie abandoned, leaving vestiges behind.[15] I doubt, however, that Rushdie would name his novel after an episode in which Satan interrupts and fabricates revelation, and then relegate to vestiges the instances where Satan interrupts and manipulates the narrative. While I do not agree with Harrison's conclusion, I find his angle on the novel insightful, especially when he observes that Rushdie provides "each narrative stream with an angelic and a diabolic presence," and when he says that this may have motivated the "half-dozen or so instances in which Satan steps forward and comments on what is happening."[16] He asks, "shouldn't the devil be allowed to have his say"? and adds, "If Saladin Chamcha qua horned beast can invade the dreams of immigrant youth, why shouldn't the original, of which Saladin is a mere parody, invade Gibreel's dreams?"[17]

Harrison also does what many critics have failed to do: draw attention to the text rather than to what people think about it. Particularly helpful is his list of six instances of satanic narration. I agree with his first five instances, which start with the occasion on which the narrator refers to himself as a Higher Power and adds, "In the matter of tumbles, I yield pride of place to no personage, whether mortal or im-. From clouds to ashes, down the chimney you might say, from heavenlight to hellfire … under the stress of a long plunge, I was saying, mutations are to be expected, not all of them random" (sv 133). The narrator also asks, "Of what type – angelic, satanic – was Farishta's song? / Who am I? / Let's put it this way: who has the best tunes?" (sv 10). In answering this question, one should keep in mind that in the novel Satan leads a devilish choir and that the song "Sympathy for the Devil" echoes in the streets of a burning London. The narrator's biased take on celestial politics can also be seen in his view that "Angels are easily pacified; turn them into instruments and they'll play your harpy tune. [Angels] don't have much in the way of a will. To will is to disagree; not to submit; to dissent. I know; devil talk. Shaitan interrupting Gibreel. Me?" (sv 92–3). Harrison's fourth reference is to the time at which, the narrator tells us, Hagar asked Ismail if leaving her alone in the desert could be God's will. The narrator says that God "replied, it is. And left, the bastard. From the beginning men used God to justify the unjustifiable. He moves in mysterious ways: men say. Small wonder, then, that women have turned to me" (sv 95). I have already discussed Harrison's fifth reference (to the narrator's statements "I'm saying nothing" and "I'm leaving now") but would here add the following two remarks by the narrator: "I, in my wickedness, sometimes imagine the coming of a great wave, a high wall of foaming water roaring across the desert, a liquid catastrophe full of snapping boats and drowning arms" (sv 94); "What evil had [Chamcha] done – what vile thing could he, would he do? For what was he – he couldn't avoid the notion – being punished? And, come to that, by whom? (I held my tongue.)" (sv 256).

There are also numerous remarks about the course and meaning of evil which suggest a suspicious intimacy with the subject: Gibreel "was the beneficiary of the infinite generosity of women, but he was its victim, too, because their forgiveness made possible the deepest and sweetest corruption of all, namely the idea that he was doing nothing wrong" (sv 26); "in fact, we fall towards [evil] naturally, that is, not against our natures" (sv 427); Chamcha "was heading for a human ruin; not to admire, and maybe even (for the decision to do evil is never finally taken until the very instant of the deed; there is always a last chance to withdraw) to vandalize. To scrawl his name in Gibreel's flesh: Saladin woz ear" (sv 433); "There is the moment before evil; then the moment of; then the time after, when the step has been taken, and each subsequent stride becomes progressively easier" (sv 438–9); "How comfortably evil lodged in [Chamcha's] supple, infinitely flexible vocal cords, those puppetmaster's strings!" (sv 445); "Is it possible that evil is never total, that its victory, no matter how overwhelming, is never absolute? (sv 467). One can also associate the above questions "Who am I? Let's put it another way: who has the best tunes?" (*sv* 10) and "Shaitan interrupting Gibreel. Me?" (*sv* 93) with the following ones: "Who am I? Who else is there?" (*sv* 4); Chamcha asks, "Oh my God. What's happening to me? What the devil? Help" (*sv* 60); "All around [Gibreel] are people hearing voices, being seduced by words. But not his; never his original material. – Then whose?" (*sv* 234); Chamcha asks himself, "Devil, Goat, Shaitan? Not I. Not I: another. Who?" (*sv* 257).

Because I see an insidious otherworldly drama being played out on a worldly stage, I cannot conclude, as Harrison does, that "the device" of a satanic narrator "is less than perfectly worked out and executed," and that "it is too infrequently used to establish a clear function for itself."[18] In order to be effective, this voice does not need to have a clear function. Indeed, its obscurity increases the level of uncertainty and insinuation in the text – all of which coincides with Satan's traditional mode of operating.

Timothy Brennan and Keith Booker also grapple to some degree with the satanic voice in the text. Brennan observes that the *Verses* "projects itself as a rival *Quran* with Rushdie as its prophet and the devil as its supernatural voice." He adds: "Or perhaps it is not the devil but only what the parasitical self-servers within the Faith call the devil by invoking God 'to justify the unjustifiable.'"[19] Booker echoes Brennan's equivocation: "the narrator of *The Satanic Verses* turns out to be none other than Satan himself but may also be God or the archangel Gabriel; it is difficult if not impossible to distinguish among such figures in Rushdie's book."[20] He observes that there "are many indications in the book that the narrator is, in fact, Satan," adding that "God and Satan are indistinguishable, irrevocably intertwined."[21] In the text itself this intertwining is suggested in the comment that Everest is "diabolic as well as transcendent, or, rather, its diabolism and its transcendence [are] one" (*sv* 303). We also find that love is "that archetypal, capitalized djinn, the yearning towards, the blurring of the boundaries of the self, the unbuttoning, until you were open from your adam's-apple to your crotch" (*sv* 314). The interpenetration of God and Satan is more directly asserted by the Rekha of Gibreel's tortured imagination, who comments in exegetical fashion that the "separation of functions, light versus dark, evil versus good, may be straightforward enough in Islam," yet if one goes back in time one finds that it is "a pretty recent fabrication": "Amos, eighth century BC, asks: 'Shall there be evil in a city and the Lord hath not done it?' Also, Jahweh, quoted by Deutero-Isaiah two hundred years later, remarks: 'I form the light, and create darkness; I make peace and create evil; I the Lord do all these things.' It isn't until the Book of Chronicles, merely fourth century BC, that the word *shaitan* is used to mean a being, and not only an attribute of God" (*sv* 323). Such comments can be taken many ways, most of which encourage readers to question the primary categories of moral and cosmic power: good and evil, God and the Devil.

Booker notes one instance in which the narrator "clearly indicates a satanic component in his identity,"[22] while Corcoran notes that the second chapter in the novel "has a suspicious narrator who may be, as in the case of the original troubling verses [of the satanic verses incident], Satan himself."[23] This fact becomes particularly striking when one learns that one of the two texts Rushdie was thinking of while writing the novel, Bulgakov's *The Master and Margarita*, contains only one chapter clearly narrated by Satan – Chapter Two! I return to Bulgakov and his *Master* later in this chapter.

Sami Naïr and Srinivas Aravamudan join the small group of critics who argue that the *Verses* is darker than it at first seems. Naïr calls it an exploration of the way evil eats away at life, evidence of "la quête rushdienne du sens dans un monde rongé par le mal (le cancer, qui traverse ce roman comme une obsession vive et déchirante),"[24] which I translate as "the Rushdean quest for sense in a world scoured by evil (the cancer which runs through this novel like a live and ripping obsession)." While many critics see Chamcha as a liberated character at the end of the novel (he is no longer possessed and he finds his Indian roots), Naïr maintains that both Chamcha and Gibreel remain caught in the Devil's trap: "Mais le mal est profond; si Chamcha, le diable, se retrouve à la fin du roman face à lui-même, sans aucune réponse véritable, condamné pour l'éternité à douter, Gibreel Farishta, lui, rongé par le cancer (le mal incurable du monde), finit par se suicider."[25] ("But the evil is deep: if Chamcha, the Devil, finds himself at the end of the novel faced with himself, without any genuine answer, condemned for all eternity to doubt, Gibreel Farishta is himself racked with a cancer – the incurable evil of the world – and ends up by killing himself.")

Aravamudan stresses that Chamcha's return to normality is especially deceptive: "The book ends with the spectacular self-destruction of Gibreel, while Chamcha's final, sudden decision to remain in Bombay (where he had gone back to reconcile with his dying father) and revive his Indian roots might contain the slyly ironical last laugh of the devil, who has conquered by fading away into innocuous moral virtue. This nagging doubt suggests itself through the book's closing lines, which painfully re-emphasize the repression of the diabolical rather than its seeming expulsion from Chamcha's personality."[26] One might even say that the satanic narrator contrives events so that his archangel meets a violent end, while his archdevil is rewarded for destroying the Edenic love between Gibreel and Alleluia. This is not to say that the satanic narrator ever makes life easy for Chamcha: his "reward" is preceded by anguish, and when it finally comes it is a mixed blessing, tarnished with alienation and doubt.

One might ask why Rushdie has not clarified his narrative strategy. One must remember, however, that those threatening his life accuse him of blasphemy and of playing the part of the Devil. Who has not seen the burning cardboard Rushdies with horns and their eyes poked out? With this in mind one cannot be surprised that he downplays the subtle or insidious moments where he lets his Satan influence the narrative. Rushdie tends to veer away from such discussion, emphasizing instead the novel's cross-cultural politics. He says that theologically charged phrases such as "the satanic verses" show the West its own insulting view of the Muslim Other. He adds, "You call us devils? ... Very well, then, here is the devil's version of the world, of 'your' world, the version written *from the experience* of those who have been demonized by virtue of their otherness" (*IH* 403). I agree that the *Verses* shows the Devil's version of the world, yet the Devil is used for two purposes, not just one. While it is true the Devil makes worldly political points à la *Shame*'s narrator, he also plays an otherworldly role, one which supersedes the worldly insofar as he uses the politics of rebellion to promote rebellion against God. In addition, he cares as little about the demonized, dark Other (Chamcha, Gibreel and Sufyan) as about the "angelized," white Alleluia.

Rushdie has also said that Gibreel's dreams "are reworkings, in a kind of nightmare way, of incidents from the early life of Islam." Since Gibreel is a Muslim, his "nightmare of religion" is naturally "a nightmare about God and the Devil."[27] Yet Gibreel's dreams are not only mental scenarios shaped by his upbringing and by his inner fears or frustrations; nor are they merely aimed at political or postcolonial targets. They are also projections or dreamscapes which the novel's Satan uses to take the upper hand in his ancient vendetta with God.

Harveen Mann notes that Rushdie "has offered contrastable interpretations" of the novel. Initially, he contended that the novel is a serious investigation of religious conflict. Then, "faced with the hard reality of the *fatwa* and after a year of life in hiding, Rushdie fell back on the fabulosity of his narrative as his key defence against the charges of blasphemy." Mann notes that Rushdie claims his audience to be "Indian migrants in Britain," while it is much more likely to be "the Western(ized), liberal cosmopolite."[28] I think Rushdie is too selective when he claims to write mainly for South Asian Muslims in England, and that he bends over backwards too far when he objects that what they perceive as blasphemy is in fact for their political benefit. No doubt he is writing in part for South Asians in Britain and no doubt certain demonic depictions illustrate the demonizations inflicted on migrants by the West. Yet the audience which most appreciates his fiction is a global, postmodern one, and much of the blasphemy in the novel reflects a satanic view of *this* world inhabited by figures such as Margaret Thatcher and *that* mythic other world inhabited by figures such as Gabriel, Satan and God. Rushdie may be expecting too much when he asks Muslims to divorce a worldly political message, which parodies their demonization, from what appears to be an attack – or at least a sinister questioning – of the otherworldly framework which has always separated them from their Christian neighbours.

What could be the purpose of writing a novel in which the figure of Satan has such a profound yet elusive influence? One possible explanation is that Rushdie is taking a narrative experiment almost as far as it can go. Unlike C.S. Lewis's *Screwtape Letters*, Rushdie's novel has no subtitle such as *Letters from a Senior to a Junior Devil*. Unlike Blake's *Marriage of Heaven and Hell*, sections have no headings such as "The Voice of the Devil" or "Proverbs of Hell." Rushdie pushes his narrator-construction close to its limit, that is, he uses the construction yet does not warn his readers about its presence or meaning. He thus allows his satanic creation to operate in the traditional satanic modes of disguise, deception and insinuation. Yet Rushdie also burdens his Satan with the Devil's archetypal flaw: pride. As a result, his Satan cannot stop himself from boasting and giving himself away: he tells readers that in "the matter of tumbles" he will "yield pride of place to no personage, whether mortal or im-. From clouds to ashes, down the chimney you might say, from heavenlight to hellfire" (*sv* 133). In supplying just as many hints as are absolutely necessary to identify a satanic voice, Rushdie puts into practice what he learns from Günter Grass: "Go for broke. Always try and do too much. Dispense with safety nets" (*IH* 277). The wisdom of such advice appears uncertain, and raises a difficult and perhaps unanswerable question: What happens when an already chaotic narrative is infused with the voice of a satanic narrator, one who is by very definition comfortable – one might even say *well-versed* – in meaninglessness and chaos?

Another question arises from Rushdie's use of a satanically invaded narrative: Will such a strategy inevitably lead to the type of clash that has characterized the Rushdie Affair? Several of the most intriguing answers are suggested in the novel itself. Sisodia's prospective film is essentially the version of events we have in chapter 2, for it is set "in an imaginary and fabulous city made of sand, and would recount the story of the encounter between a prophet and an archangel; also the temptation of the prophet." Countering an interviewer's objection that this film could "be seen as blasphemous, a crime against ...," the tycoon Billy Battuta responds, "Certainly not ... Fiction is fiction; facts are facts" (*sv* 272). Such naiveté is not left unchallenged, however. When the poet Baal suggests to the Madam of a brothel that a prostitute use the name of Mahound's favorite wife in order to give customers a forbidden thrill, the Madam replies, "If they heard you say that they'd boil your balls in butter." The Madam then allows her girls to use the names of the prophet's wives, observing that it "is very dangerous" but "it could be damn good for business" (*sv* 380). The Madam's words are strangely prophetic, both of the danger in which Rushdie lives and of the book sales his notoriety has encouraged outside the Muslim world.

The career of the poet Baal serves as the strongest warning to those who would play with sacred ideas in satiric ways. Because Baal both pens devotional verses to the goddess Al-Lat and scribbles poems against Mahound and Allah, and because he plays the role of "the Prophet" with his twelve "prostitute wives" in the brothel, it comes as no surprise that he bears the brunt of Mahound's anger. Routed from the Curtain and condemned to death, Baal shouts at his monotheistic opponent: "Whores and writers, Mahound. We are the people you can't forgive." Eerily anticipating Khomeini's unforgiving position, Mahound retorts coldly, "Writers and whores. I see no difference here" (*sv* 392). While Khomeini did not say this about writers in his condemnation of Rushdie (Khomeini was well aware of the poetic Sufi tradition of attacking dogma and piety – he even wrote a poem in this vein),[29] he did say that "Even if Salman Rushdie repents and becomes the most pious man of [our] time, it is incumbent on every Muslim to employ everything he has, his life and his wealth, to send him to hell."[30] A grim irony presents itself, given that Rushdie's existence in hiding resembles that of the novel's exiled Imam – a clear stand-in for Khomeini. For both, paranoia "is a prerequisite of survival" (*sv* 207).

Rushdie's satanic narration creates a problem for general readers and for Rushdie himself, yet it presents a particularly difficult problem for the orthodox reader who wishes to steer clear of the satanic and the demonic. Aravamudan notes that if "we wish to spot the ruses of the devil, we are in a catch-22 ... as we have to proceed in a vein more diabolical than the devil himself."[31] This is particularly difficult for Muslims, who by and large are taught to shun anything that involves the Devil. While certain strains of Islamic tradition allow Satan a tragic, even noble stature, by and large Muslim cultures do not condone interest in, let alone any detailed exploration of, the diabolic.[32] While orthodox readers may not take a close enough look at the novel to see the satanic narrator, they can nevertheless ascertain numerous points of view which are antithetical to those promoted by the God of the Koran. In the West the problem of reading the novel is by and large different: readers either do not realize what blasphemous things the satanic narrator is saying, or they are conditioned to separate the narrator from the author, whose message, they assume, lies deeper than that of his narrator.

HELL RAISER: THE SATANIC PUPPETEER

Fundamental to the otherworldly design of the text is the way the satanic narrator possesses Chamcha and then uses him to manipulate Gibreel. With great deftness and duplicity, the novel's Satan figure inundates both of their minds with hellish visions and turns them into puppets which act out a cosmic drama they neither see nor understand.

The text can be read from the very beginning on both worldly and otherworldly levels. On the worldly level, it begins when the plane Bostan explodes after the Canadian Sikh terrorist sets off her bomb-girdled body. On the otherworldly level, Bostan represents the Muslim heaven of the same name. Significantly, the plane explodes at exactly the height of Everest, the mountain at the top of which Alleluia hears angels and almost sees the face of God. The explosion of the plane, and the miraculous landing of Chamcha and Gibreel, revises the myth of Satan's rebellion in Heaven and his subsequent fall to Hell.

While the opening scene is entertaining in many ways, one should note that Satan grabs hold of Chamcha and possesses him as he falls, and that both the good angel (Gibreel) and the bad angel (Chamcha) fall onto the plains of Hell – the "cozy sea-coast" on which "danced Lucifer, the morning's star" (*sv* 198–9, 131). Thus the novel begins with a revision of the myth in which only bad angels fall. Having brought both angels with him onto his home turf, the satanic narrator proceeds to replay his victory in Eden: he uses his devilish, Iago-like Chamcha (or chump) to sow the seeds of division in the heavenly, Edenic garden of love inhabited by Gibreel and Alleluia. The narrator also sows the seeds of doubt, arguing that fallen angels merely exercise the freedom to dissent from God's tyranny, and that humans ought to follow their example by doubting revelation and by exploring the doubt which lies between belief and disbelief (*sv* 92). The cosmic drama reaches its climax when Gibreel Farishta ("Gabriel Angel") murders Alleluia Cone ("Praise God Mountain") before the latter can climb Everest and see the face of God a second time.

Chamcha's possession in the opening scene has been overlooked by critics (except Corcoran) and tends to be seen merely as a magic realist episode. Yet when one looks closely at the last two pages of the opening scene one finds that the satanic narrator is in the process of lodging himself – in the form of a "will to live," a will to survive his own fall from Heaven – in the stomach and vocal cords of Chamcha. Treating Chamcha in much the same ruthless way as the Beast treats Sufiya in *Shame,* he takes over the inner parts of Chamcha's body, wanting "nothing to do with his pathetic personality, that half-reconstructed affair of mimicry and voices." Chamcha finds "himself surrendering" to this will to live, and the narrator adds, "yes, go on, as if he were a bystander in his own mind, in his own body, because it began in the very centre of his body and spread outwards, turning his blood to iron, changing his flesh to steel, except that it also felt like a fist that enveloped him from outside, holding him in a way that was both unbearably tight and intolerably gentle." The Satan figure then uses Chamcha's vocal cords as if they were his strings, working them so that Chamcha can in turn take control of Gibreel's vocal cords: once the will to live "had conquered him totally and could work his mouth, his fingers, whatever it chose, and once it was sure of its dominion it spread outward from his body and grabbed Gibreel Farishta by the balls. 'Fly,' it commanded Gibreel. 'Sing'" (*sv* 9). Rushdie here takes great advantage of the notion that in mythology the angel Gabriel never lost his angelic wings, for Chamcha forces Gabriel's parodic stand-in to produce a flight of song that will land them both safely on the ground. Even more important in the larger scheme of the novel is that by forcing Chamcha to command the "Archangel," Satan usurps God's position in the cosmic chain of command. This usurpation anticipates the all-important reworking of the satanic verses incident, in which Satan substitutes his own voice for that of God's archangelic messenger.

Readers ought to note the insidiousness of the words, "yes, go on" in the opening scene, for they are slyly inserted in a passage which suggests possession, euphemistically called "dominion." Is the satanic narrator urging Chamcha to surrender to his power? Or is he urging the reader to accept, even enjoy, this possession? The opening scene ends on a particularly suspicious note, the full import of which is developed by Corcoran:

In a command much like the archangel gave to Muhammad to 'Recite,' the will-to live commands Gibreel to 'Sing.' … A narrator who claims, 'I know the truth, obviously,' comments on this chain of inspiration, and questions its type:

> Chamcha willed it and Farishta did what was willed.
> Which one was the miracle-worker?
> Of what type – angelic, satanic – was Farishta's song?
> Who am I?

By asking 'Who am I?' this narrator poses for the novel the same question Muhammad asked of the dubious "Satanic verses": who is their narrator?[33]

One should also note the narrator's use of multiple questions here, for these often accompany satanic innuendo. The rhetorical question "Who am I?" at the end of the possession scene ought to be kept in mind throughout the novel. One should note that the rhetorical answer, "Let's put it this way: who has the best tunes?" (sv 10) is also laced with satanic innuendo, given that the narrator later quotes from The Rolling Stones's "Sympathy for the Devil," and extols the "sweet songs" Satan sings "from hellbelow" (sv 286, 91).

The possession of Chamcha results in horns and a tail as well as the inward forms of heart palpitations, black water lapping at his heart, and evil thoughts rising from some hitherto unknown place within him. Chamcha experiences heart palpitations, which echo with the sound of "doom," at early moments in the novel when he appears to undergo possession (sv 34, 57, 63, 65). The narrator tells us that Chamcha's palpitations are the result of his heart wanting "to metamorphose into some new, diabolic form" (sv 253), yet this is clearly not what Chamcha wants. While one might say that deep down in his heart Chamcha desires "to substitute the complex unpredictability of tabla improvisations for [his heart's] old metronomic beat" (sv 253), Chamcha does not desire the "black water" of evil to lap at his heart. He has no choice but to give in to it.

In the hellish hospital, bitterness overcomes Chamcha, who reflects, "Once I was lighter, happier, warm. Now the black water is in my veins." Immediately after this he thinks to himself, "What the hell," and the narrator comments, "That night, he told the manticore and the wolf that he was with them, all the way" (sv 170). Also, in the protected environment of the Shaandaar Café he feels that the "grotesque" has taken hold of him and that he's "sliding down a grey slope, the black water lapping at his heart." He feels there's "no-way-back" to his old life, and he tells himself, "Leave your nail-marks in the grey slope as you slide" (sv 260).

Chamcha's demonization makes a political statement about the way immigrants are mistreated or demonized in Britain, yet this demonization also fits into an otherworldly plot in which Satan possesses and manipulates an innocent victim. Rushdie makes use of the association between the culturally demonized Other (the "dark foreigner," especially "the Muslim") and the otherworldly Other (the Devil), an association which is unfortunately part of the Western intellectual heritage. In *Orientalism* Edward Said notes how Dante positions Muhammad "in the eighth of the nine circles of Hell," one circle "before one arrives at the very bottom of Hell, which is where Satan himself is to be found." Said then goes on to argue that the "discriminations and refinements of Dante's poetic grasp of Islam are an instance of the schematic, almost cosmological inevitability with which Islam and its designated representatives are creatures of Western geographical, historical, and above all, moral apprehension." He also says that Orientalism and its "self-reinforcing" system of representation "turned Islam into the very epitome of an outsider against which the whole of European civilization from the Middle Ages on was founded."[34] Rushdie emphasizes this association between the Devil and the Muslim Other when he has his Prophet adopt "the demon-tag the farangis hung around his neck ... the Devil's synonym: Mahound" (*sv* 93).

As a demonized Other with hooves, the Devil is sympathetically and at times humorously present in the body of Chamcha, yet as the demonizing otherworldly Other who puts these hooves on Chamcha's feet, the Devil is neither so obvious nor so comic. While Rushdie sides with the demonized Other (and consequently criticizes the demonizing West), he does not necessarily side with the demonizing otherworldly Other; the former struggles for cultural and political equality *in this world* while the latter does whatever necessary *to this world* in order to take revenge on God. While much in the narrative suggests a concern for the plight of immigrants, the satanic narrator plays immigrant politics for all it is worth, that is, for all it is worth *to him.* He is only concerned about those who are marginalized and demonized insofar as they can be used to further his own case against God and the cosmic status quo. In this sense, the novel's postcolonial politics and its cosmic politics are worlds apart. Perhaps this is why the novel is not a complete success. Or, to put it another way, this may be the reason why the author cannot convince his postcolonial Muslims that he is on their side.

While Chamcha learns to sympathize with the people for whom he becomes a rallying symbol, he is terrified by the cause of his outward and inward changes: he feels radically "alarmed by the hostile violence of the images arising from his unconscious." These images are not as much the result of a Freudian psychodrama in which unwanted thoughts rise from the suppressed unconscious as they are the result of psychological and spiritual invasion. Chamcha remains totally alienated from the larger metaphysical machinery in which he is caught: he thinks to himself that forgiveness "seems to be out of [his] control; it either operates or it doesn't and [he finds] out in due course" (*sv* 402–3). This extreme alienation occurs just before his heart palpitations worsen, and an unseen force kicks him in the chest (*sv* 466). Significantly, the palpitations subside *after* he whispers the "satanic verses" which eventually lead Gibreel to kill Allie. Is Chamcha thus being rewarded for playing the role of the snake? Equally suspicious is that the *bad doom* or "badoom" in his chest disappears once he receives a heart by-pass. On the worldly level, this "by-pass" is a medical operation, yet on the otherworldly level it is a satanic trick or "operation" which dismisses Chamcha's evil in a superficial manner.

From the beginning to the end of the novel, Chamcha is both the immigrant worldly Other, who is defined and manipulated by the British status quo, and the stand-in and chump of the satanic otherworldly Other, who transforms and manipulates him without his knowledge. Chamcha's name is craftily chosen, for as Aravamudan explains, it "combines the romanticized enemy of Richard the Lionheart in the Crusades with a shortened version of his family name, 'Chamchawala,' literally, 'seller of spoons.' Just as 'Saladin' was originally 'Salahuddin,' Chamcha contracted his name from 'spoon-seller' to 'spoon,' in order to better serve English palates. The etymology hints at an elaborate crosscultural intellectual joke, because Chamcha has no long spoon to sup with the devil; he is both devil and spoon at once."[35]

While Gibreel is not possessed in the same ruthless and direct manner as Chamcha, his fate is perhaps worse, for his mind becomes the landscape through which the narrator moves. Moreover, he becomes twice a puppet, once in the hands of the unknowing devil-puppet, Chamcha, and once in the hands of the all-too knowing satanic puppeteer.

Gibreel's hallucinatory dreamworld initially appears to be a "fabulous world beneath" in comparison to the "dense, blinding air" above (*sv* 22), yet it soon takes on nightmarish qualities. The hidden watery bulk of this submerged world, seen in terms of hot icebergs, becomes associated with a rage and hatred directed at Allie and her symbolic ice replicas of God. The image of hot icebergs is appropriate to satanic rage since icebergs are mostly hidden (like the id) and since hell is characterized by fire. Gibreel's hot icebergs thus constitute an effective contrast to Allie's cold mountains, which represent God's transcendent overworldly realm. The two realms are brought into close juxtaposition when Allie sees "the ten highest mountains in the world" as "icebergs" floating up the Thames (*sv* 302–3). The satanic narrator's Iago-like scheme then comes into play when Allie's mountains (or icebergs) become representative in Gibreel's confused mind of a diabolism he must destroy.

Once the green-eyed monster of jealousy rises in Gibreel, he hacks to pieces Allie's "priceless whittled memento" of Everest, and he thaws "the ice-Everest she kept in the freezer." Given that Allie's Everest stands for Heaven and Qaf, Gibreel's attack is an attack on God – even though Gibreel himself does not see it this way (he is hardly the one to consult about the meaning of his own visions). Gripped by a Shakespearean rage, Gibreel pulls down and rips "to shreds the parachute-silk peaks that rose above her bed" (*sv* 446). On the otherworldly level this act expresses Satan's jealousy of Gabriel in a most insidious manner, that is, by having the "Archangel" destroy his own heavenly bliss. The degeneration of Gibreel's mind is almost total, for he calls Allie a "whore" and he cannot string together a coherent sentence: "So I called down the wrath of God I pointed my finger I shot [Sisodia] in the heart but she bitch I thought bitch cool as ice ... I pointed my finger at her ... Bloody hell I loved that girl" (*sv* 545). The satanic narrator's antagonism to the cool, glacial Himalayas, and to whoever remains devoted to the God-mountain of Everest, thus plays itself out consistently in terms of Chamcha's jealousy and hatred of Gibreel and Alleluia, and in terms of Gibreel's increasingly violent relationship with Alleluia. The satanic narrator, playing that old Garden of Eden game, thus succeeds in taking heavenly unity and love and turning it into hellish division and hate.

Gibreel's increasingly violent mental condition can be seen as a satanic fantasy or dreamscape, one which mirrors the narrator's imagined flood in the Arabian desert, that sadistically dreamed "liquid catastrophe full of snapping boats and drowning arms" (*sv* 94). Not surprisingly, the narrator revels in Gibreel's urban vision of a wasted "Brickhall," a "concrete formlessness [in] the howling of a perpetual wind, and the eddying of debris" (*sv* 461). (Brickhall is most probably a mix of Brixton and Southall – predominantly African and South Asian parts of London). The demonic element in this cityscape is made explicit on numerous occasions. For instance, the "screaming city" mirrors "the dark fire of evil" in Chamcha's soul (*sv* 463), and Gibreel sees London as "that tortured metropolis" in which the Devil is everywhere: "Gibreel with open eyes and by the light of the moon as well as the sun detected everywhere the presence of his adversary, his – to give the old word back its original meaning – *shaitan.*" Even with his eyes closed Gibreel "instantly see[s] clouds of minuscule demons surrounding every man and woman on earth" (*sv* 320–1). In the narrator's empty apocalypse, in this Final Hour which has no genuine theophany and no convincing redemption, he portrays London as an even more violent place than the London of Hanif Kureishi's *Sammy and Rosie Get Laid,* a movie which appeared just before the novel and which highlights racial tension amid the fires of immigrant London.

The narrator's fantasy of destruction becomes ever more violent, lurid, diabolical. He revels in the flames that "are every colour of the rainbow," in the "garden of dense intertwined chimeras," and in the transformation of the Shaandaar Café's doorway into "the maw of the black hole." As fire devours Chamcha's soul and the "screaming city," the narrator pretends to be horrified: "Truly these are 'most horrid, malicious, bloody flames, not like the fine flame of an ordinary fire'" (*sv* 462–4). The use of quotations parodies religious language, and thus inverts his point: rather than being horrified, he finds these flames delightful, suggesting as they do the sort of revenge dreamt of by Milton's Moloch, "Armed with Hell-flames and fury."[36]

One must remember that in Islam Satan is born of fire, he commands legions of fiery djinn, and any mention of fire betrays his presence. Iblis's admission of his fiery origin in the Koran is seen as proof of his evil nature: "And when Iblis, in the Kur'anic text, declares himself to be 'created from fire' (*nar*) and not from light (*nur*), this is because God intended that, by a *lapsus linguae*, he should in a sense utter his own condemnation."[37] By suggesting that the flames devouring London are not "ordinary" and that they display "every colour of the rainbow," the satanic narrator may be making a similar slip. This may also fit with Satan's condescending view of angels, who are created from light; in the *Verses* he depicts them as airheads and spineless lackeys who could benefit from the fire of his thoughts and the fire of his rebellious acts.

Consistent with his reversed codes of morality and behaviour, the narrator claims that fire and brimstone cleanses England's capital. The voiced spelling of London, "Ellowendeeowen," suggests "Halloween," which is appropriate since London becomes a town presided over by pagan spirits – the Devil, the hybrid shapes in the hospital (*sv* 164–71), the demons Gibreel sees everywhere (*sv* 321), and the ghost of Rekha Merchant (*sv* 323–6). The narrator ingenuously suggests that believers desire this sort of apocalyptic wasteland: Gibreel "proclaims to the riotous night, 'that men be granted their heart's desires, and that they be by them consumed'" (*sv* 461). Again, the narrator twists religious language, this time to suggest that bloody flames could be a magical way of fulfilling human desires. Yet the scene he paints is clearly one of horror, one of Hell on Earth: "In the High Street [Gibreel] sees houses built of flame, with walls of fire, and flames like gathered curtains hanging at the windows. – And there are men and women with fiery skins strolling, running, milling around him, dressed in coats of fire. The street has become red hot, molten, a river the colour of blood. – All, all is ablaze as he toots his merry horn, *giving the people what they want*, the hair and teeth of the citizenry are smoking and red, glass burns, and birds fly overhead on blazing wings" (*sv* 462). The "men and women with fiery skins" adds a hellfire element of torture to Chamcha's nightmarish dreams of cracking glass skin (*sv* 34). The birds flying "overhead on blazing wings" also suggest scary djinns and afreets, as well as the three high-flying birds which hover over Mount Cone (*sv* 122–3).

In addition to inundating Chamcha's body with his black water and engulfing Gibreel's vision in flames, the narrator steers his two puppets into a spiritual world which is characterized by vengeance and violence. Gibreel acknowledges "this world and another that was also right there, visible but unseen" and he feels that "the splitting [of these two worlds] was not in him, but in the universe" (*sv* 351). Two pages later he interprets the devil horns below him on the Earls Court stage as "the adversary's sign" and then "in that instant when he saw the adversary's sign he felt the universe fork and he stepped down the left-hand path" (*sv* 352). Chamcha also perceives a split in the universe, and he too chooses the "left-hand path." In the Brickhall community centre he feels "the kind of blurring associated with double vision," and he seems "to look into two worlds at once; one was the brightly lit, no-smoking-allowed meeting hall, but the other was a world of phantoms, in which Azraeel, the exterminating angel, was swooping towards him, and a girl's forehead could burn with ominous flames" (*sv* 416). Three pages later we find Chamcha in a taxi cab, insanely jealous of Gibreel and ready to embark on his satanic revenge: "A new, dark world had opened up for him (or: within him) when he fell from the sky; no matter how assiduously he attempted to re-create his old existence, this was, he now saw, a fact that could not be unmade. He seemed to see a road before him, forking to left and right. Closing his eyes, settling back against taxicab upholstery, he chose the left-hand path" (*sv* 418–19).

The implication behind these left-handed paths, which are versions of the *via sinistra*, becomes less obscure when one sees that not only the Devil (Chamcha) but also the Archangel (Gibreel) choose the *sinister* path of destructive violence over the *right* path of justice and constructive love. This is of course similar to the opening scene, where both the good and the bad angels fall from heavenly heights. Rushdie further links the choices of the two by having Gibreel opt for the left-handed path at the moment he decides he is Azraeel, the Angel of Doom, and by having Chamcha opt at the moment he accepts his transformation into an agent of darkness, an agent that willingly tortures his friend Gibreel. This moment for Chamcha has echoes not only of *Othello* and of the scenario in the Garden of Eden, but also of the moment in *Midnight's Children* where Saleem decides to follow the advice of the snake and "strike from cover."

The satanic narrator has parallel yet nevertheless distinct strategies in dealing with Chamcha and Gibreel: while he possesses Chamcha and transforms him into a confused version of his demonic self, he creates gaps in Gibreel's consciousness and takes advantage of what transpires during these gaps. While both become puppets, Gibreel is most puppet-like in that he often appears empty-headed and without a will of his own. Gibreel first lacks volition when he stands at the top of Rosa Diamond's stairs and says nothing while Chamcha (who is growing horns) is taken away by the police. On the otherworldly level, this scene suggests that the angel Gabriel collaborates with the tyrannical Powers That Be, that he demonstrates no solidarity with the "rebel hero" Satan. The narrator prepares us for this conclusion earlier on, when he interrupts Gibreel with his "devil['s] talk," arguing that angels are merely God's lackeys, without the gumption and free will to dissent (*sv* 92–3). Such a view of angels goes some way in explaining why Gibreel is so easily manipulated: his malleability and empty-headedness express in parodic form the disdain of the rebellious fallen angel.

It is essential to note who benefits from what transpires when Gibreel evinces no will of his own. At Rosa's, Gibreel's blank-mindedness and subsequent inaction thrust Chamcha into the role of the forsaken, unjustly accused angel, a role which makes Satan appear justified in his resentment against Gabriel and God. Chamcha is of course ignorant of his rebellious stature; he even tells the officers that he has a "lovely, white, English wife" (*sv* 141). This superimposition of a power struggle between cosmic figures onto a power struggle between worldly characters anticipates a parallel situation during the party at Shepperton Studios, where Chamcha bitterly resents "the great injustice of the division" between Gibreel (with his stardom and his "glacial" English Alleluia) and himself, who has lost both job and wife (*sv* 425). Chamcha sees Gibreel's "celebrity, and the great injustice of the division" (*sv* 425), yet he does not see that Gibreel and Alleluia are also in pain. He fails to see that "Gibreel the embodiment of all the good fortune that the Fury-haunted Chamcha so signally lacked, was as much the creature of his fancy, as much a fiction, as his invented-resented Allie" (*sv* 429).

Chamcha and Gibreel are not aware that they are merely puppets in a far removed, otherworldly drama being shaped in favour of the fallen angel. Chamcha is however conscious that he pulls Gibreel's strings: in devising his plan to destroy Gibreel, he becomes a "tyro puppeteer" studying Gibreel's "strings, to find out what was connected to what" (*sv* 432). After Chamcha delivers the "little, satanic verses" which drive Gibreel mad with jealousy, the narrator exclaims: "How comfortably evil lodged in those supple, infinitely flexible vocal cords, those puppetmaster's strings!" (*sv* 445). At this point, the distinction between the sentiments of the narrator and those of his devil-puppet/puppeteer is difficult to gauge. What is relatively clear, however, is that the narrator has managed to execute his diabolic plan by using his devil-puppet to pull the strings of his angel-puppet. The *coup de grace* (or *coup de feu* rather) occurs when Gibreel enters his final gap of consciousness, during which Allie is shot and/or pushed, and plummets from Everest Vilas.

Another incident in which Gibreel remains inactive, yet during which actions or words are attributed to him, occurs when he unintentionally lies next to the Indian Ayesha, at which point she "conceives" the idea of leading a pilgrimage across the Arabian Sea (*sv* 226, 234–5). He protests he "never laid a finger on her," and in his dream he sees her "receiving a message from somewhere that she called Gibreel." In exasperation, he exclaims: "Damn me if I know from where that girl was getting her information/inspiration. Not from this quarter, that's for sure" (*sv* 226). Not long after this, the narrator uses the suspiciously echoing short query to direct readers to the source of his unbidden voices: "All around him, he thinks as he half-dreams, half-wakes, are people hearing voices, being seduced by words. But not his; never his original material. – Then whose?" (*sv* 234). Ayesha's "being seduced by words" appears doubly suspicious in light of the earlier "soft seductive verses" Satan sings "from hellbelow" (*sv* 91).

The most problematic instance in which Gibreel remains puppet-like during a moment of diabolic intervention occurs during the scenes on Mount Cone. Immediately prior to hearing the voice which is ascribed in legend to Satan, Gibreel hangs in suspension, "held up like a kite on a golden thread" (*sv* 112). Here Gibreel hovers much as he does when he abandons Chamcha on Rosa's stairs, or when he agrees to go on a "motor tour" which leads to his being murdered in serial and surreal fashion in Rosa's Argentina (*sv* 151–5). His hovering over Mount Cone also resembles the hovering of the three high-flying birds (*sv* 123), the same birds who are Satan's "fiendish backing group," and who giggle "behind their hands at Gibreel" because they have a trick in store for him "and for that businessman [Mahound] on the hill" (sv 91). Just as the satanic narrator works Chamcha's strings, making him whisper satanic verses over the telephone, so he may work Gibreel's strings, making the latter recite satanic verses to Mahound.

The notion of a hidden satanic puppeteer helps to make sense of Gibreel's two following statements, both of which can be taken to mean that it is God's opposite who manipulates the drama or "picture"[38] on Mount Cone: "Being God's postman is no fun, yaar. / But-butbut: God isn't in this picture. / God knows whose postman I've been"; "*it was me both times, baba, me first and second also me. From my mouth, both the statement and the repudiation, verses and converses, universes and reverses, the whole thing, and we all know how my mouth got worked*" (*sv* 112, 123). It is not at all obvious how his mouth gets worked, yet if one accepts that the first of the above statements implies that it is the opposite of God who is "in this picture," and if one follows the trail of possessions, heart palpitations, blanked-out minds, puppet strings and dangling threads, one can conclude that it is the satanic narrator who works his mouth. Important to remember is that Satan is the author of the spurious verses in the original, quasi-historical satanic verses incident, which Rushdie clearly refers to when Mahound tells himself that "the Devil came to him in the guise of the archangel" (*sv* 123).

A reworking of the original incident also allows the narrator to dwell on the momentary victory he once appears to have gained over the Prophet. After accepting the three high-flying birds as intercessors, Mahound endures a hellish night full of "phantasmagoria and lust." The narrator lingers on this victorious moment by having Mahound go over in his memory the events of the night before: he wakes up with the memory of "his wild anguished walk in the corrupt city, staring at the souls he had supposedly saved, looking at the simurgh-effigies, the devil-masks, the behemoths and hippogriffs" (*sv* 117, 120).

One cannot, however, say for sure that the Gibreel who hovers over Mount Cone is puppeteered by Satan. Mahound either hears the words of Satan disguised as the words of Gabriel/Gibreel or he hears what he wants to hear, that is, he hears the words he forces from Gabriel/Gibreel's mouth. The latter possibility – that Mahound works Gibreel's mouth – is strengthened by what appears to take place at the beginning of the next chapter, in Gibreel's oneiric Argentina. Here the dream-blasted angel "was being held prisoner and manipulated by the force of Rosa's will, just as the Angel Gibreel had been obliged to speak by the overwhelming need of the Prophet, Mahound"; "As with the businessman of his dreams, [Gibreel] felt helpless, ignorant … [Rosa] seemed to know, however, how to draw the images from him. Linking the two of them, navel to navel, he saw a shining cord" (*sv* 150, 154). This shining cord appears to be the "golden cord of light linking [the soul] to the body." The narrator tells us that "it is known to archangels" (*sv* 322), although Rosa and Mahound also appear to "know" it.

Rushdie's meaning becomes so slippery here that I hesitate to conclude anything, except perhaps that this confusion as to who pulls whose vocal cords might be counted among what Alex Knönagel calls the "numerous tactics" which the narrator uses "to confuse the reader's insights into the novel's structure."[39] If, however, one sees Mahound as the one who works Gibreel's mouth, the satanic narrator still advances his position in his battle against Allah and his Prophet by suggesting that Muhammad is either self-deluded or an impostor. The satanic narrator thus urges us to believe that the Koran is not purely the word of God, but rather shares in the diabolic imagination of Satan or in the limitations and self-interests of humans. Or, by insinuating that both Satan *and* Mahound are the sources of revelation, the satanic narrator prompts readers to conclude that Mahound could not distinguish between the voices of Gabriel and the Devil, and also that Mahound sometimes hears what he wants to hear. Again, both conclusions suggest that God is not always the source of what later becomes known as His revelations.

TOO MANY SATANS

In attempting to grasp the cosmic politics in the novel, the reader must get at what kind of Satan is doing the politicking. Does the satanic voice which invades the narrative come from a Muslim or a Christian Satan? Is he a traditional Satan, the embodiment of evil, or is he a Sufi or Romantic Satan, one who has redeeming qualities?

While there are similarities between Islamic and European versions of the Devil,[40] readers cannot go beyond the title of Rushdie's novel before differences cause divergent interpretations. Corcoran observes, "On one hand, non-Muslim readers are unlikely to know what the title means. They are therefore in the position of someone who picks up an English Romantic poem championing Satan without having read any earlier versions of the Fall. On the other hand, Muslims may recognize the title and find themselves systematically insulted throughout the novel."[41] While there are many works which help to contextualize the diverse figure of Satan, I would recommend Jeffrey Russell's series, especially his third volume, *Lucifer: The Devil in the Middle Ages*, and the concise and comparative chapter within this, "The Muslim Devil." Another concise account can be found in Schimmel's "Good and Evil: The Role of Satan" in *Mystical Dimensions of Islam*. Finally, in *Satan's Tragedy and Redemption: Iblis in Sufi Psychology*, Peter Awn gives an extensive view of the Devil in both orthodox and mystical Islam.

Schimmel notes that in Islam Satan (Iblis, Shaitan, Azazeel)[42] has a variety of personalities, many of which are reflected in Muhammad Iqbal's "multicoloured picture of Satan." Iqbal's Satan is a lover, an intellectual, a monotheist, and an evil being who longs to be "broken in order to find salvation." Yet Iqbal also employs "the more common image of Satan the seducer, the materialist, and the destroyer."[43] Rushdie's Satan pretends to many of the finer qualities Iqbal attributes to Satan, yet he never attains the status of a Sufi or Romantic Satan. For to some Sufis Iblis is a proud, tragic figure who loves God so passionately that he disobeys His command to bow before humanity, that is, to bow before anyone but God. According to al-Hallaj, Sana'i, Ahmad Ghazzali, Attar, Sarmad and Shah Abdul-Latif, Iblis remains a devout monotheist, a great lover of the one and only Deity.[44] We do not, however, see anything of this side of Satan in Rushdie's novel. Notwithstanding, Rushdie's Satan figure does promote himself as a Promethean, Romantic hero who helps humans shake off the supposed tyranny of God. While he succeeds in evoking the plight of Prometheus, he does not display the type of compassion one finds, for instance, in Shelley's Prometheus. Rather, he brings to mind the gods Gloucester speaks of in *King Lear* – especially when he brags that "Higher Powers" such as himself "have a mischievous, almost a wanton attitude to tumbling flies" (*sv* 133).[45]

Rushdie's Satan resembles both the Christian and Islamic Satan insofar as he is the fallen angel (or djinn)[46] who attempts to lure humans away from God. Christianity and Islam, by and large, share the notion that Satan's insidious counsel in Eden led to the expulsion of Adam and Eve, yet the two religions differ in the way Satan subsequently tempts their chief human figures, Christ and Muhammad. In Matthew 4: 8–10 and Luke 4: 5–8, Satan offers Christ dominion over the world and Christ immediately rejects this offer. This type of temptation is not employed by the satanic narrator, who follows instead in the footsteps of the Muslim Iblis. According to several *hadith* (accounts of Muhammad's life), Iblis, pretending to be Gabriel, tempts Muhammad to gain followers by offering three already popular goddesses as intercessors between humans and the Divine. Muhammad first accepts, then rejects this idea when he realizes it comes from Satan. Daniel Pipes notes that Tabari, ibn Saad, al-Bukhari and Yaqut all cite different wordings of the following verses which, according to Tabari, "Satan threw on [Muhammad's] tongue": "These are the exalted birds, / And their intercession is desired indeed."[47] The Koran does not directly refer to these "satanic verses," yet the koranic verses which are believed to put an end to the satanic verses incident are as follows: "Have you thought on Al-Lat and Al-'Uzza, and thirdly, on Manat, the other? Are you to have the sons, and He the daughters? This is indeed an unfair distinction! / They are but names which you and your fathers have invented: God has vested no authority in them."[48] Also relevant are the following verses: "Never have We sent a single prophet or apostle before you with whose wishes Satan did not tamper. But God abrogates the interjections of Satan and confirms His own revelations."[49] The title of Rushdie's novel occasions insult because "the satanic verses" can be read as both "Satan's verses" and "the satanic Koranic verses," given that "verses" in this context means verses from the Koran.[50] The title not only suggests that the novel is about verses by Satan but also that the Koran was written by Satan. The religious politics surrounding the novel are extremely involved and I refer readers to several of the numerous critics who have ventured explanations as to why the novel and its title have insulted Muslims.[51]

My argument takes a different direction, for I contend that much of the novel, including its title, are naturally blasphemous since they are the product of a narrative strongly influenced by a satanic narrator. The novel's title also makes sense in this context, for the novel itself can be seen as yet another attempt by Satan to justify his verses, his words, his logic.

In addition to borrowing from Islamic versions of Satan, Rushdie borrows from the diverse Satans that populate Western literature – from the charismatic Satan of Milton's *Paradise Lost* to the good-hearted Satan of Mikhail Bulgakov's *The Master and Margarita*. In his 1990 essay "In Good Faith" Rushdie gives a few clues about the nature of the Devil in the *Verses:* "the two books that were most influential on the shape this novel took do not include the Qur'an. One was William Blake's *Marriage of Heaven and Hell*, the classic meditation on the interpenetration of good and evil; the other *The Master and Margarita* by Mikhail Bulgakov, the great Russian lyrical and comical novel in which the Devil descends upon Moscow and wreaks havoc upon the corrupt, materialistic, decadent inhabitants and turns out, by the end, not to be such a bad chap after all" (*IH* 403). I have two problems with Rushdie's statement. First, I find it hard to believe that the Koran and the related *hadith* are not among the two most important influences on the novel. The title, as well as the numerous reworkings of the incident the title refers to, attest to this. Second, when one compares the actions of the Devils in Blake and Bulgakov to those of the satanic narrator, one finds that Rushdie's Satan is thoroughly insidious and destructive. He is not at all the poetic rebel or the good chap Rushdie suggests.

Blake's *The Marriage of Heaven and Hell* (1790–93) is referred to directly and indirectly in the novel: the narrator quotes from Blake's second "Memorable Fancy" and compares the visible Oopervala to Blake's abstract God (*SV* 304–5, 338, 318). Yet on one hand Blake's "diabolical" poet uses what is conventionally thought of as evil to liberate the imagination, while on the other Rushdie's satanic narrator uses evil to trap souls. Blake's daemonic genius uses the inversion of moral categories to demonstrate that everything is holy and that the flux of energy (the fire of Hell) is eternal delight. Blake's poet can argue this successfully since he is cast in the starring role of a scenario which proves his argument. In the *Verses*, however, a crucial gap exists between the satanic narrator and Gibreel, the puppet-like protagonist who is led into a confusing and tormenting labyrinth in which he destroys his own delight. Because Gibreel cannot fathom what is happening to him and because he cannot reconcile the heaven and hell within him, he cannot see that the supposedly evil woman he calls a whore is in fact holy. While Blake inverts cosmology and morality in order to liberate the imagination, the satanic narrator inverts cosmology and morality without allowing his characters – including the Blake-reading Allie – to take any sort of meaningful flight.

Blake sends his poet on a journey that confirms the value of the imagination while the satanic narrator sends Gibreel on one that ends in nightmarish hallucination. The journey Blake describes in his fourth "Memorable Fancy" demonstrates that one can experience the eternal delight of genius by opening one's mind: the Analytical Angel takes the poet down through a church vault into an Abyss containing fire, darkness, spiders, a cataract of blood and "the scaly fold of a monstrous serpent." The poet then uses his imagination to change this hell of "raging foam" and "beams of blood" into "a pleasant bank beside a river by moonlight."[52] As with Flapping Eagle in *Grimus*, Blake's poet uses the destructive or "Devouring" power of his mind to destroy the reptiles lurking within it, and he uses the creative or "Prolific" to create new and more liberating perceptions. In contrast, Gibreel's journeys enact only the destructive power of the imagination: he travels down from the Edenic garden of his love with Alleluia, and plummets into a hellish world of confusion, violence, deception and disturbing revelations. Gibreel's visions do not become the basis of what Blake's Isaiah calls "firm perswasion" [*sic*], or of what Blake's poet calls "the enjoyments of Genius."[53] Instead, his visions lead to a state of mind in which he kills the woman whose aim in life is to see God, and whose very name expresses the joy of spiritual intoxication.

Gibreel's dreams may link the temporally and geographically disparate settings in the novel, and they may tie together "the satanic verses" theme for the reader, yet Gibreel remains unable to reconcile or marry the basic physical and metaphysical layers of his reality. Unable to tell if he is being overwhelmed by otherworldly forces or going insane, and powerless to close the doors of apocalyptic perception which have somehow been opened inside him, he kills Sisodia, Alleluia and then himself. The narrator sees this suicide as liberating: "Gibreel put the barrel of the gun into his own mouth; and pulled the trigger; and was free" (*sv* 546). Yet looking at Gibreel's suicide in light of a satanic revenge on God via His angelic and human creations, one might ask the following question: What greater pleasure could the Devil imagine than to drive his archangelic rival into such a state of jealousy and schizophrenia that he murders himself as well as a woman who represents love, self-sacrifice, and return to the otherworldly Mountain of God?

The other avowed influence on the *Verses* is Mikhail Bulgakov's *The Master and Margarita*. Like the *Verses*, the *Master* was subject to censorship: though written between 1928 and 1940, it "first appeared in *Moskva* in late 1966 and early 1967."[54] Rushdie comments that "*The Master and Margarita* and its author were persecuted by Soviet totalitarianism," and that it "is extraordinary to find [the *Verses's*] life echoing that of one of its greatest models" (*IH* 404). Mirra Ginsburg's remarks concerning censorship of the *Master* are uncannily apropos here: "Another element is [Bulgakov's] lasting concern with the relation of the artist, the creative individual, to state authority, and with the fate of the artist's work – the manuscript, the created word – which, he came to feel, must not, cannot be destroyed. As Satan says in his novel, 'manuscripts don't burn.' Alas, a metaphysical statement."[55]

The two novels also resemble each other because they are written on two levels, the worldly and the otherworldly, and because they shift back and forth between contemporary secular settings and ancient religious settings. Ginsburg observes that Bulgakov's novel "is built essentially on two planes. On the transcendent, the towering figures of Yeshua, Satan, his retinue, even in its clownish incarnation, and, yes, Pilate are accorded the full dignity of their immortal being – of myth. On the earthly plane, few escape the author's satiric barbs. And even the tale of the Master and Margarita, who are perhaps of both worlds, being closest to myth, is tinged with irony. The four principal strands in the novel's astonishing web – contemporary Moscow, the infernal visitors, the story of the Master and Margarita, and the events in Yershalayim – are each distinct in style."[56] Settings in the *Verses* are likewise distinct, and also contain interplay between "earthly" and "transcendent" forces. Moreover, the "transcendent" level becomes violent in both novels: in the *Master* Woland (the Devil) wreaks havoc in Moscow, and Pilate has visions of fire and bloody streets[57]; in the *Verses* the satanic narrator delights in the fiery chaos of London, he dreams of a tidal wave in the desert, and he revels in "the festival of Ibrahim," during which Hind's followers, represented by "the red manticore with the triple row of teeth," attack Mahound's followers (*sv* 116–17).

The violence in both novels is followed by a redemption of sorts. After inflicting punishments on Muscovites, Woland leads his familiars across the sky into the oblivion of a strangely redemptive Night.[58] In the *Verses*, Chamcha is saved by Gibreel after multicoloured flames devour "the screaming city," and after "the universe shrinks" and the doorway of the Shaandaar Café becomes "the maw of the black hole" (*sv* 463–4). Mirza too experiences an ambiguous sort of mystical union with Ayesha: he joins her in an afterlife pilgrimage across the Arabian Sea after the tree-village of Titlipur explodes "into a thousand fragments, and the trunk crack[s], like a heart" (*sv* 506).

Most uncanny is the fact that the *Verses* and the *Master* both contain second chapters which are more clearly narrated by Satan than are any other chapters. In the *Master*, Chapter 2 is the only one narrated directly by Woland, and in the *Verses* the first four pages of the Chapter 2 make it relatively clear that Satan is narrating. And in both novels the second chapters are set in ancient, religiously charged locations which reappear: Pilate's dilemma continues in Chapters 16, 25 and 26, and Mahound's story continues in Chapter 6. The events in the second chapters can also be felt throughout the novels: Woland's narrative, together with the effect of his prediction of Berlioz's death, casts a strange light over the whole text, much as the satanic narrator's trickery in Jahilia reverberates throughout the

Verses. Rushdie follows Bulgakov in that he gives a strong indication of Satan's presence early in the novel and then allows this satanic narrative presence to become less obvious. The major difference in this regard is that Bulgakov eventually delineates the Devil's personality whereas Rushdie keeps his satanic narrator shadowy and elusive.

The second chapters of both novels also insinuate that errors have crept into what has become sacred scripture. In the *Master* Matthu Levi follows Yeshua (Jesus) and "writes things down incorrectly,"[59] and in the *Verses* Salman the Persian changes Mahound's verses. The most significant difference between the two novels in this regard is that the *Verses* contains harsh criticism of Muhammad and grave doubts about his holy words, whereas the *Master* contains a very sympathetic portrait of Jesus and does not heap irreverent doubt on his history-shaping utterances.

Two more crucial differences lie in the way Woland and the satanic narrator torment humans and affect the endings of the novels. The satanic narrator relishes inflicting pain whereas Woland becomes weary of his scourging chores. In addition, Woland eventually unites the Master and Margarita, whereas the satanic narrator drives a fatal wedge between Gibreel and Alleluia. Bulgakov's Satan "turns out, by the end, not to be such a bad chap after all," while Rushdie's Satan only fades away once Alleluia falls to her death and Gibreel commits suicide.

Another, far different, influence on Rushdie's narrative is the demonic songster of Mick Jagger's "Sympathy for the Devil." While the narrator does not come out and say, "just call me Lucifer," both Devils are proud of their cosmopolitan sensibilities (they are both men of wealth and taste) and of their ability to sow the seeds of doubt (they love to puzzle us with the nature of their games). Like Jagger's Lucifer, the satanic narrator puzzles readers by reversing moral categories and by making them guess the nature of his "game." A weird twist of fate surrounds both song and novel: just as Jagger was shocked when, during a rendition of "Sympathy for the Devil" at Altamont Freeway, the Hell's Angels beat fans with pool cues and knifed a gun-wielding fan to death, so Rushdie was shocked by the riots and deaths in Pakistan and India, resulting from the reaction to his book. Also, "outcry that 'Sympathy for the Devil' had in some way incited the violence led the Stones to drop the tune from their stage shows for the next six years"[60]; and, similarly, at the end of 1990 Rushdie temporarily dropped the notion of publishing his novel in paperback.

SATAN UNBOUND

In addition to constructing a complex satanic narrator with all sorts of mythic and literary ancestries, Rushdie constructs two of his characters along fairly specific satanic lines. The depictions of Chamcha as a Devil with strong Promethean traits and Mirza as the Iblis of the satanic verses incident further corroborate a satanic slant in the narrative, one in which the satanic narrator fashions them both into heroic, sympathetic, and eventually liberated versions of his devilish self.

Chamcha takes on the aspect of the rebel angel by revolting against Changez, his God-like father, and by falling into physical and moral hells. He repeatedly accuses his father of *"becoming* [his] *supreme being."* For at least twenty-five years Chamcha feels an "implacable rage" boiling away "his childhood father-worship," until at last he learns to be a "secular man," to "live without a god of any type" (*sv* 41, 43). While there are indications that Changez is the type of God/Devil figure with which the narrator often tries to confuse his readers, Chamcha sees his father mostly as a God or Zeus figure. He rejects the tyranny of his father, replacing it with the weight of being English: "On winter nights he, who had never slept beneath more than a sheet, lay beneath mountains of wool and felt like a figure in an ancient myth, condemned by the gods to have a boulder pressing down upon his chest; but never mind, he would be English" (*sv* 43). Changez is likewise a resented God-figure when his "letter of forgiveness" is felt to be more insulting than his "earlier, excommunicatory thunderbolt" (*sv* 47).

Chamcha rebels against this *supreme being*, who in turn repudiates him, calling him "a *ghoul*, a *hoosh*, a demon up from hell." Changez also accuses his son of having his "own bad djinni" (*sv* 48), an accusation which echoes in the various hollows of the text and which has no clear meaning, since djinns can be understood in various ways: they can be good or bad, although their fiery nature often prompts them to be mischievous and evil. Given Rushdie's interest in *The Arabian Nights*, it is not surprising to make numerous genie-sightings in the novel. Even the butterfly cloud which hovers over the pilgrims in India and the giant who crushes Titlipur vaguely suggest djinns. More important is the fact that Gibreel sees himself as "the genie of the lamp" and feels "his master is the Roc" (*sv* 461) when he is in his destructive or apocalyptic mode. Since Gibreel appears to shoot Allie and clearly shoots himself, there appears to be a link between gunshot violence and genies. This link is strengthened when the gun which pops out of Changez's lamp (and which Chamcha dismisses all too easily) is seen explicitly in terms of a genie. Taking into account that Iblis is considered the father of the djinn, Chamcha's ostensible freedom becomes increasingly doubtful. Can Chamcha really dismiss such a subtle, powerful, violent force? Or will it resurface to hound him in the future, like Gibreel's jealousy which erupts in gunshot, or like the Beast in *Shame*, which takes the form of the panther, Madame Guillotine, Kali and who knows what else to come?

Without understanding what is happening to him, Chamcha feels the floor give way beneath his feet and he stares "into the inferno" (*sv* 68). While he tries to convince himself that he is not in Hell, the sky above him is "blood-orange flecked with green," he enters a "void," and he wakes into "the most fearsome of nightmares" which becomes "ever more infernal and outré" (*sv* 132, 141, 160). In making Chamcha's devilish appearance unmistakable and Gibreel's angelic appearance ambiguous, the satanic narrator may be implying that the Devil clearly exists while God and His angels are only figments of the imagination. This is not of course beyond question, for police at Rosa's see Gibreel's halo, but only for an instant; the only characters who see it clearly are John Maslama (John the Baptist?) and Maslama's three clerks (the three wise men?). To make matters worse, Maslama sees himself as "the chief herald of the returned Celestial and Semi-(Godlike) Being," whom he immediately recognizes as Gibreel (*sv* 447, 191). If the mocking of theophanies is not the aim here, then one can ask the following question: Why does God give prophetic visions to someone who cannot put these visions into perspective and to someone who kills himself? Why does the world not end as the visions prophesy?

Chamcha takes on the physical likeness of the Devil as a result of the possession which I described earlier, and as a result of the viciousness of authoritarian powers linked to religion: he grows horns and starts to bleat while he is being abused by policemen in "the black Maria of his hard fall from grace" (*sv* 162), and he undergoes complete transformation in a hospital in which immigrants succumb to the tyrannical and self-serving definitions of the West. The racist and fascist State – which supposedly parallels the Heaven which God rules "by terror" – exacerbates Chamcha's demonic state, and it is only after he submits to the diabolic force within him that he can escape the tyranny of the hospital: once the "black water" seeps into his veins, he joins the wolf and the manticore, travelling "without hope, but also without shame" on one of "the low roads to London town" (*sv* 170–1). The manticore is of course the symbol of Jahilia's Hind, the fiercest opponent of Mahound and his one God. Thus Chamcha's identification with the manticore takes on a specifically anti-Islamic association. Chamcha's partnership with the wolf may also have mythic ties to Loki, who fathers the wolf

Fenrir and who appears obliquely in the fall of the Yggdrasil-like Titlipur. This association remains conjectural, although Chamcha's partnership with the wolf suggests that he, like the wolf, is a wild and peripheral threat to established culture.

While critics tend to see Chamcha's transformation as heroic, and hence echo Mishal Sufyan's enthusiasm for this victimized rebel who learns to fight back, the Promethean elements should not blind readers to the evil which destroys Chamcha's moral fibre, or to the cruelty which characterizes Chamcha's subsequent actions. Readers initially have sympathy for Chamcha, which is understandable on the worldly level (where he is being persecuted by the racist police) and on the otherworldly level (where he is being possessed and manipulated by Satan), yet readers also feel increasingly uneasy as his thoughts and actions follow darker and darker paths. The narrator gloats over the "dark fire of evil" which continues "perniciously to spread" in Chamcha and which he says "springs from some recess in his own true nature" (sv 463). In two gross parodies, one of them of misappropriating God's words to Moses in Exodus 3: 14 ("I am that I am"), and the other distorting the submission to God from which Islam derives its name, Chamcha "submits" to the dark angry force which is transforming his habitually peaceful and tolerant state of mind into one that is violent and aggressive: "Bitterness, too, and hatred, all these coarse things. He would enter into his new self; he would be what he had become: loud, stenchy, hideous, outsize, grotesque, inhuman, powerful. He had the sense of being able to stretch out a little finger and topple church spires with the force growing in him, the anger, the anger, the anger. *Powers*. He was looking for someone to blame. ... *I am*, he accepted, *that I am*. Submission" (sv 289). Evil lodges "comfortably" in his vocal cords and the narrator likens the easy, natural movement of evil in him to the confidence of "a handsome man in a perfectly tailored suit!" (*sv* 445) – an image which calls to mind the Devil as sophisticate, as Mick Jagger's man of wealth and taste (these images contrast markedly with the image of God as a bumbling, myopic, dandruff-flaked old man.) The narrator gives a particularly sick twist to Chamcha's evil when his devil-puppet cloaks his "profoundly immoral" verses in children's rhymes, in an "infernal, childlike evil" (sv 444–5).

We are then privy to the delight the narrator and Chamcha take in separating Gibreel from the real world and in warping Gibreel's mind so that Allie appears to be covered in a slimy green film: one by one Chamcha's satanic verses "dripped into Gibreel's ears, weakening his hold on the real world, drawing him little by little into their deceitful web, so that little by little their obscene, invented women began to coat the real woman like a viscous, green film, and in spite of his protestations to the contrary he started slipping away from her; and then it was time for the return of the little, satanic verses that made him mad" (*sv* 445). Chamcha takes a satanic delight in constructing his "deceitful web" and in destroying Gibreel's strongest link to reality, Allie's love.

Mirza Saeed is also modelled on Satan, particularly the Iblis of the satanic verses incident. Given that everything happening in the India of Mirza and Ayesha is dreamt by Gibreel, one might see the two poles of Mirza's skepticism and Ayesha's certainty as the same two poles that rip Gibreel apart in London. One might also see Mirza's eventual union with Ayesha at the moment of his death as Gibreel's inability to keep these poles apart or as his belief that only in death can he escape his torment. In any case, the portrayals of Mirza and Ayesha are both slanted in favour of the Devil: Mirza is the diabolic, reasonable, compassionate counterpart to the angelic, unreasonable, hard-hearted Ayesha. Rushdie plays a complicated game here, for Mirza plays Iblis's role in tempting the pilgrims away from Ayesha's God, yet Ayesha, with her sexual and polytheistic associations, also brings to mind the three goddesses who tempt Mahound away from his God.

Mirza clearly behaves in the manner of the Iblis who tempts the faithful to revolt: he rejoices in his "first convert" when Muhammad Din enters his "station wagon of scepticism"; he gives people a choice between himself (the Devil) "and the deep blue sea" into which Ayesha leads the pilgrims; he laughs an "echoing laughter of revenge" when he hears that Ayesha's Archangel sings to her in pop songs; he offers Ayesha a "compromise" which echoes both the compromise offered by Satan to Mahound and the "compromise solution" offered by Rekha to Gibreel (curiously a "compromise solution" is also offered by Mick Jagger's feisty persona in "Street Fighting Man"); and finally, he tells himself that "Revenge is sweet" when he feels that Ayesha's hold over the pilgrims will "be destroyed forever" (*sv* 481, 484, 497–9).

Mirza resembles Chamcha in that both initially resist figures associated with religious authority (Ayesha and Changez) and both eventually reconcile themselves to these figures – yet on terms which emphasize the sensual or irreligious sides of these "religious authorities": Mirza unites with Ayesha at the moment of his death, at which time it is not clear what appeals to him more, her spiritual or her sexual qualities; Chamcha makes peace with his father only after Changez loses his God-like status. Changez resembles *Shame*'s old Mr Shakil with his death-bed blasphemies when he denies the afterlife and when he refuses to pronounce the name of God in the hour of his death (*sv* 529, 531). Chamcha admires his father for his resistance to religious rites and he acts in his father's behalf by violently rejecting the mullah's sacred cloth (*sv* 532). Chamcha's reconciliation with his erstwhile *supreme being* becomes yet another excuse to reject God and religion.

The images used in the "liberations" of the Promethean Chamcha and Iblis-like Mirza also suggest continued demonic influence. While Gibreel's rescue of Chamcha seems to purge the latter of his evil, Chamcha finds that the fire of love had not "driven those devils out into the consuming flames" (*sv* 540). Mirza's "liberation" is even more ambiguous, for he is "set free" by a burning wind which has at least two demonic associations. First, the burning wind which "frees" Mirza may derive from Iblis as Al-Jann, who is closely associated with "the fierce heat of a smokeless fire," the "hot winds that blow at night" and the "whirlwind capable of stifling a person."[61] It seems appropriate that since Mirza plays the role of Iblis, he should be "set free" by the fiery wind of his exemplar. Mirza's potential for bliss with Ayesha might also be seen in light of Saleem's embrace with the *houris-cum-apsaras* in the Kali temple, an embrace which becomes the opposite of what it first appears to be. Second, because the village of Titlipur takes the form of a giant tree, its burning and fall suggests the drama in which Loki precipitates the fall of Yggdrasil and Sutr sets fire to Earth and Heaven. The Norse element may seem peripheral, yet it enters explicitly into *Grimus* and *Shame*, the conflation of Loki and Satan is well established, and it fits with the general notion of assault on the powers that be – whether these be Odin in his mystic frenzy or God behind his buttressed gates of Heaven.

KNOCKING DOWN HEAVEN'S DOOR

The onslaught of diabolic forces is sometimes covert, as in the persona of the satanic narrator, and at other times overt, as in the diabolic personas of Chamcha and Mirza. While we rarely get glimpses of why the narrative works overtly or covertly – certainly we never get a Miltonic phrase such as "by what best way, / Whether of open Warr or covert guile, / We now debate"[62] – the same mix of the two strategies can be seen in the narrator's blatant antireligious rhetoric and in his subtle and convoluted use of the satanic verses incident.

While the *Verses* contains the harshest, crudest, most blasphemous and most insulting of attacks, the severity of these attacks is in keeping with the notion of a satanic narrator, for such a narrator is the sworn enemy of God and Islam. As such, he indulges in blasphemy, in attacks on his former Ruler, and in attacks on God's chief links to humanity: Muhammad and Gabriel. In one of the novel's most infamous assaults on Islam's exemplar, Salman the Persian claims that Mahound justifies polygamy (and frustrates his young wife Ayesha) by obtaining "God's own permission to fuck as many women as he liked." Salman also makes the cynical observation that Mahound exonerates Ayesha from suspicions of impropriety (she spent a night in the desert without Mahound) by calling upon "his pet, the archangel," after which "the lady didn't complain about the convenience of the verses" (*sv* 386–7). While this passage has occasioned outrage, the most gratuitous instance of irreverence occurs when the prostitutes in the Curtain take the names of Mahound's twelve wives, a narrative playfulness which is obscene to many Muslims. The narrator takes this irreverence to the depths of blasphemy when one of these prostitutes then panders to necrophilia by mimicking Mahound's deceased wife (*sv* 382).

What readers hear about Islam's holy prophet is often sifted through the narrator's favourite Jahilia setting, the brothel, which is "ruled over by the ancient and nameless Madam of the Curtain whose guttural utterances from the secrecy of a chair shrouded in black veils" are "the profane antithesis of Mahound's sacred utterances" (*sv* 376). Within the confines of the brothel, the narrator gives voice to extremely crude language. For instance, Mahound's soldiers refer to women as "cunts" and "slits." In *A Brief History of Blasphemy* Richard Webster observes that such extreme language "is potentially the most violent and the most insulting of all the registers available to Western writers." Moreover, it "is brought into conjunction with some of the most sacred traditions of Islam."[63] This chapter of the novel is also focused on Baal, who succumbs to "the seductions of becoming the secret, profane mirror of Mahound" (*sv* 384). The verses he writes are, like the words of the Madam, "the profane antithesis of Mahound's sacred utterances."

The narrator also draws a sympathetic portrait of Salman Farsi, who calls Mahound a "conjurer" (*sv* 363) and who admits to playing a diabolic role when he alters Mahound's recitation: "I went on with my devilment, changing verses, until one day I read my lines to [Mahound] and saw him frown and shake his head as if to clear his mind, and then nod his approval slowly, but with a little doubt" (*sv* 368). In "The Two Salmans: Salman Farsi and Salman Rushdie," Abedi and Fischer say that the above derives "from Tabari's account of Muhammad's scribe, 'Abdullah ibn Sa'd, who lost his faith after the Prophet failed to notice a deliberate mistake in his transcription." They say that the "figuration here is of the secular Muslim, Salman

Rushdie, adapting the Islamic message to the contemporary world, and at some point becoming subject to the repressive wrath of fundamentalist brethren whose sense of Islam is violated."[64] They also suggest that an "interesting undercurrent thematic in Rushdie's work is a redemption of a cosmopolitan Persian sensibility ('I must say I'm very taken with the idea of being a Mughal'), against both political or Arabicized ('pure') Islam and against European cultural colonialism."[65] No doubt they are correct here, yet what needs to be added is that in Chapter 6 Rushdie pushes this sensitivity from refinement to crudeness, and places it in a context that cannot but be insulting to devout Muslims. It is particularly offensive if these Muslims get the impression that Rushdie himself is on the attack here (and how can they do otherwise, given the use of the name Salman?) and not some shadowy Iblis figure. Yet I doubt that the backlash against the novel would be much less severe even if the blame were shifted from Rushdie to a satanic narrator, for the question of why Rushdie creates such a narrator may be a fascinating one in Western literature, with its Satanic, Promethean and Faustian heroes, but is not likely to find much of a sympathetic audience in the Muslim world.

In addition to allowing his Salman the Persian to pervert the purity of Mahound's words, Rushdie employs a derogatory name for the exemplar of Islam. The name *Mahound* carries strong anti-Islamic baggage: "Mahound – with his variants Mahum, Mahun, Mahoune, Macon, Machound and so forth – is a medieval European version of Muhammad, whom Christians presumed the infidel Muslims worshipped as God. For poets from Langland to Burns, Mahound is synonymous with the devil – an expletive by which people swear, or a false god."[66] For instance, in H. White's 1865 textbook, *Elements of Universal History*, he says the Koran "is filled with stories from the Old Testament and parables borrowed from the New. [Muhammad] asserted that it was brought in fragments from heaven by the Angel Gabriel, and appealed to the pure classical style of the work as a proof of its divine origin. It comprises a mass of tales, visions, discourses, laws, precepts, and counsels, in which truth and falsehood, the sublime and ridiculous, meet side by side."[67] I quote this textbook account of "universal history" to supply an inkling of the anti-Muslim views which continue well past the Middle Ages. Although Muhammad is not portrayed as White's "impostor" who "formed that mighty scheme of fraud, which, under the name of *Islamism*, he at length proclaimed to the world,"[68] he is nevertheless presented as an opportunist who seizes upon revelations that are suspiciously close to what he desires to be true – as when it is revealed to him that polygamy will help him win converts. Once again, it can be asserted that attributing these depictions to the fictional narrator, rather than to Rushdie himself, will not serve to exonerate the author. For if the narrator is biased but more or less reliable – like the narrator of *Shame* – devout Muslims will blame the human narrator and his human author. And if the narrator is satanic, they are not likely to appreciate the work in a Western Romantic or postmodern light; instead, they are likely to question the motive for allowing narrative rein to a figure totally opposed to Allah and his word.

The *Verses* gives great prominence to the incident of the satanic verses, treating it both in its original form and in reworkings set in London and India. One should preface a closer examination of this incident with the insistence that Muslim interpreters do not view it as casting doubt on Muhammad or the Koran. Rather, they see it in light of the Koranic verses in which God says that, while every prophet is tempted by Satan, God always "abrogates the interjections of Satan and confirms His own revelations."[69] Shabbir Akhtar comments that "the incident of the satanic verses is actually a tribute both to the scrupulous honesty of a Muslim tradition that recorded such a potentially damaging event and also to the integrity and sincerity of Muhammad as God's spokesman."[70] It is, however, only the "potentially damaging" aspects which the satanic narrator emphasizes.

In the novel's version of the original scenario, Mahound responds eagerly to Abu Simbel's proposal that the three goddesses "be given some sort of intermediary, lesser status":

"Like devils," Bilal bursts out.

"No," Salman the Persian gets the point. "Like archangels. The Grandee's a clever man."

"Angels and devils," Mahound says. "Shaitan and Gibreel. We all, already, accept their existence, halfway between God and man. Abu Simbel asks that we admit just three more to this great company. Just three, and, he indicates, all Jahilia's souls will be ours."

(sv 107)

The narrator puts Mahound in a questionable light by suggesting that he tries to sell the goddesses to his followers in order to win souls. Mahound's language is ambiguous, for example when he asks, "The souls of the city, of the world, surely they are worth three angels?" (*sv* 111). While it ought to be clear that Mahound is thinking of winning souls for God, the narrator makes Mahound sound less like a prophet than a materialistic entrepreneur. Hence the narrator's view that Mahound is *profit*-motivated rather than *prophet*-motivated. Just as the narrator suggests that God is a manipulative manager, so he suggests that His Prophet is a greedy accountant. Within this context, it is hard to credit Rushdie's notion that Mahound's derogatory name derives from a desire to "turn insults into strengths" (*sv* 93). While I would not discredit this motive altogether, the use of "Mahound" has clearly backfired both politically and culturally. Moreover, this use fits all too well with a demonic agenda that has nothing to do with raising the status of the majority of Muslims, who believe that Muhammad is the exemplar of human thought and action. In his essay "In Good Faith" Rushdie argues that Muhammad is called Mahound in order to reclaim "language from one's opponents" (*ih* 402). Or, as he puts it in the novel, Muhammad is given "the Devil's synonym," "the demon-tag the farangis hung around his neck" in order to "turn insults into strengths" (*sv* 93). If this is the reason Rushdie uses the name, he miscalculates the effect of using it, for Muslims have clearly not joined him. Arguing through analogy, Webster points out that "blacks have not attempted to reclaim and wear with pride the word 'nigger' and Margaret Thatcher is unlikely to call herself 'Mrs. Torture.'"[71] In any case, whatever Rushdie says about trying to reverse the demonized status of Muhammad is not clearly backed up by the way he depicts "Mahound" in the novel.

Although the author allows for a certain amount of ambiguity in the depiction of Mahound (he may be opportunistic and greedy yet he also struggles with himself), there is no mistaking the negative portrayal of God in the novel. Disguising himself as a balding "God" with dandruff, the narrator suggests that God is a bumbler who is either indifferent to human confusion and suffering or does not know His own nature. "Oopervala" tells Gibreel: "Whether We be multiform, plural, representing the union-by-hybridization of such opposites as *Oopar* [up] and *Neechay* [down], or whether We be pure, stark, extreme, will not be resolved here" (*sv* 319). The narrator also has his Archangel Gibreel remember telling God, "at the very beginning" of time, that it was a mistake to allow "criminals and evildoers" to live on earth, to which "the Being, as usual, replied only that he knew better" (*sv* 336). Because Gibreel is filled "with resentment at the nonappearance" of God both at the moment of his illness and during his "persecuting visions," he thinks to himself: "*He* never turns up, the one who kept away when I was dying, when I needed him. The one it's all about, Allah Ishvar God. Absent as ever while we writhe and suffer in his name" (*sv* 111). The narrator also indirectly suggests God's absence when, after Gibreel and Chamcha fall "from the Everest of the catastrophe to the milky paleness of the sea," he asks "Who am I?" Readers cannot answer this question unless they have read the novel at least once. Puzzling them further, he answers his question with the rhetorical question, "Who else is there?" (*sv* 4), implying that he exists while God does not. Just because God is marginalized by the satanic narrator does not mean, however, that readers will conclude that Satan is the only one who exists, who "is there." God's absence from this world is also stressed in Babasaheb's psychic experiment: the question "*Is there a God* [?]" remains unanswered (Babasaheb's "glass medium" does not move, "not a twitch") while the question "*Is there a Devil* [?]" provokes a response (the glass falls off the table and shatters "into a thousand and one pieces") which strongly suggests that the answer is *Yes* (*sv* 21). The satanic narrator portrays himself as the dominant and victorious Higher Power and he does his best to keep God both out of the picture and out of the running.

The attack on God's angels, particularly Gabriel, is an integral part of the attack on God and His otherworldly chain of command. The satanic narrator maligns his archangelic rival Gabriel by creating a Gibreel who is extremely fallible and "fallable," as well as schizophrenic and prone to homicidal rages. The narrator constructs such an "angel" and then prompts him to think bitter satanic thoughts: Gibreel thinks to himself that the Deity lacks confidence since "It" does not "want Its finest creations to know right from wrong" (*sv* 332). Gibreel also thinks that God reigns "by terror" and that "It" insists "upon the unqualified submission of even Its closest associates, packing off all dissidents to Its blazing Siberias, the gulag-infernos of Hell" (*sv* 332). These are, of course, variants of the argument made by Milton's infernal Serpent, who says that God "Sole reigning holds the tyranny of Heav'n" and that he upholds his "Empire" by "strength or Chance, or Fate."[72]

The narrator also depicts God and His control over angels in terms of a tyrannical manager and servile workers. He contends that just as workers should doubt and rebel against managers, so angels ought to doubt and rebel against God (*sv* 92). Above all, he wants to cast doubts on the entire chain of command which puts Muhammad, Gabriel and God in positions of power. He does this by making Mahound, "that businessman on the hill" (*sv* 91), seem opportunistic, and by promoting skepticism toward Gabriel and God, toward the "very businesslike archangel" who hands down "the management decisions of this highly corporate, if non-corporeal, God" (*sv* 364). Hence, of course, the recurrent, relentless use of the satanic verses incident.

At the root of the satanic verses incident lies *shirk*, the association of something with God other than God Himself. Glassé notes that the "sin of *shirk* ("association") is a name for paganism; pagans are called "the associators" (*mushrikun*). But *shirk* is the fundamental state of being in revolt against God, irrespective of any professed belief in other gods. It is also atheism, or the putting of nothingness in the place of God."[73] In terms of myth or religious cosmology, Satan most strongly stands for revolt against God, and it comes as no surprise that he would use various forms of polytheistic temptation to lure souls from the strict monotheism upon which Islam – which literally means the submission to Allah's power – is based.

The satanic narrator reworks the satanic verses incident so as to cast doubt on the cosmic power structure of Islam, yet the incident is also reworked elsewhere and for parallel reasons – both in India, where Mirza tempts Ayesha to compromise her faith, and in London, where Gibreel's rejection of Allie mocks Mahound's rejection of the three goddesses. This mockery is not straightforward, for it is complicated by Gibreel's rejection of Rekha. Echoing Muhammad's triumph over Satan and the goddesses in the original satanic verses incident, Gibreel spurns Rekha, who tells him that a "compromise solution is always possible," who asks him to say "just three-little-words," and who tells him, "I can take for you any form you prefer" (*sv* 333–4). Gibreel's rejection does not necessarily create mockery (or at least not a *clear* instance of mockery), yet it does set up the conditions for mockery by running parallel to Gibreel's unjust, harmful rejection of Allie. Infected by a puritanical and misogynistic fervour, Gibreel thinks of Allie as a "temptress" and a "creatrix of strife." He feels that he has become "enmeshed by her in the web of a love so complex as to be beyond comprehension," and that in loving her "he had come to the very edge of the ultimate Fall" (*sv* 321). Because Rekha is recognizably fiendish, Gibreel's rejection of her more or less follows the model of Mahound's rejection of the goddesses. Yet because Allie incarnates a mystical, Sufi devotion to the Mountain of God, and because she wants to "salvage him so that they could resume the great, exciting struggle of their love" (*sv* 341), Gibreel's rejection of her mocks Mahound's rejection.

At the risk of complicating an already complex scenario, I will reiterate that the rejection of Rekha's verses only *might* suggest mockery, for Gibreel rejects them even though they have a soothing effect – at least compared to the torture they inflict on Mahound as he walks through the nighttime streets of Jahilia. Gibreel's walk is not an anguished one, nor is the city transformed into a violent carnival of demonic spirits: "All that night [Gibreel] walked the city streets, which remained stable, banal, as if restored to the hegemony of natural laws; while Rekha – floating before him on her carpet like an artiste on a stage, just above head-height – serenaded him with the sweetest of love songs" (*sv* 334). These "sweetest of love songs" bear striking resemblance, both in the context where they are found and in the words used to describe them, to the "sweet songs" of Satan and his "fiendish backing group" (*sv* 91). Despite their soothing effect, Gibreel follows in the footsteps of the exemplar of Islam: he rejects the compromise solution offered by Rekha. In so doing he feels he is breaking the tyranny of "all the women who wished to bind him in the chains of desires and songs" (*sv* 336). Thus while Gibreel's rejection of the fiendish Rekha mostly parallels Mahound's rejection of the three goddesses, it also suggests – as does his rejection of Allie – that he rejects what might calm his severely over-heated mind.

The narrator also promotes the sin of *shirk* by setting up a self-serving distinction between tyrannical monotheistic "purity" and liberating polytheistic "impurity." In his portraits of Tavleen and the Imam, he provides examples of those who resemble Mahound in their uncompromising religious stance and in their desire to impose an otherworldly scheme on the world around them. While the narrator infuses a certain amount of heroism into the ruthless Tavleen, her overriding character is one of austerity and refusal to compromise. The Imam is equally uncompromising and ruthless, yet his depiction does not contain a shred of heroism or dignity. A caricature of the late Ayatollah Khomeini, the Imam sees the West as a place where people know little – and care less – about God. As a result, he sees London as "the Sodom in which he had been obliged to wait." Consciously attempting to remain "ignorant, and therefore unsullied, unaltered, pure," he blocks the London light with thick curtains, "because otherwise the evil thing might creep into his apartment: foreignness, Abroad, the alien nation" (*sv* 206–7). The "devilish" Chamcha's struggle to transform himself according to his environment is the opposite of the "holy" Imam's struggle, which is to maintain cultural difference and "purity" at all costs. The Imam also forces political change on the world around him, while at the same time attempting to turn back the hands of time. He wants Iran to return to a pre-Westernized Islamic era, an "Untime." The Imam's version of a return to old-time Islamic religion is one in which he smashes clocks and in which history is the forbidden "intoxicant, the creation and possession of the Devil, of the great Shaitan" (*sv* 215, 210).

While on one level Rushdie is expressing his antagonism to Khomeini's vision of Islam, on another he is allowing his satanic narrator to benefit from the distinction between the coercive, tyrannical figure of the Imam and the liberating figures of Al-Lat, Hind and the Empress. The latter two are linked through Al-Lat: Hind worships Al-Lat, and her revenge against Mahound leads to the appearance of Al-Lat in Mahound's bedroom (*sv* 393–4); the Empress takes the form of the goddess when the Imam storms her palace: "Then the golden dome of the palace bursts open like an egg, and rising from it, glowing with blackness, is a mythological apparition with vast black wings, her hair streaming loose, as long and black as the Imam's is long and white: Al-Lat, Gibreel understands, bursting out of Ayesha's shell. 'Kill her,' the Imam commands" (*sv* 214). Al-Lat, Hind and the Empress are associated with what in the Muslim subcontinental context might be called the "threat" of Hinduism, or, in particular, the "threat" of Kali, the black goddess of Time. Abedi and Fischer observe that "Abu Simbel's Queen is that other great threat, Hind, India, land of female goddesses par excellence: from Kali to Indira Gandhi, exalted females, 360 idols and more, polymorphous perversity and fecundity run riot."[74] The references to Kali and Indira Gandhi are appropriate given the related spellings of *Hind*, *Hindu*ism, *Ind*ia and *Ind*ira, and given the resemblance between the Kali-like Widow in *Midnight's Children* and the Empress with her black wings and loose streaming black hair. One could object that there is nothing threatening, let alone demonic, in suggesting that polytheism provides multivocal and therefore liberating forms of theology; yet the context is all-important here, for the novel is steeped in Satan's promotion of *shirk*, in the otherworldly power struggle of the satanic verses incident. The narrator champions polytheistic female figures not because he believes in gender equality or cultural pluralism, but because these figures are alternatives to monotheism in general, and to the monotheism of Islam in particular. He is, of course, the self-professed leader of these alternatives.

The narrator champions the goddesses and – lest they get the glory and not he – suggests that these goddesses are his daughters, his pride and joy. For after being (in Milton's words) "Hurl'd headlong from th'Etherial Sky,"[75] he says that he and his daughters sang their verses. One should keep in mind his earlier question, "Who has the best tunes?" (*sv* 10), when he says they "sang from hellbelow his soft seductive verses" and when he reminisces, "O the sweet songs that he knew. With his daughters as his fiendish backing group, yes, the three of them, Lat Manat Uzza, motherless girls laughing with their Abba, giggling behind their hands at Gibreel, what a trick we got in store for you, they giggle, for you and for that businessman on the hill" (*sv* 91). Besides noting that the popular tune, "Sympathy for the Devil," has a backup chorus, and that the three goddesses here appear to join the campaign of psychological terrorism which the satanic narrator wages against Gibreel, one should observe the ambiguity of the narrative voice. Is the voice Satan's, or simply that of someone who appreciates Satan's verses, his "sweet songs"? Also unclear is whether or not Rushdie is here influenced by legends in which Satan and Satan's wife hatch daughters from eggs: "Allah created al-Shaitan, perhaps another name for Iblis, who then produced eggs from which other demons were hatched. In a variant legend, Allah created not only al-Shaitan, but a wife, who produced three eggs. When hatched, the children were all ugly, having hoofs instead of feet."[76] Such legends might associate the Devil's daughters with the Empress, who bursts from the shell of her palace once the Imam takes power (*sv* 214). While Satan is created by God in both of the above legends, the satanic narrator does not mention having such a father. And while the three hatched daughters in the second legend have a mother, the three daughters of the narrator are "motherless." The narrator admits to no matriarchal equal, although he does make his daughter Al-Lat "Allah's opposite and equal": Hind tells Mahound that Al-Lat "hasn't the slightest wish to be [Allah's] daughter. She's his equal, as I am yours" (*sv* 91, 100, 121). Manipulating mythic genealogy, he allows himself – but not God – to be Al-Lat's father, and he allows Al-Lat to be God's equal. He thus positions himself above the three goddesses and above the "God" who is, according to his revised cosmogony, equal to a goddess.

In his bid to usurp power from God, the narrator argues that he deserves to take God's place because God is unjust to women. Referring to Ibrahim's belief that God wanted him to leave Hagar alone in the desert, he comments: "From the beginning men used God to justify the unjustifiable. He moves in mysterious ways: men say. Small wonder, then, that women have turned to me. – But I'll keep to the point; Hagar wasn't a witch" (*sv* 95). This notion of a tyrannical and unjust God is consistent with the suffering Chamcha endures under the yoke of a father who is his "supreme being" and that the angels endure under the yoke of a business-like, sweat-factory God. While it is not too hard, given Promethean and feminist schemas, to see how the narrator might get readers to agree that women suffer under the yoke of a patriarchal God, it is rather more difficult to credit the notion that Satan is the cosmic power who sympathizes with their plight. This is especially the case when he daydreams about genocide in the desert and admits to treating humans as wanton boys treat flies, and when he possesses Chamcha, drives Gibreel into homicidal insanity, and turns Allie's potentially mystical ascent of Everest into a sordid scene in which she is pushed from the roof of an apartment. It therefore seems unlikely that his cosmic leadership would prove any more compassionate than that of the "God" he depicts as aloof and tyrannical.

The narrator also tempts humanity from strict monotheism by making the sensual and polytheistic aspects of the Indian Ayesha seem more appealing than her austerity and devotion. Corcoran sums up as follows the feminine, polytheistic attraction of the Indian Ayesha, whom she considers to be "the most powerful female figure in all of Rushdie's fiction": "Her erotic magnetism is clear from the moment we see her, through the eyes of Mirza Saeed, a man who, standing in the bedroom he shares with his beloved wife, looks out the window at Ayesha and is overcome with lust. The compelling call of Ayesha is erotic, but not only carnal. Ayesha is married to the archangel, and her desire is for the holy city. Is she a female version of the true Prophet, or a return of the banished goddesses of the 'Satanic verses'?"[77] Readers are left to wonder whether or not Ayesha's appeal may include something of the polytheism of Srinivas, who sees her as the Hindu goddess of wealth, Lakshmi. Mirza tells Srinivas that goddesses are "abstract concepts only," yet Srinivas proceeds to see Ayesha as Lakshmi despite Mirza's objections: " 'I am no philosopher, Sethji,' he said. And did not say that his heart had leapt into his mouth because he had realized that the sleeping girl [Ayesha] and the goddess in the calendar on his factory wall [Lakshmi] had the identical, same-to-same, face." (sv 476). While the vision of Srinivas is no doubt beatific, it must be remembered that the real issue in this context is monotheism, and that the praise of goddesses is exactly what the Devil tempts Muhammad with in the incident that gives the novel its title.

GUNFIRE ON QAF'S PEAK

The satanic narrator uses the three goddesses and associated female figures to promote the *shirk* of polytheistic compromise and to place himself in a position of power. This is not, however, the strategy he uses in his treatment of Allie, who is arguably his most challenging opponent, as well as one of the few characters over whom he does not seem able to exert a victorious demonizing influence. For Allie represents a very deep, yet in no way unattractive devotion to the God-Mountain, Everest. Allie's temperament is antithetical to the violent and puritanical zeal of characters such as Tavleen and the Imam, and she avoids the dogmatism and intractability of Eugene Dumsday, Mahound or Hind. Indeed, she remains closest to Sufyan in her open-minded sympathy.

In order to see the extent to which the narrator goes in attacking Alleluia, one must note the links between the events which occur at the start, middle, and end of the novel: the explosion of the plane Bostan at the height of Mount Everest, the gunshot Allie hears at the peak of Mount Everest, and the shots which appear to be fired on the roof of Everest Vilas. Also, one must recall that Chamcha's antagonism to Allie is couched in terms of a jealousy which derives from Satan's jealousy of the good angel Gabriel, and that Chamcha's revenge combines the actions of the snake in the Garden of Eden with those of Iago in *Othello*. While the satanic narrator is successful in keeping Allie from her angel Gibreel and from her God-Mountain (which is twenty-nine thousand feet high, just one thousand feet short of Attar's thirty), he nevertheless fails to eradicate the traces of Sufi yearning and unity which Allie leaves behind.

Rushdie subtly associates the explosion of Bostan at the height of Everest with the explosive sound, the "sharp report, like a gun," which occurs when Allie nears the peak of Mount Everest. Her visions begin with "rainbows looping and dancing in the sky, the radiance pouring down like a waterfall from the sun," and she becomes convinced that she is in the presence of angels. She says that she would gladly die there, except that she hears "a noise, a loud, sharp report, like a gun." This sharp noise changes positive to negative, upwards to downwards: "That snapped me out of it. I had to yell at Pem [the Sherpa] until he, too, shook himself and we started down. The weather was changing rapidly: a blizzard was on the way. The air was heavy now, heaviness instead of that light." (*sv* 199).

Despite the immense pain of her fallen arches, Allie yearns to make a second ascent of Everest, an effort mirrored in her yearning to climb the mountain of Gibreel's love: "Denied mountains by my weak-boned feet, I'd have looked for the mountain in him: establishing base camp, sussing out routes, negotiating ice-falls, crevasses, overhangs. I'd have assaulted the peak and seen the angels dance" (*sv* 314). After forgiving Gibreel for smashing her miniature mountains, Allie returns to India in the hopes of climbing Everest again. Yet before she can do this she visits Gibreel in Bombay, only to be shot or pushed to her death after being brought by him to the roof of his apartment tower, Everest Vilas. Given that Gibreel earlier pointed his finger at Sisodia and shot him, his admission that he pointed his finger at Allie before her death suggests that he shot her as well (*sv* 545). Gibreel may thus have entered his most disastrous gap in consciousness. The text, however, is ambiguous: Allie may have been pushed by Rekha, the angry, jealous spirit who says (unconvincingly) that she is not jealous of Alleluia and that she would be happy to be Gibreel's mistress. If Allie is pushed by Rekha, one still has to ask, Why did Gibreel bring her to the roof of his apartment? Another possibility is that Satan pushes her – a possibility not far removed from the previous two, for if Gibreel is possessed or if the witch-like Rekha pushes her, both cases suggest strong satanic intervention.

Alleluia's association with angels and mystical unity makes her the perfect target of the satanic narrator, who depicts her in the same negative way in which he depicts God, that is, as cold and self-serving. Allie's description at the Shepperton film studio party suggests God's frosty indifference (a theme on which the satanic narrator often harps), and highlights Satan's jealousy of both Gabriel and the human spirit that can ascend to God's icy realm: "The moment Saladin Chamcha got close enough to Allie Cone to be transfixed, and somewhat chilled, by her eyes, he felt his reborn animosity towards Gibreel extending itself to her, with her degree-zero go-to-hell look, her air of being privy to some great, secret mystery of the universe; also her quality of what he would afterwards think of as *wilderness*, a hard, sparse thing, anti-social, self-contained, an essence. Why did it annoy him so much? Why, before she'd even opened her mouth, had he characterized her as part of the enemy?" (*sv* 428). Allie's spiritual "essence," her celestial visions and her yearning to climb the Mountain of God, make her a figure of envy, for in Islam Iblis once enjoyed the plenitude of being which comes from proximity to God. As was noted earlier, the narrator transmits his jealousy of Gabriel to Chamcha, his hoofed double. The narrator notes how Chamcha "struggles alone through that partying throng," while Farishta is "beset with admirers, at the very centre of the crowd." It is in this setting that the "glacial presence by Farishta's side of Alleluia Cone" makes him feel "the entirety of his loss," and, "at its bottom, his own anonymity, the other's equal celebrity, and the great injustice of the division" (*sv* 425). To avenge the "great injustice" of this division, the narrator gets his hoofed double to drive his Archangel into a homicidal jealousy, thus torturing both Chamcha and Gibreel with the very emotion that he himself longs to escape.

The primal, mythic source of this jealousy surfaces after the narrator tells us that he will not shrug off the question of why evil exists: "It's not unknown for literary-theatrical exegetes, defeated by the character [of Iago], to ascribe his actions to 'motiveless malignity'. Evil is evil and will do evil, and that's that; the serpent's poison is his very definition. – Well, such shruggings-off will not pass muster here" (*sv* 424–5). The narrator does not then give us a clear explanation of why evil exists, although he does illustrate his implicit meaning (that envy lies at the root of his evil) by depicting Chamcha's jealousy of Gibreel during the Shepperton party. Implicitly, he is arguing that Satan's evil is a reaction to divine injustice, and that Satan's motives have little in common with the supposed motivelessness that gives evil a bad name. Chamcha "has destroyed what he is not and cannot be; has taken revenge, returning treason with treason;

and has done so by exploiting his enemy's weakness, bruising his unprotected heel. – There is satisfaction in this" (*sv* 466). The narrator here charges his fellow angels with treason, and claims that they too deserve to have their heels bruised. The logic is demonic, for while in the ancient myth the serpent is allowed by God to exact punishment on the first couple, here the narrator is saying that he is justified in inflicting punishment on an angel who would not rise with him against God, on an angel who still enjoys the bliss of God's icy realm.

In addition to having Allie murdered, the satanic narrator contrives events so that Sufyan's life is snuffed out and so that Sufyan's views are marginalized. We do not hear Sufyan's views about *Othello*, but instead we hear the views of his wife, who is far more concerned about money than ideas: "And what was it that made them a living in this Vilayet of her exile, this Yuké of her sex-obsessed husband's vindictiveness? What? His book learning? His *Gitanjali, Eclogues,* or that play *Othello* that he explained was really like Attallah or Attaullah except the writer couldn't spell, what sort of writer was that, anyway?" (*sv* 248). Sufyan's views on important questions, such as the motives of Iago, are thus left unexplored. Readers only know that Sufyan's wife has distorted something Sufyan appears to have said into the contours of her own misunderstanding. One can only wonder what her husband might say about Shakespeare's tragedy, given his love of Tagore's *Gitanjali,* Virgil's *Eclogues* and a thousand other philosophic things. For Sufyan "swallow[s] the multiple cultures of the subcontinent," and he has a "pluralistic openness of mind" which allows him to "quote effortlessly from Rig-Veda as well as Quran-Sharif, from the military accounts of Julius Caesar as well as the Revelations of St John the Divine" (*sv* 246, 245). Add to this his status as "least doctrinaire of hajis" (*sv* 243), his name, and his sympathy for the wool-covered Chamcha, all of which associate him with the Sufis. Schimmel notes that the derivation of Sufism "from *suf,* 'wool,' is now generally accepted – the coarse woolen garment of the first generation of Muslim ascetics was their distinguishing mark."[78] Rushdie goes to some pains to bring in this association when he has the goat-like Chamcha wrapped in a "sheepskin jacket" (*sv* 244). Sufyan also immediately accepts Chamcha in his fallen, transformed state (*sv* 243–4), which perhaps suggests that Sufyan holds an unconventional Sufi view of Satan.

Just as Rushdie allows his Hind to frame, to edit, and to omit Sufyan's opinion on a matter which has direct import on the theme of the novel, so Rushdie allows his satanic narrator the freedom to frame his own case, to plead his own cause, to define his own terms, and to marginalize or eliminate whatever or whoever does not help him attain his goals. Clearly, the narrator does not encourage readers to contemplate Allie's fate in light of Sufyan's implicit Sufism.

Interestingly, the mysticism suggested by Allie and Sufyan is not something critics have spend much time examining. Hélène Kafi refers to Qaf and to several other Sufi ideas in a creative essay, yet she does not show where Sufi motifs enter the text.[79] Abedi and Fischer suggest that Everest and Qaf can be associated with "the ice-woman," that is, the English Allie and Pamela.[80] Syed suggests a correspondence between Calf, Qaf, Kailasa and Alleluia's "mystical Himalayas."[81] David Myers calls Rushdie a "free-thinking mystic," and contends that the ending of the novel suggests that the only way out of the maze created by loss of faith is "through unorthodox, mystic faith or intellectually open discussion in a framework of altruistic socialism."[82] It is difficult, however, to see why in an article in which he calls Rushdie a mystic, he ignores Sufi mysticism – especially when it might go some way in explaining the liberation he detects. Sara Suleri offers a provocative reading which, although not specifically focused on mysticism, suggests that Rushdie has a religious sympathy not alien to iconoclastic mysticism: "Even before the fundamentalists descend to burn the published text, the book itself inflames, unfolding as an act of archaic devotion to the cultural system that it must both desecrate and renew"; Rushdie's use of the *ghazal* links him "to a highly wrought tradition in which a recurrent trope is the rejection of Islam for some new object of epistemological and erotic devotion."[83] Suleri argues that just as poets such as Ghalib (whom Rushdie quotes in the novel) take on the "burden of devotional blasphemy" (in which "irreligion compels" and "faith retards"), so Rushdie's religious renunciation "is figured as a taut and ironized submission to the alterities represented by an Islamic culture in a colonial world."[84] While these comments offer avenues of possibility, they do not take into account the overwhelming diabolism of the text. Critics tend to see Rushdie's mystical or iconoclastic moments as rays of light in a prism of many colours. I on the other hand see the mysticism of Allie and Sufyan as two thin shafts of wavering light in an ingeniously constructed prison of darkness.

One might ask, What is the point of marginalizing Allie and Sufyan and allowing evil to dominate? And what is the value of a drama in which a devil-figure drives an angel-figure to homicide and suicide, and in which the devil-figure walks away scot-free? I would argue that this scenario is meaningless in the same way that the evil Satan and Iago stand for is without any positive or redeeming features (and

I am here of course not talking about any Romantic or Promethean Satan). Nevertheless, while the text is meaningless on the level of the satanic narrator's vision – as is *Othello* on the level of Iago's vision – it affirms the value of love and tolerance on a symbolic and mystical level. The suffering caused by the satanic narrator gains meaning when readers recognize his divisive scheming, when they sympathize with the victims of his manipulations, and when they see that the initial explosion of the plane Bostan is echoed in the gunfire that twice stops Alleluia from climbing to God and thus actualizing the deepest meaning of her name. In this sense the novel can become everything the satanic narrator does not mean it to be.

7 Post-*Verses*

O! wither'd is the garland of the war,
The soldier's pole is fall'n; young boys and girls
Are level now with men; the odds is gone,
And there is nothing left remarkable
Beneath the visiting moon.

Antony and Cleopatra, IV.15.64–8

BY THE LIGHT OF THE MOON

While it would be too dramatic to insist on Ophelia's "what a mind is here o'er thrown," Rushdie's fiction post-*Verses* is disappointing in various ways. Apart from *Haroun*, which is in a category of its own, his last two novels lack the kind of new trajectory, both in terms of idea and language, which lends excitement to his earlier work. This fall from literary brilliance is particularly noticeable in the areas of cosmology, mythology and mysticism, for only on occasion do the *Moor* and *Ground* rework other worlds in startling ways. In general, they display neither the primordial spark of *Grimus* nor the sustained artistic fire of *Midnight's Children*, *Shame* and the *Verses*. They dismiss rather than explore the complexities of other worlds, and they set up otherworldly expectations they do not fulfill.

In their beginning chapters, the *Moor* and *Ground* push readers to expect that Edenic and infernal worlds will work their way into the mindscapes of the characters and onto the landscapes of their worlds. Yet unfortunately this never happens. I find this disappointing, for it seems like telling us that Saleem has a lower house of parliament in his head, and then asserting that these diverse voices were a whim, and that their silencing has no meaning because they never meant anything to begin with. It is like saying that Omar has a mystic void in his spirit and then, afterwards, that this was just an analogy, and that any peopling of this void by witches or monsters would not make sense because such places and figures do not exist. While it is not entirely fair to thrust the antireligious moral of Rushdie's later novels onto the religious complexity of his earlier ones, he himself invites such an exercise by setting up expectations.

One might object that Rushdie has all along been skeptical about, and even antagonistic toward, the otherworldly. Yet, as I hope this study has shown, cosmology, mythology and mysticism are deeply embedded in the structures of his narratives and in the depictions of his characters – even the ones who reject religion most vehemently. For example, Aadam Aziz's struggle to reject a God in which he could not wholly disbelieve works because it operates in a universe in which beliefs are both confirmed and debunked. Yet in the *Moor* and *Ground* Rushdie's rejection of belief takes place in a fictional universe which precludes the possibilities of myth, magic and mysticism. Thus he proves his point in an almost tautological manner.

In the last two books there is not so much a shift in his attitude toward mixing politics and religion as there is in the way he goes about portraying the otherworldly within the individual. For characters like Grimus, Saleem, Padma, Raza, Omar, Allie and Gibreel religion is very real; it has palpable beauties and terrors as well as a susceptibility to being used for political gain. In the *Moor* and *Ground* he no longer explores the deeply engrained and often puzzling beliefs and superstitions of his characters. He no longer delves very far into the paradox of religion in the secular and postmodern world, be it that of London or Bombay. He now neither inspires nor frightens with the dervish pirouettes and the snake-pit vortexes of his strange other worlds.

It is as if Rushdie has given up on a more difficult literary exploration, and fallen back on some general antireligious view, one that his earlier fiction examined within a larger panoply of belief, disbelief and doubt. He once left a space for belief despite his skepticism; he once explored "a form which doesn't prejudge whether your characters are right or wrong," "a form in which the idea of the miraculous can coexist with observable, everyday reality."[1] In the *Moor* and *Ground*, on the other hand, he gives up on this "form." And, to speak quite frankly, he prejudges.

Given the personal repercussions of the disastrous Affair which bears his name, it is not surprising that Rushdie stops confronting religion and those who promote it. Nor is it surprising that in *Haroun* – this jolly novel written amid the scariest of his days – he uses other worlds in an intensely idealistic fashion, projecting them as an escape from the real-world threats of dogma and fatwa.

In some ways *Haroun* has common ground with its predecessors: it fuses other worlds à la *Grimus* and it attacks authoritarianism just as

Rushdie does in every novel he writes. In addition, its two-dimensional villain, its cardboard Cultmaster, is the same villain we find in Chapter 3 of the *Verses*. Yet this common ground is also deceiving, for *Haroun* is more fabulous and fairytale-like than any of Rushdie's previous novels, including *Grimus*. Also, its cardboard Cultmaster inhabits an equally cardboard universe. This is different from the *Verses*, where the two-dimensionality of his Imam contrasts with the depth of the other characters, thus making the Imam's obsession with cultural and religious purity an object of ridicule. In this sense the Imam is the exact opposite of Sufyan – just as the evangelist Eugene Dumsday is the opposite of Allie. In *Haroun*, on the other hand, neither the two-dimensional Cultmaster nor the two-dimensional world around him are real enough to care about in the same way that we care about Allie or Sufyan in London, Saleem in Bombay, or even Flapping Eagle in the town of Calf. Moreover, all personal and political problems in *Haroun* are solved with the touch of a magic wand. This is appropriate, for *Haroun* is after all a novel for children. Yet this fact can also hide the shift in Rushdie's oeuvre, away from a serious and problematic use of other worlds.

Coming down from *Haroun*'s fantastic lunar flight, the Rushdie reader lands in the *Moor*'s Bombay, a city which serves (as it did in *Midnight's Children*) as a microcosm of Indian diversity and the tension that comes along with it. In particular, Rushdie zeroes in on the tension and alienation caused by the anti-Muslim sentiments of Hindu fundamentalists. The theme of alienation applies to Muslims as a group both in India and in the broader sweep of history: they are pushed from Ayodhya and Bombay just as the last Moorish ruler is pushed from the Alhambra and Granada in 1492. This communalist theme echoes that in *Midnight's Children*, where Ahmed is mistreated by the Hindu Ravana gang on the one hand and by the new Indian government on the other. In exploring this theme the *Moor* is not nearly as engaging as *Midnight's Children*, however, and this for at least two reasons. First, while the *Moor* touches on Ayodhya, it does not chronicle this event in the same haunting way as *Midnight's Children* chronicles the Hindu-Muslim conflicts of Partition or the several wars between Pakistan and India. And while Rushdie does make something of an Indian-Iberian link, the analogy with the Spanish Moors remains a rather awkward one, rendered only slightly more meaningful by the initial eastern migration of the novel's Portuguese families and by the eventual westward migration of the protagonist to Andalusia. Second, the novel's coverage of communalist tension is rather shallow, at least in terms of characterization. The main problem is that the communalists themselves seem to care little about the religions for which they are fighting. Rushdie may of course be making the point that for such people the politics of belief is more important than belief itself, yet he did this effectively in *Midnight's Children* with the Ravana gang and the Muslim mob while *also* rounding out the picture with characters such as Padma and Naseem – characters for whom religion matters more than money or political gain.

The *Moor* takes jabs at Hindu fundamentalism, yet by and large it declaws or secularizes the demons or *rakshasas* of that religion. One might object that Rushdie makes much the same point as he does in *Midnight's Children*, where the Hummingbird's Convocation and Saleem's Conference are destroyed by forces very much like the gangs of Abraham and Mainduck. Yet in *Midnight's Children* the forces and figures of religion are embedded deep in the psyches of the main characters, and there are complex connections between these depths and their social, allegorical and political expressions – be these in the form of advocacy (as in Convocation and Conference), distortion (as in Padma and Shiva), or manipulation (as in the Widow and General Ayub). Later in this chapter I will show that this kind of depth and complexity is not *entirely* absent in the *Moor*, but I will also suggest that what little depth we get in the novel only points to how much deeper Rushdie could have dug beneath the surface.

The Ground Beneath Her Feet also avoids taking other worlds seriously or portraying them profoundly. This is more frustrating in the recent novel than in the *Moor*, since Rushdie insistently promises some ontological chasm in which Rai and Ormus might lose themselves à la Omar and Chamcha, yet he never takes us into this subterranean realm. We never get any interesting irruption of the sacred or the diabolic, despite the narrator's speculation that "Ormus's doubts about reality might be a kind of revenge of the spirit, an irruption, into a life dedicated to the actual and the sensual, of the irrational, the incorporeal. He, who had rejected the unknowable, was being plagued by the unknown" (G 184). The possibility of an opening dimension – especially of the Rekha variety we find in the *Verses* – arises many times, yet it is never fully realized. Here *Ground* is leagues from the kind of exploration we get with Aadam Aziz and Omar, who are seduced and tortured by an other world controlled by a God and a Devil they do not want to believe in. Moreover, Omar's fears are but one entry point into an other world of unpredictable and shifting figures of retribution. Likewise, Aadam's fight with God is only one entry point to the novel's many other worlds – from Ramram Seth's prediction and Saleem's telepathy to the purgatorial magic of the Sundarbans Jungle. In *Ground*, on the other hand, Ormus's other world opens up only long enough to confirm our suspicions that he is entering the strange days of a less talented Jim Morrison. And for Rai the other world yawns open long enough to be rendered tedious and ineffectual, if not laughable.

The *Moor* and *Ground* lack the high stakes which make otherworldly tension worth betting on. Rarely does magic or myth erupt from the surface of normal life, and never does a fifth dimension seriously disrupt the moving contours of our four-dimensional world. Rushdie's otherworldly magic realism becomes metaphoric magic realism, expressed succinctly in the disappointing maxim of *Ground*'s Rai: "Life's bruises demythologise us all" (*G* 154). In this formulation, the perplexing notions people have about God and the Devil, Heaven and Hell, rapture and possession, become mere symptoms of something else – most often delusion. While this message crops up in Rushdie's previous novels, there it clashes with the way other worlds come alive and are thus not delusional – as in the afterlife world and the mythic implosions of *Grimus*, the web of myth, magic and mysticism of *Midnight's Children*, the satanic possessions and mythic scourges of *Shame*, and the demonic incursions and crushed mystical visions of the *Verses*.

As in his personal life, where open celebrity becomes overshadowed by secretive notoriety, Rushdie's fiction post-*Verses* inhabits a radically different space. He no longer urges us to look at Forster's "huge scenic background of stars, fires, blue or black air." He no longer projects us into that great religious game of Rushdie Roulette, the one in which he pits demons against gods and angels, the legions of darkness against the royalty of light. In brief, the odds are gone and there is not as much that is remarkable under his visiting moon.

HAROUN AND THE *MOOR:* SEA CHANGES

Before rejecting other worlds as mere fantasies, Rushdie first indulges in a novel that is total fantasy. *Haroun* operates, like many a good children's novel, on two levels: one for children and one for adults. On the former, it is a lively, light story, complete with an ending in which the villain vanishes (with none of the violence of the Grimm brothers) and everyone lives happily ever after. On the adult level, the novel works more like *Grimus*, in that it is a masterful fusion of cosmological and mystical paradigms.

The fabulous world of *Haroun* may partly derive from a desire to fabricate a happy ending to the unhappy story of Rushdie's life during the first year of the fatwa, yet it more certainly derives from the fact that he wrote the book with children in mind, especially his son Zafar. While he touches on serious conflicts in the story (the

Cultmaster is a reincarnation of the *Verses's* censorious Imam; Snooty Buttoo manipulates the Kashmiri electorate; the Gups and Chups represent cultures at war; Rashid and Soraya are on the verge of divorce), he does not go into the kind of detail or realism we see in his previous novels. The problems in *Haroun* remain by and large on the Disney level.

There is even a crucial difference in the way he fuses his paradigms, for in *Haroun* he does so neatly. While *Haroun* is not simplistic, it is far less complex than *Grimus*, the most idealistic and syncretic of his previous novels. *Grimus* uses the same syncretic mode to highlight the ideal of multidimensionality, yet also contains a profusion of myths and loose ends, complex characters like Deggle, Virgil and Grimus-Eagle, and delves into dark and problematic visions of the universe. Finally, *Grimus* ends in paradoxes and conundrums, while *Haroun* ends with a neat fusion of paradigms, a happy ending that is clearly in the comic and fairy tale mode. That *Haroun* operates purely in the realm of the fabulous becomes doubly clear when, returning to a more realistic exploration of subcontinental politics in his short story "Chekov and Zulu," Rushdie drops the idea of a happy ending: the politics of the subcontinent (in this case Sikh separatism) become as many-headed as the politics surrounding Aadam's Free Islam Convocation or Iskander's Popular Front. And in the *Moor* optimism takes an equal beating, as Abraham the Overlord of the Semitic Underworld engages in a mutually destructive communalist street battle with Hindus led by the Battering Ram.

One of the more interesting aspects of *Haroun* is the way Attar's twelfth-Century Persian paradigm slides into Somadeva's eleventh-Century Sanskrit one. Initially Attar's schema is dominant. His Hoopoe even does double duty: he first takes the form of Butt the speed-possessed bus driver and then of Butt the mechanical bird who flies Haroun to the moon and back. The name Butt appears to derive from the conference-given right to differ, to say *but*, and in this sense it complements Iff, which is both the name of the water genie on the moon and an indicator of the conditional tense. Extended politically, Iff also signals the proposals and initiatives that enliven the conference or body politic. The Sufi paradigm of flight toward unity gives way to the Hindu paradigm of multidimensionality when Butt transports Haroun to the Sea of Stories on the moon. Rushdie knits Somadeva's conceit of a great sea containing many currents of narrative into his own story on many levels, all of which suggest that problems and contradictions can be resolved by opening them up into new ways of configuration, into new ways of telling. Once conflicts are mixed into the great sea in this way, positive transformation occurs in society, where division turns into unity (Chups unite with Gups), in the political sphere, where coercion turns to conference (the Cultmaster and Snooty Buttoo are defeated) and on the emotional level, where alienation turns into sympathy (there are multiple reconciliations, culminating with the reunion of Rashid and his wife). Attar's unity is thus injected into the chaotic profusion, the many-currented sea of Somadeva. It is impossible to say exactly where the Hindu conceit takes over from the Muslim, or which remains the stronger in the end, and this impossibility strengthens the pro-unity moral Rushdie is aiming at.

The division between Chupwalas and Gupwalas can represent any religious, cultural or political division, and as such it brings to mind the division between *us* and *them*, *pure* and *impure* made by the Axonans in *Grimus*, Bariamma in *Shame*, and the Imam in the *Verses*. In light of *Haroun*'s subcontinental settings (probably Bombay and certainly Srinagar), the division suggests the great Muslim-Hindu divide. The same division is represented in *Midnight's Children* in terms of flight and the diversity of Bombay. Yet in *Midnight's Children* Saleem's unifying flight is grounded, whereas Haroun and Rashid succeed in unifying the dark and light sides of the moon, and, consequently, in restoring harmony to the earthly city by the sea. Father and son also come together, in that Haroun rediscovers his faith in his father's stories and in the imaginative Ocean of Notions which supplies them. Thus Haroun and Rashid regain the unity from which their names derive, that is, from the historical and legendary Haroun al-Rashid (764–809), the Caliph celebrated in tales from *The Arabian Nights* such as "Khalifah the Fisherman" and "The Porter and the Three Girls of Baghdad."

Haroun and Rashid defeat the Cultmaster and succeed in making the lunar poles spin, an action which suggests a union of opposites, a commingling of the infinite number of things symbolized by light and dark, force and counterforce, us and them. And as new stories flow into the lunar ocean, so the waters of creativity flow into Rashid's Ocean of Notions. This liberating chain of events affects both otherworldly and worldly settings: on the moon the Cultmaster's idol of sewn lips topples from its place in the Citadel of Chup and on Earth the politician who urges Rashid to turn his creativity into propaganda slinks out of town. Buttoo's departure from Kashmir leaves "the people of the Valley free to choose leaders they actually liked" (*H* 207). In this sense the dynamic parallels that in *Grimus*, where Eagle's defeat of Grimus – a Cultmaster of sorts – liberates the citizens below.

Haroun may be light fare, yet it helps to clarify the ideals which from *Grimus* to the *Verses* are increasingly difficult to discern amid a tangled web of mythic figures, narrative ambiguity, demonic possession, oneiric shifts, diabolic innuendo, and outright satanic invasion. While *Haroun's* intricacies require a certain amount of concentration on the reader's part, they are nowhere near as perplexing as those in *Grimus*, *Midnight's Children* or the *Verses*. Once one identifies Rushdie's Muslim and Hindu sources as well as the novel's subcontinental setting, the moral becomes rather easy to see. While there is some complication involved in the dream shared by Haroun and Rashid, one should remember that the two names come from the name Haroun al-Rashid and that therefore a certain amount of commingling is appropriate. Moreover, as Aklujkar notes, the sharing of dreams is "in keeping with the treatment of names and dreams" in the Sanskrit collection of tales from which Rushdie draws.[2] Whereas in the *Verses* dreams lead Gibreel into dark, entangling webs (and lead readers into confusion), in *Haroun* they suggest what Aklujkar calls Rushdie's "general concepts of freedom of speech, growth of language, dialogue between the binary oppositions" and "the life-line of good literature."[3]

The *Moor* initiates a double break in Rushdie's adult fiction, away from using otherworldly motifs and paradigms to structure his novels, and away from allowing otherworldly dimensions to break through the surface of the real. While the *Moor* contains many of the usual Rushdean motifs drawn from myth and cosmology, these remain on the level of metaphor and analogy. They do not constitute versions of reality which are sustained or which are ontologically challenging to the realism of a common, practical, material universe. The *Moor's* "four sequestered, serpented, Edenic-infernal private universes" (*M* 15) remain private, personal and societal analogies rather than cosmic or metaphysical realms. Eden, Lucifer and Hell are effective indicators of a fall from a happier or powerful state, but not of any separate dimension or demonic possession. The diabolical Vasco tells the Moor that to be "the offspring of the daemonic Aurora" is "to be, truly, a modern Lucifer" (*M* 5), yet neither Aurora nor the Moor ever demonstrate a satanic nature or any satanic power. The Moor is hurled from Aurora's Paradise, her "fabulous garden, and plunged towards Pandaemonium" (*M* 5), yet his expulsion does not parallel Aadam's fall into a violent world, Saleem's fall into his two-headed possession, or Chamcha's fall into a London of raging fires and cloven hooves.

This is not to deny Rushdie's great use of otherworldly motifs and metaphors. Especially effective is his portrayal of the Moor's father, Abraham, the cold-blooded Over Lord of an Under World filled with gang wars and communal hatred. Yet Abraham's gangsterism, with its thuggery, extortion and drugs, in no way poses a challenge to God or pokes a malevolent finger through the fabric of a positivist universe. The *Moor*'s malign figures may operate analogously to the "base deeds" which lead to "the destruction of the ethical nexus" postulated by Francisco (*m* 20), but they do not suggest that Rushdie is reworking cosmology, mythology or mysticism in any earth-or heaven-shattering way.

Despite the lack of any deeply penetrating other world, Rushdie does make effective use of magical blue tiles, which suggest Somadeva's Ocean, the god Vishnu, who takes the form of a Battering Ram, and the figure of Satan. All of these contribute to shaping the novel and help Rushdie to develop his points about cultural diversity, communalism and identity. These magical and otherworldly borrowings are not tightly interwoven in the same way that cosmology, mythology and mysticism are fused in *Grimus*, nor are they pushed into precarious juxtaposition as they are in *Midnight's Children*. Yet they nevertheless complement the overall point Rushdie has always made and continues to make: while the unity of cultures, like the unity of the self, is destroyed by self-interested individuals or groups, the ideal of such unity remains a beautiful and transcendent thing.

With their Chinese, Jewish and Keralan origins, the Cantonese tiles in the Cochin Synagogue represent a flow of divergent histories or stories: "Some said that if you explored for long enough you'd find your own story in one of the blue-and-white squares, because the pictures on the tiles could change, were changing, generation by generation, to tell the story of the Cochin Jews. Still others were convinced that the tiles were prophecies, the keys to whose meanings had been lost with the passing years" (*m* 75–76). The blue tiles stand for multiple versions of history, and they are among the few elements in the novel which shift ever so slightly from metaphor to magic. One might imagine that Rushdie would use these blue tiles to suggest a mystical plurality, just as he used the Stone Rose in *Grimus* or the inlaid lapis-lazuli spittoon in *Midnight's Children*. Yet the opposite happens: when Flory stares into "the ceramic encyclopedia of the material world that was also a bestiary, a travelogue, a synthesis and a song," she realizes that God is "missing from the hyperabundant cavalcade" (*m* 84). Underscoring his point, Rushdie makes a statement that is more emphatically worldly than any he has made before: "'What you see is what there is,' Flory mumbled under her breath. 'There is no world but the world.' And then, a little louder: 'There is no God. Hocus-pocus! Mumbo-jumbo! *There is no spiritual life*'"(*m* 84). While one might be tempted to see this as a repetition of Aadam Aziz's refusal to bow in *Midnight's Children*, there are here no rubies or diamonds dropping in silent symbolic protest; there is no suggestion that Flory is losing something by declaring that there is no God. And while one might see something of Mirza Saeed's disdain for the "mumbo-jumbo" of religion (*sv* 232), there is no subsequent parting of the waters, no quasi-miraculous event which confounds the reader and casts perplexing ambiguity onto the God who has been dismissed.

The blue tiles of Cochin may not induce mystical visions, yet they do suggest an Ocean of Stories. In *Haroun* this ocean blends with Attar's mysticism, but in the Bombay of Aurora, Abraham, and their son "the Moor" it becomes a more worldly ocean, swelling with the currents of humanity. And while in *Midnight's Children* Bombay is seen through the mystic eyes and telepathic mind of Saleem, here it is seen with the more jaded eyes and far less imaginative mind of the Moor. Nevertheless, some of the "highly-spiced nonconformity" which characterizes Saleem's Bombay (*mc* 308) and which gives taste to his stories also flows into the *Moor*'s version of that great port city on the western coast of India: "Bombay was central; all rivers flowed into its human sea. It was an ocean of stories; we were all its narrators, and everybody talked at once" (*m* 350).

Saleem sees his Bombay in Muslim, Hindu and occasionally Christian and Parsi terms, yet the Moor tells his tale from the marginal and hyphenated perspective of a Portuguese/Keralan/Maharashtrian family of Jewish and Christian background. Some of what Rushdie has to say about this family's identity strikes a chord with the poetry of the Jewish Bombay poet Nissim Ezekiel, who often explores the alienation of Indian Jews. In "Background, Casually" he writes, "I went to Roman Catholic school, / A mugging Jew among the wolves. / They told me I had killed the Christ, / That year I won the scripture prize. / A Muslim sportsman boxed my ears." // "I grew in terror of the strong / But undernourished Hindu lads ..."[4] Ezekiel also sees from a non-Hindu and non-Muslim point of view the problem Rushdie focuses on in the *Moor*: Hindu fundamentalism, which can be seen as a clash between Hindu ideals of openness and the narrower practices of ethnocentric Hindus. In "The Patriot" he gingerly mocks this contradiction by writing in a voice which betrays its own religious bias: "In India also / Gujaratis, Maharashrians, Hindiwallahs / All brothers – / Though some are having funny habits. // Still, you tolerate me, / I tolerate you, / One day Ram Rajya is surely coming."[5] It is this desire for the Rule of Ram, promoted by religious political movements such as Bombay's powerful Shiv Sena, that Rushdie takes issue with in the novel.

The Jewish and Christian backgrounds of his families are interesting in themselves, yet Rushdie leaves off any exploration of them so that he can focus in on the same religious conflict which dominates much of his oeuvre – that between Hindus and Muslims. To do this he takes two of their most powerful figures, Vishnu and Abraham, and has them stand for Hindu and Muslim gangs. While what happens in the *Moor*'s Bombay mirrors to some degree what happens in the Agra and Delhi of *Midnight's Children's*, where the *muhalla* mob and the Ravana gang form the many-headed monster of communalism, the *Moor* is easier to follow in this regard, since the communalist factions are not represented by amorphous monsters. They are, instead, focused into well-known and fairly clearly delineated figures from their respective religions.

In shifting from the metaphor of the Ocean of Bombay to the mythic figures which divide this Ocean, Rushdie suggests that the violence of the Hindu-Muslim conflict at Ayodhya seeps south and into Bombay. To appreciate what Rushdie has to say here one should remember that Ayodhya's famous Mosque "was built in the early 16th century by the Mughal emperor Babur on a site traditionally identified as Rama's birthplace and as the location of an ancient Hindu temple." The site took on increasing importance to both sides, and "on Dec. 6, 1992, the three-story mosque was demolished in a few hours by a crowd of Hindu fundamentalists. It was estimated that more than 1,000 people died in the rioting that swept through India following the mosque's destruction."[6] In Rushdie's novel, Zeenat comments caustically: the "followers of one fiction knock down another popular piece of make-believe." While Rushdie makes his secular point obvious through Zeenat – "I'd rather die fighting over great poets than over gods" (*M* 351) – the shift from oceanic metaphor to mythic figure is less obvious: the "corrosive acid of the spirit" which is strongest at Ayodhya is seen in terms of a liquid which, like the liquid the Cultmaster pours into *Haroun*'s Sea, poisons the great sea of human stories. Even with all its diversity, Bombay is not strong enough to withstand it: "even the great city's powers of dilution could not weaken it enough" (*M* 351).

It is at this point that the Hindu ideal of Rama, the seventh incarnation of Vishnu, is betrayed by Hinduism's most zealous devotees. In making his point, Rushdie foregoes metaphor, discarding many-headed monsters and doublebills of destruction for unambiguous clarity: "Lord Ram was an avatar of Vishnu; Vishnu, most metamorphic of the gods. The true 'rule of Ram' should therefore, surely, be premised on the mutating, inconstant, shape-shifting realities of human nature – and not only human nature, but divine as well. This thing being advocated in the great god's name flew in the face of his essence as well as ours" (*M* 351).

Against the degradation of Vishnu/Rama into a dogmatic and violent "Battering Ram," Rushdie pits the figure of the Moor's father, who is seen chiefly in terms of Satan. Just as Rushdie juxtaposes the ideal and the betrayal of Vishnu, so he brings together the revered figure of Abraham with the malevolent figure of Satan. That the Moor's father has this double identity does not cause the type of confusion generated by the God/Satan figure of Changez in the *Verses*; rather, the *Moor*'s Abraham/Satan suggests what the Battering Ram signifies even more explicitly: a religious ideal twisted for selfish, coercive, violent purposes. Rushdie does not complicate these mythicized figures further by casting them onto the type of densely populated mythic battlefield one finds in *Midnight's Children*. Rather, the betrayal of Hinduism is clearly focused in the creation of a Battering Ram, and the betrayal of Islam is clearly focused in the figure of Abraham, the Over Lord of the Bombay Under World.

In having Abraham lose the battle for Bombay turf, Rushdie adroitly symbolizes the alienation of Muslim India. Mainducks's comment on the destruction of the Ayodhya mosque displays the type of intolerant, "unoceanic" spirit which reminds one of bloody Partition and of that most hideous of phrases, "ethnic cleansing": "When such alien artifacts disappear from India's holy soil, let no man mourn"; "if the new nation is to be born, there is much invader-history that may have to be erased." The Moor responds to this stupidity by concluding, "After two thousand years, [Muslims] still did not belong" (*M* 364), and by an equal and opposite stupidity: he proceeds to kill for the Muslim side, thus adding fuel to the fire that scorches the soul of nation and city. The Moor's account is of course written during his last days in Andalusia (another echoland of Islamic glory), and thus he can see his own stupidity, as well as the culpability of both sides: "There comes a point in the unfurling of communal violence in which it becomes irrelevant to ask, 'Who started it?' The lethal conjunctions of death part company with any possibility of justification, let alone justice." Rushdie then combines the ocean motif with allusions to *Romeo and Juliet*, when he writes, "They surge among us, left and right, Hindu and Muslim, knife and pistol, killing, burning, looting, and raising into the smoky air their clenched and bloody fists. Both their houses are damned by their deeds; both sides sacrifice the right to any shred of virtue; they are each other's plagues" (*M* 365).

While no Kali or Satan springs into the world to enact retribution, the plague on both Hindu and Muslim houses takes a figurative shape. The plague becomes an avenging demon, bestriding the horizon and raining fire upon the heads of all Indians (M 372). Vaguely reminiscent of the Beast in *Shame*, this demon topples the contingents of Muslim power represented by Abraham and his Cashondeliveri Tower. This destructive force evokes Ravana, the Hindu extortionist gang of *Midnight's Children*, when the Tower falls into "clouds of ravenous black smoke," and Rushdie hints at the fallen beauties of Islamic mysticism when he says that the "feathers of un-Indian birds went on drifting through the air for days" (M 375). One should note the word *un-Indian*, for it reminds readers of the virulent prejudice of Mainduck. Rushdie's oblique evocations of Ravana and Sufism are also followed by the political irony that he is so fond of establishing. In attacking the Muslims, the Hindus wound their fellow citizens: "the great atrium at the top of Cashondeliveri Tower burst like a firework in the sky and a rain of glass knives began to fall, stabbing the running workers through the neck the back the thigh, spearing their dreams, their loves, their hope" (M 375).

The atrium holds the ill-gotten luxury of Abraham as well as an Edenic garden filled with the trees and birds of mystical possibility – all of which are betrayed by Abraham, the "God in paradise" who operates not for the good of others but for his own wealth and power. Reminiscent of Raza with his appropriation of God's power, and of Chamcha with his fantasy of toppling church spires with his finger ("*I am*, he accepted, *that I am*" – SV 289), Abraham damns himself by defining himself: "'I am a business person,' he said. 'What there is to do, I do.' *YHWH. I am that I am*" (M 336). This blasphemous reference to Exodus 3: 14 reinforces the notion that Abraham is a "shadow-Jehovah," an "anti-Almighty" (M 336–7), an "overlord in his hanging garden in the sky," "rich beyond rich men's richest dreams" and "of course above the Law as well" (M 317). Abraham is the worst of both worlds: in worldly terms he rules an empire of crime and thus sacrifices the well-being of society for his own gain; in otherworldly terms he so hates this world that he sacrifices his only son for no good reason at all.

The Over Lord of the Under World may live up to his dual nature of fascist God and vengeful Satan, yet the Moor hardly lives up to anything at all, being a rather listless and directionless figure. His state of mind mirrors only weakly the complex fears and yearnings found in characters such as Saleem, Omar and Chamcha. Like Chamcha, he is caught in – and acts out – evil plots he barely understands. A crucial difference between the two lies in the way forces act upon and within them: whereas Chamcha is possessed by Satan and then plays the Devil's part, the Moor is undermined by his rather evil

parents yet he is never possessed. The result of his parents' cruelty is
nevertheless similar to that experienced by Chamcha, who dreams
that a man (probably a projection of himself) has glass skin that
cracks and rips the flesh from his bones (*sv* 34); the Moor's fall from
parental grace leaves him "emptied, invalidated ... the horror of it
shattered the universe, like a mirror. I felt as though I, too, had shattered; as if I were falling to earth, not as myself, but as a thousand and
one fragmented images of myself, trapped in shards of glass"
(*M* 279). This image of a fragmented, splintering self goes back to
Saleem, whose cracks threaten not only to dry up his body but also to
invalidate him, to plunge him into absurdity (*MC* 9).

The Moor's alienation is somewhat poignant because he has no
spiritual terms, metaphors or structures to fall back on. In his early
dreams he tells his mother that he is being flayed, and she responds,
"We will never gain our humanity until we lose our skins" (*M* 95). In
a later dream his loss of an outer covering or identity hints at a hypothetical freedom: "I would be able to peel away more than skin, I
would float free of flesh, skin and bones, having become simply an
intelligence or a feeling set loose in the world, at play in its fields, like
a science-fiction glow which needed no physical form" (*M* 136). In
this version of alienation the Moor does not accept mystical succour,
yet receives a sort of existential or postmodern freedom instead. This
is not as liberating as it first seems, however, for he remains without
fulfilling attachment to others (at least Chamcha hooks up with
Zeeny at the end of the *Verses*). Rushdie drives this home in the final
scene, when the Moor refuses to sacrifice one moment of his life for
one moment of his fellow captive's. Moreover, he remains unable to
mine any hidden seam of maternal affection: "she never spoke to me,
never made confession, never gave me back what I needed, the certainty of her love" (*M* 432).

Against this stark alienating background Rushdie casts one of the
rare magic spells in the novel. Scrambling over the terrain outside
Vasco's Alhambra, the Moor sheds his skin as a Sufi might shed his
self: "*Thorns, branches and stones tore at my skin. I paid no attention to
these wounds; if my skin was falling from me at last, I was happy to shed that
load*" (*M* 433). This quasi-mystical liberation is succeeded by a homage
to the real Alhambra, the "*triumphant masterpiece*" of the once victorious Moors. The architectural masterpiece is a "*palace of interlocking
forms and secret wisdom,*" and it testifies to everything the Moor needs:
"*to lost but sweetest love, to the love that endures beyond defeat, beyond annihilation, beyond despair; to the defeated love that is greater than what defeats it, to that most profound of our needs, to our need for flowing together,
for putting an end to frontiers, for the dropping of the boundaries of the self*"

(*M* 433). This eulogy to what he never sees, "*to that monument to a lost possibility,*" very subtly, very indirectly alludes to Attar's Impossible Qaf and to the annihilation that gives meaning to the spirit once it has transcended the boundaries of the skin or self. It is also fitting that the Moor's last sigh is couched in poetic terms which include the image of the Ocean, a symbol which earlier in the novel held out the possibility of people living together in harmony: "*Yes, I have seen it across an oceanic plain, though it has not been given to me to walk in its noble courts. I watch it vanish in the twilight, and in its fading it brings tears to my eyes*" (*M* 433). One must stress, however, that this final quasi-mystical note does not complete any mystical pattern in the novel. It cannot, therefore, supply anything like the regenerative and spiritual depth we find in Picture Singh's flute, Saleem's thirty pickle jars, or Allie's precipitous flight from the thirtieth floor of Everest Vilas.

The Moor's final moments bring with them curious disparate allusions, to Arthur in Avalon, the dream-time of the Australian aboriginals, Finn MacCool in the Irish hills, Rip Van Winkle, Barbarossa in his cave, and "Ouroboros in the bed of the Sundering Sea" (*M* 433). In suggesting multiple literary and mythical contexts into which the Moor may dream, and out of which he may wake "into a better time," Rushdie takes pages from his first two novels: from *Grimus*, where allusions to Paradise and Qaf fuse with those suggesting a new start in Gimle or some other new universe created by Shiva, and from *Midnight's Children*, where Shiva and the Black Angel threaten to tear Saleem apart, while in another possible ending Saleem marries his Hindu lover and they enjoy a honeymoon with Aadam in the re-imagined Paradise of Kashmir. The *Moor* thus leaves us where we are left so often by Rushdie: in an indeterminate space, one redolent with options, possibilities, and alternate dimensions of story.

This open-endedness does not, however, mean that the *Moor* stands head to head with Rushdie's previous novels. While its characters and literary style make it superior to *Grimus*, its overall conception is not nearly as complex or challenging. And in its treatment of Indian communalism and alienation in Bombay it comes far short of *Midnight's Children*. Some of the problem lies in the level of exuberance in the writing yet much of it comes from the fact that otherworldly paradigms are evoked yet never supply a provocative insight into the structure of the universe (the novel's setting) or into the structure of the mind (the novel's protagonist). Here, again, it is helpful to compare the Moor with Saleem. Much of the interest generated in *Midnight's Children* comes from the way Rushdie uses other worlds as integral and complex functions of Saleem's psychological make-up. For instance, Saleem's internal struggle with his two-headed-demon is not an isolated personal problem; rather, it is deeply and subtly linked to other demons of division: the singing knives which scatter the Free Islam Convocation and scare the wits out of Nadir; the many-headed monsters that stalk his mother in the muhalla and in the old city; and the many-headed Ravana that stalks his father in the Old Fort. Saleem's desire to punish his mother for her affair creates a divided or two-headed monster within him, one which reverberates with the previous monsters and which also divides Lila from Homi Catrack, Hanif from his life, and Saleem from his dream of living the kind of life Hanif wanted to realize in his screenplay.

When compared with this kind of complexity, the *Moor* seems rather straightforward and even a bit dull. In it Rushdie says the following about those who would make of the great god Vishnu a Battering Ram to pound Muslims: "A single, martial deity, a single book, and mob rule: that is what they have made of Hindu culture, its many-headed beauty, its peace" (*M* 338). While this idea of the Battering Ram has a number of links to Hindu culture and religion in the novel, the many-headed beauty-cum-monster does not take the kind of complex, many-sided form it does in *Midnight's Children*, where at the Old Fort Ahmed is tormented by Ravana and Hanuman – both necessary adjuncts in the same mythology of Vishnu and Rama – and where Saleem's revenge against Amina boomerangs as a result of listening to the two-headed demon inside him which tells him to strike from cover. The Moor's interior world is so much less fascinating than Saleem's because for the Moor other worlds never come alive, either around him or within him. For him, Hell is just a prison and religion is just a fight-club to which he belongs. For Saleem, however, religion is a gate which leads downwards and upwards – to the demons which threaten Lifafa and which make him want to punish his mother, and to visions of thirty birds, the microcosm inside Lifafa's peepshow, the Convocation beloved of Aadam and Nadir Khan, and the Conference predicted by Ramram's mystic visions. Saleem's psyche is linked to the otherworldliness that religion may not be *all* about but is *also* about: such things as yoga, tantra, magic and mysticism, represented parodically in Ramram's meditation yet not parodically in his prediction of Saleem's life, and represented in Shiva's eroticism and destruction as well as in Parvati's magic, her affair with Shiva and her trans-religious love for Saleem. While the *Moor*'s point about "the Battering Ram" is fascinating and remains consistent with Rushdie's other writings, it lacks such a complex other world of force. In this sense it leads us to what is perhaps Rushdie's most disappointing production, his most recent novel.

THE GROUND BENEATH HER FEET:
MEET JIM MORRISON

Rushdie's latest is a strange brew of a novel. It starts off strong, yet takes a fall not unlike those of Jimi Hendrix, Curt Cobain, or that most archetypal of decadent rock stars, Jim Morrison. Indeed, *Ground*'s emphasis on sex, drugs and drug-induced rock and roll visions makes one wonder if Rushdie has not boarded the bluest of buses; not just blue as in Delta or Chicago blues, or in the historical line from blues to rock and roll (a recurrent theme in the novel), but also blue as in Morrison's blue bus which plunges into a psychotropic underworld, a dark realm of Greek mythology and death. One finds particularly strong traits of Jim Morrison in the rock star Ormus, with his drug addiction, his Roman wilderness of pain, and his dogged attempt to break on through to the other side – to the underworld in which he tries to resurrect the spirit of his dead love, his Indian Eurydice. This "heavy" or "deep" drama cannot, unfortunetely, avoid being seen in terms of melodrama, given that it is surrounded on all sides by love affairs so tepid or unlikely that the reader loses interest, and by a parallel dimension theme that is quite frankly trite. While there are brilliant patches in the novel the only parts that match the author's previous writing are the opening chapters.

The early chapters set in Bombay are particularly vibrant, and Rushdie manages to work in much of the double-edged humour for which he is famous. One of the best examples is the cricket match between the British, Hindus, Parsis, Muslims and "the Remainders." The scene is comical as well as politically incisive: the players are harassed by protesters who feel the match is yet one more British ploy to divide and conquer Indians. It is humorous as well as tragic: the pro-British Parsi batter tries to hit the protesters but brains his own son instead.

Those looking for echoes of Rushdie's earlier work find plenty: there are references to the *Moor*'s Aurora and to the comically stuttering Sisodia of the *Verses*. Rushdie also casually – yet eerily – refers to the *Verses's* Everest Vilas – that twenty-nine floor skyscraper from the top of which Allie is pushed or shot. The skyscraper in *Ground* "sits like a squat missile and fills that territory with its grey, discolouring concrete." Rai says that it is "twenty-nine stories high, but mercifully those are stories [he does] not need to tell" (*GB* 169). We also get a rare peek into the life of the enigmatic British overlord from *Midnight's Children*, Sir William Methwold. We find out that Methwold's "myth world" of a British India is complemented by an obsession with the parallels between Greek and Hindu myth. This comparative mythology remains somewhat superficial, yet it works well throughout the novel and it ties in with the Orpheus and Eurydice theme.

The novel also contains a weak version of the same parallel dimension idea Rushdie handles with dexterity in *Grimus, Shame* and the *Verses*. The theme starts off interestingly enough, for Ormus receives telepathic songs from the future and takes on aspects of Elvis before his time. Rushdie also plays with an eerie doppelganger theme when Ormus's brother dies and seems to enter the same realm as his dead twin. His brother haunts him necromantically, to the point where Ormus fears that he has stolen his beloved Vina and is keeping her for himself in the underworld. Yet the idea takes a turn for the worse when a woman from a parallel dimension shows up in Rai's photographs. Then another woman from the parallel dimension explains to Rai that the first woman is in fact insane, that she is having delusions of belonging in our dimension. Finally, the parallel dimension disappears altogether, defeated by the strength of ours. Such convolutions are reminiscent of the *Verses*, yet they do not come with that novel's larger and more provocative challenges. The parallel dimension theme in *Ground* is – except when it intersects with the doppelganger theme, which unfortunately fizzles out – about as gripping as the parallel Rushdie draws between seismic and political activity.

More effective than the romances and the parallel dimension theme, the myth of Orpheus and Eurydice supplies the novel with some coherence, initially at any rate. It too, however, fails to fulfill expectations or challenge readers with anything startling or new. After Vina's death in a Mexico earthquake Ormus falls into a rock and roll wilderness of pain and self-destruction. Wasting away on strong drugs and vain hopes of Vina's return from the dead, he enters a metaphoric hell. But Vina's return in the guise of Mira, the Italian-American diva, takes on a fairy-tale note which deadens the mythic strain. She is "the Mira on the wall" who steps out of the frame, in typical fairytale fashion to make everything right – at least for Rai, who finds in her a lover more devoted to him than Vina ever was. (One should also note that the love between them is not convincing: one moment the beautiful young woman is about to kill the aging Rai, and the next she hops into bed with him). Ormus' painful search and Mira's fortuitous appearance hardly fulfill the classical design that Rushdie builds up with some urgency throughout the novel. Even though Rushdie crowds his final pages with references to Greek mythology, the overarching myth becomes deflated and quotidian. All that is left of the grand plan is "Cerberus, a grateful old stray whom [Rai and Mira] seem to have adopted" (*GB* 574).

In the *Moor* we have Rushdie's first novel which does not have a strong overarching otherworldly structure. As a result, his references to an Edenic Cochin, a satanic Abraham, a Battering Ram, and the hell of prison in Bombay fail to take on deeper meaning. In *Ground* he supplies every hint of a strong overarching meaning – from Sir Darius' Hindu-Greek studies à la Sir William Jones, to the incessant allusions to Virgil, Ovid and Hades. Yet he does not complete this meaning: he does not make it integral to the experiences of his main characters – except insofar as Ormus plummets into his own hell and Vina returns as Mira.

The tension between the use and the refusal of mythic frameworks in *Ground* tells us a great deal about the way Rushdie has come to feel about other worlds. While one cannot of course equate Rai with Rushdie, the narrator's comments, especially toward the end of the novel, confirm the type of antagonism one finds in the Aadam of *Midnight's Children*, the Mirza of *Verses*, and the Flory of the *Moor*. Rai comments that when "we stop believing in the gods we can start believing in the story" (*GB* 458), a sentiment which takes on the form of a rant when he is saved by chance from Indian thugs: "Thank god? No, no, *no*. Let's not invent anything as cruel, vicious, vengeful, intolerant, unloving, immoral and arrogant as god just to explain a stroke of dumb, undeserved luck. I don't need some multi-limbed Cosmic Dancer or white-bearded Ineffable, some virgin-raping metamorphic Thunderbolt Hurler or world-destroying flood and fire Maniac, to take the credit for saving my skin. Nobody saved the other fellow, did they? Nobody saved the Indochinese or the Angkorans or the Kennedys or the Jews" (*GB* 242).

Rai's anti-religious ardour takes a milder, more philosophic slant when he contemplates his happy yet unspectacular life with Mira: "In all the old stories, in different ways, the point is always reached after which the gods no longer share their lives with mortal men and women, they die or wither away or retire." Apart from noting that this is not the case in *all* the old stories, I would add that Rai's words also hint, albeit unintentionally, at the novel's faltering bulk: the gods "vacate the stage and leave us alone upon it, stumbling over our lines. This, the myths hint, is what a mature civilization is: a place where the gods stop jostling and shoving us and seducing our womenfolk and using our armies to lave their proxy quarrels in our children's blood; a time when they move back, still leering, still priapic, still whimsical, from the realm of the actual to the land of so to speak – Olympus, Valhalla – leaving us free to do our best or worst without their autocratic meddling" (*GB* 575). What I find particularly interesting about these sentences is that the notion of gods leaving the stage coincides with the novel's weakness, that is, with its mythic build-up without a climax. I want to emphasize that it is not the complete absence of otherworldly design which makes *Ground* falter, but rather the departure of the mythic once it has been established. In this case the departure of the gods hardly seems to have left Rushdie free to complete his best work.

The final pages also convey telling insight into Rushdie's recent views on mysticism. While in *Midnight's Children* Rushdie parodied Attar's schema in old Aziz sahib's blissful death, he nevertheless used it as a model for the conferences of both Aadam and Saleem. And while in the *Verses* Mirza attacks the mumbo jumbo of revelation, he has a death-bed vision of his own. Moreover, Allie's tragic death does much to resuscitate Attar's ideal.

A striking example of Rushdie distancing himself from such mysticism occurs when Rai enters the Towers of Silence in Bombay, where Sir Darius' corpse awaits dismemberment by vultures, in accordance with Parsi tradition: "*There are plenty of birds today, thirty birds, like the thirty in Attar's great poem who made the journey to the Simurg and became the god they sought. The thirty vultures joining together and becoming Vulture. That is the kind of thought my father might have had, the kind of connection he might have made*" (*GB* 199). Attar's schema no longer structures the narrative in any overt or subtle way. Instead, it becomes a passing analogy, one attributed to a mode of comparative, orientalist, mythopoetic thinking that is foreign to the narrator.

In chapter 2 I used the notion of a Common Law of the Unknown to refer to the power of larger systems of belief which have penetrated deeply both historically and culturally, and I opposed these to individual instances of magic amid realism. The larger systems present a sort of structural weight – superstructure or infrastructure – which is not easy to ignore, whereas an instance of magic can be fairly quickly shrugged off. Ormus's visions of another world promise to be profound and challenging, yet because they are not marked by sign posts that might enable one to chart a formidable otherworldly terrain, they fail to offer provoking challenges to already held visions of the universe. Perhaps if Ormus had taken a trip to Hell, or if Vina got past portals guarded by Cerberus, readers would be confronted with another world which presented some sort of larger challenge. This is not to say that one must write in a mythopoetic manner. Indeed, Rushdie's point seems to be that of Sir Darius, who with the myth of Prometheus in mind believes that each bite of the vulture "shows us why we should turn aside from gods & take the rational path" (*GB* 199). Yet one can hardly put a three-headed Cerberus on the dustjacket and then expect readers to find the debunked mythic world inside anything but anticlimactic.

Since no complex other worlds are structured in Rushdie's last two novels, there can be no large-scale or exciting collision of worlds with their different epistemologies. The fifth dimension which breaks into the vision of Ormus and Rai simply carries no conviction. It becomes a mere oddity, photographed and thus verified by Rai (whose sanity also verifies it), but incapable of affecting him in any profound or interesting way. In terms of ontology and epistemology the dimension has a limited interest (it challenges neither positivism nor otherworldly systems) and in terms of plot and narrative it presents little because the stakes are so low.

Rushdie's earlier work is more interesting, not because in it he promotes a mythopoetic view of the universe (his myths contradict as much as they support each other), but because he presents other worlds which are integral to his characters' situations and because these other worlds play off against the real world and against each other. The psychological predicaments of the characters trapped in these worlds become both complex and integrated into larger questions of ontology and epistemology. This may not be the only reason his earlier novels are his strongest, yet it does at least partly explain why in the *Moor* and *Ground* he loses his edge.

Notes

CHAPTER ONE

1 Borges, *Labyrinths*, 52.
2 Whitman, *Complete Poetry*, 63–4.
3 Hamilton, "The First Life of Salman Rushdie," 92.
4 Ibid., 92.
5 Ibid., 90.
6 Ibid., 94.
7 Ibid., 92.
8 Ibid.
9 Ibid.
10 Ibid., 93.
11 Ibid.
12 Sharukh Husain in *Cambridge Encyclopedia of India, Pakistan, Bangladesh, Sri Lanka* 486.
13 Hamilton, "The First Life of Salman Rushdie," 94.
14 Weatherby, *Salman Rushdie: Sentenced to Death*, 18.
15 Hamilton, "The First Life of Salman Rushdie," 96.
16 Ibid., 105.
17 Ibid., 97.
18 Rushdie with Phillips 17–18.
19 Hamilton, "The First Life of Salman Rushdie," 100.
20 Weatherby, *Salman Rushdie: Sentenced to Death*, 33.
21 Ibid., 37.
22 Whitman, *Complete Poetry*, 64.

CHAPTER TWO

1 Forster, *A Passage to India*, 212.
2 Dipple, *The Unresolvable Plot*, 66.
3 Baudelaire, *Les Fleurs du Mal et autres poèmes*, 155.
4 Durix, "The Artistic Journey in Salman Rushdie's *Shame*," 454.
5 Slemon, "Magic Realism as Postcolonial Discourse," 409–10.
6 Byron, *Don Juan*, Canto I, stanzas CXXXIII-CXXXIV.
7 Rushdie with Wachtel, 149.
8 Khayyam, *Ruba'iyat*, 62.
9 Rushdie with Cronenberg 24. In addition to changing his mind, Rushdie withdrew the essay "Why I Have Embraced Islam" from the 1991 edition of *Imaginary Homelands*.
10 Avery in Khayyam, *Ruba'iyat*, 17.
11 Eliade, *The Sacred and the Profane*, 21.
12 Jasper, *The Study of Literature and Religion*, 129.
13 Kliever, "Polysymbolism and Modern Religiosity," 178.
14 Kliever, 178.
15 Dante, *Inferno*, xxxiv, 55–6.
16 Ziolkowski, "Religion and Literature in a Secular Age: The Critic's Dilemma," 20.
17 *Rig Veda*, 26.
18 O'Flaherty *Dreams, Illusions and Other Realities*, 244.
19 Ibid., 138–9.
20 Ibid., 240, 244.
21 Chuang Tze, *The Writings of Chuang Tze*, 245.

CHAPTER THREE

1 Borges, *Labyrinths*, 58.
2 Attar, *The Conference of the Birds*, 33.
3 Schimmel, *Mystical Dimensions of Islam*, 421.
4 Ibid., 260.
5 Mercantante, *The Facts on File Encyclopedia of World Mythology and Legend*, 590–1.
6 Keats, *Complete Poems*, 608.
7 Ibid., 587.
8 Ted Hughes, *Crow*, 41.
9 Attar, *The Conference of the Birds*, 194, 184.
10 Basham, *The Wonder That Was India*, 51.
11 Eliot, *Collected Poems*, 199.
12 Ibid., 191.
13 Ibid., 219.

14 Borges 58.

15 Dante, *Inferno* IX, 1–15, XXIII, 1–57.

16 Cundy, "Rehearsing Voices': Salman Rushdie's *Grimus*," 133.

17 Attar, *Conference*, 191.

18 Ibid., 192.

19 Ibid., 201, 200, 197, 196.

20 Ibid., 198.

21 Puhvel, *Comparative Mythology*, 193.

22 Puhvel 218.

23 Eliade, *A History of Religious Ideas, Vol.II: From Gautama Buddha to the Triumph of Christianity*, 160–1.

24 Puhvel, *Comparative Mythology*, 198.

25 The cosmic tree of Germanic myth has an ambiguous fate: it falls yet it also brings humanity from the cataclysmic present to the post-Ragnarok future by harbouring the primordial couple (Eliade, *A History of Religious Ideas, Vol.II*, 157, 169).

26 Eliade, *A History of Religious Ideas, Vol.II*, 158.

27 Russell, *The Devil: Perceptions of Evil from Antiquity to Primitive Christianity*, 75.

28 *The Flyting of Loki* or the *Lokasenna* is the eighth poem in *The Poetic Edda*. Lee Hollander calls the *Lokasenna* "the product of a witty and clever skald who conceived the idea of showing the solemn and glorious gods from their seamy side. As interlocutor he uses Mephistophelian Loki, who engages the various gods and goddesses in a *senna* (a *flyting*, or running dialogue of vituperation) of at times very spicy quality in which each and every one gets his or her share of defamation, until the disturber of the peace is finally put to flight by Thor's threat of violence" (*Poetic Edda*, 90).

29 *Poetic Edda*, 10.

30 The eagle eating the leaves of Yggdrasil (Eliade, *A History of Religious Ideas, Vol.II*, 157) also recalls the Simurg felling the branches of Gaokerena (Mercantante, 590–1), although it remains unclear whether or not Rushdie intends any reference to Gaokerena.

31 Eliade, *A History of Religious Ideas, Vol.II*, 157.

32 Ibid., 168–9.

33 *Poetic Edda* 11.

34 Ibid., 12.

35 Glassé, *The Concise Encyclopedia of Islam*, 91.

36 *Vathek* in *Three Gothic Novels*, 195. Ronald Hatch of The University of British Columbia drew my attention to this use of Deggial.

37 Fairclough in *Three Gothic Novels*, 501.

38 Thomas Hughes, *Dictionary of Islam*, 328.

39 Glassé, *The Concise Encyclopedia of Islam*, 91.

40 Vitray-Meyerovitch, *Rumi and Sufism*, 43.

41 Schimmel, *Mystical Dimensions of Islam*, 178.
42 Vitray-Meyerovitch, 49–51.
43 O'Flaherty, *Shiva: The Erotic Ascetic*, 10.
44 Attar, *Conference*, 57.
45 Pourjavady and Wilson, *The Drunken Universe; An Anthology of Persian Sufi Poetry*, 73.
46 Blake, *William Blake*, 104.
47 Ziolkowski in Hesse, *Magister Ludi*, xii-xiii.
48 Borges, *Labyrinths*, 58.
49 Ibid., 56.
50 Attar, *Conference*, 185–6.
51 Schimmel, *Mystical Dimensions of Islam*, 299.
52 Parameswaran, *The Perforated Sheet: Essays on Salman Rushdie's Art*, 61.
53 Kinsley, *Hindu Goddesses*, 48.
54 Rao, *The Serpent and the Rope*, 42.
55 Daniélou, *The Myths and Gods of India*, 190.
56 Kinsley, *Hindu Goddesses*, 49–50.
57 Daniélou, *The Myths and Gods of India*, 206.
58 Ibid., 190.
59 Ibid., 203.
60 Schimmel, *Mystical Dimensions of Islam*, 5.
61 O'Flaherty, *Hindu Myths*, 12–13.
62 Ibid., 13.
63 Johansen, "The Flight from the Enchanter: Reflections on Salman Rushdie's *Grimus*," 29.
64 Ibid., 24.
65 Cundy, "'Rehearsing Voices': Salman Rushdie's *Grimus*," 134.
66 Johansen, "The Flight from the Enchanter," 27.
67 Parameswaran, *The Perforated Sheet*, 55–6.
68 Ibid., 64–5.
69 Kinsley, *Hindu Goddesses*, 43.
70 Puhvel, *Comparative Mythology*, 220.

CHAPTER FOUR

1 Khayyam, *Ruba'iyat*, 39.
2 Goonetilleke, *Salman Rushdie*, 26.
3 Parameswaran, *The Perforated Sheet*, 23.
4 Rushdie in *Kunapipi* 3.
5 Daniélou, *The Myths and Gods of India*, 309–10.
6 Esposito, *Islam: The Straight Path*, 25.
7 In his Introduction to Marx's *Grundrisse* David McLellan observes that the "thousand-page manuscript" of *Grundrisse der Kritik der politischen*

Ökonomie is "the most fundamental of all Marx's writings" (Marx, *Marx's Grundrisse*, 14). It is thus a canonical or fundamental text, as are the various texts of the Hadith and the Puranas.

8 Like Nadir, who hides in the depths of Aadam's Agra basement, Ahmed suffers as a result of the Hummingbird's failure to keep Muslims firmly within the fabric of India: Ahmed is persecuted not only by the criminal Ravana gang, but also by the legitimate Indian government, which seizes his assets after the State Secretariat "got the whiff of a Muslim who was throwing his rupees around like water" (*MC* 134).

9 Goonetilleke, *Salman Rushdie*, 42.

10 Parameswaran, *The Perforated Sheet*, 11.

11 Ibid., 54, 40.

12 Kinsley, *Hindu Goddesses*, 27.

13 Ibid., 26–7.

14 Rushdie in *Kunapipi* 7.

15 Rushdie with Wachtel, 149.

16 Brennan, *Salman Rushdie & The Third World: Myths of the Nation*, 105.

17 O'Flaherty, *Dreams, Illusions and Other Realities*, 214.

18 Attar, *Conference*, 77, 34.

19 Walker, *The Hindu World*, 155.

20 Rawson, *The Art of Tantra*, 184, 186.

21 Walker, *The Hindu World*, 155.

22 Stutley and Stutley, *A Dictionary of Hinduism*, 219.

23 Cotterell, *A Dictionary of World Mythology*, 49.

24 Perhaps Saleem sees Ibn Sina (the Andalusian physician and philosopher, Avicenna) as a Sufi because of his "unified study of Plato, Aristotle, and Neoplatonism" and because of his being "one of the prime targets of al-Ghazzali," who "was obliged, in the name of religious orthodoxy, to denounce the philosophers … in order to forestall a neopagan renaissance within Islam" (Glassé, *The Concise Encyclopedia of Islam*, 176, 311).

25 Rushdie with Haffenden, 239.

26 Harrison, *Salman Rushdie*, 46.

27 Swann, " 'East Is East and West Is West'? Salman Rushdie's *Midnight's Children* as an Indian Novel," 251–2.

28 Durix, "The Magician of History: Salman Rushdie's *Midnight's Children*," 126.

29 Kanaganayakam, "Myth and Fabulosity in *Midnight's Children*," 91–2.

30 Rushdie with Haffenden, 239.

31 Glassé, *The Concise Encyclopedia of Islam*, 160.

32 Daniélou, *The Myths and Gods of India*, 305.

33 Ibid., 220.

34 Kinsley, *Hindu Goddesses*, 122–3.

35 Rushdie, *The Wizard of Oz*, 33.

36 Kinsley, *Hindu Goddesses*, 116.

37 Ibid., 116.

38 Daniélou, *The Myths and Gods of India*, 273.

39 Daniélou, ibid., 338–41.

40 Swann, " 'East Is East and West Is West'? 257.

41 Kinsley, *Hindu Goddesses*, 97.

42 Goonetilleke, *Salman Rushdie*, 39–40.

43 Kanaganayakam, "Myth and Fabulosity in *Midnight's Children*," 92.

44 Daniélou, *The Myths and Gods of India*, 249.

45 Ibid., 144–5.

46 Rushdie in *Kunapipi* 10.

47 Eliade, *A History of Religious Ideas, Vol. III: From Muhammad to the Age of Reforms*, 142.

48 Rushdie in *Kunapipi*, 7–8.

49 Iyengar, *Indian Writing in English*, 390.

50 Rushdie with *Scripsi*, 118–19.

CHAPTER FIVE

1 Khayyam, *Ruba'iyat*, 39.

2 Shahid Burki in *Cambridge Encyclopedia of India, Pakistan, Bangladesh, Sri Lanka, Nepal, Bhutan and the Maldives*, 213.

3 Rushdie with *Scripsi*, 108.

4 Rushdie with Phillips, 18.

5 Rushdie with Phillips, 17.

6 Rushdie with Haffenden, 255.

7 Rushdie with *Scripsi*, 109.

8 Rushdie with *Scripsi*, 111.

9 Rushdie with Chaudhuri, 46.

10 Zakaria, *The Struggle Within Islam; The Conflict Between Religion and Politics*, 9.

11 Glassé, *The Concise Encyclopedia of Islam*, 214.

12 Daniélou, *The Myths and Gods of India*, 264.

13 Goonetilleke notes that "the surname Harappa is doubly appropriate because the site of the Harappan civilization borders Bhutto's family estate in the Sind province" (*Salman Rushdie*, 59–60).

14 Shahid Burki in *The Cambridge Encyclopedia of India, Pakistan, Bangladesh, Sri Lanka, Nepal, Bhutan and the Maldives*, 203.

15 Helen Watson-Williams suggests that Rushdie's Mahmoud alludes to the historical Mahmud of Ghazni. She observes that Mahmud was "the founder of the Ghaznawid dynasty" and that he led Islamic Turks "into Peshawar, crossed the Indus in 1005 A.D. and took Lahore in 1010" ("An Antique Land: Salman Rushdie's *Shame*" 44). In this case, Rushdie may

be applying the name "Mahmoud" ironically, given that the historical Mahmud was warlike and orthodox, and that the Mahmoud of the novel is a pacifist who confronts Muslims and Hindus alike with their prejudice.

16 At this point in the story Raza is Iskander's general. It is Raza who quells the Baluchi revolt in Needle Valley and who leads the party which shoots Babar.

17 *The Hutchinson Encyclopedia*, 97.

18 Burki in *Cambridge Encyclopedia*, 213.

19 Hutchinson, 97.

20 Thomas Hughes, *Dictionary of Islam*, 136.

21 In studying medicine, Omar Khayyam takes after his namesake, who resided in the Persian city of Nishapur in the eleventh and twelfth centuries, and who was influenced by Greek science as well as by the language of Sufi mysticism.

22 Khayyam, *Ruba'iyat*, 49; Attar, *Conference*, 192.

23 Khayyam 81, 47.

24 Avery in Khayyam, 17.

25 See Abedi and Fischer, *Debating Muslims: Cultural Dialogues in Postmodernity and Tradition*, 451–4, for Khomeini's poem, notes on it, and "The Counter Poem" which attacks it.

26 Rushdie with Haffenden, 256.

27 Rushdie with *Scripsi*, 111, 110.

28 Rushdie with Haffenden, 254–5.

29 Van der Veer, "Satanic or Angelic? The Politics of Religious and Literary Inspiration," 102.

30 Mathur, "Sense and Sensibility in *Shame*," 87–8.

31 Fletcher, "Rushdie's *Shame* as Apologue," 130.

CHAPTER SIX

1 Elements of satanic narration were first suggested to me in 1990 by Ken Bryant at The University of British Columbia.

2 Aravamudan, " 'Being God's Postman Is No Fun, Yaar': Salman Rushdie's *The Satanic Verses*," 15.

3 Ibid., 16.

4 Glasse, *The Concise Encyclopedia of Islam*, 210.

5 Ibid., 210.

6 Awn, *Satan's Tragedy and Redemption: Iblis in Sufi Psychology*, 49.

7 Ibid., 49.

8 Othello asks Iago why he has ensnared his soul and body, to which Iago responds, "Demand me nothing, what you know, you know, / From this time forth I never will speak word" (*Othello*, ii, 304–5).

9 Knönagel, "*The Satanic Verses*: Narrative Structure and Islamic Doctrine," 73.
10 Ibid., 73.
11 Ibid., 71.
12 Ibid.
13 Ibid.
14 Ibid., 70, 73.
15 Harrison, *Salman Rushdie*, 114.
16 Ibid., 99.
17 Ibid., 115.
18 Ibid.
19 Brennan, *Salman Rushdie & The Third World: Myths of the Nation*, 152.
20 Booker, "*Finnegans Wake* and *The Satanic Verses*: Two Modern Myths of the Fall," 195.
21 Booker, "Beauty and the Beast: Dualism as Despotism in the Fiction of Salman Rushdie," 988.
22 Booker, "*Finnegans Wake* and *The Satanic Verses*," 195.
23 Corcoran, "Salman Rushdie's Satanic Narration," 156.
24 Naïr, "Comment lire *Les Versets Sataniques*," 22.
25 Ibid., 23.
26 Aravamudan, "'Being God's Postman," 15.
27 Rushdie with Ball, 35–6.
28 Mann, "'Being Borne Across': Translation and Salman Rushdie's *The Satanic Verses*," 288, 290.
29 Abedi and Fischer take a cynical view of Khomeini's literary sensibility when they supply two Iranian poems, one in which he employs Sufi metaphors and ideas, and another (which they say fits with Rushdie's "cosmopolitan Persian sensibility") in which his Sufi stance is ridiculed (*Debating Muslims* 451–4).
30 Pipes, *The Rushdie Affair: The Novel, the Ayatollah, and the West*, 30, quoted from Islamic Revolution News Agency, February 19, 1989.
31 Aravamudan, "'Being God's Postman," 16.
32 For further information on the Devil in Islam, consult Schimmel's *Mystical Dimensions of Islam* or Awn's *Satan's Tragedy and Redemption: Iblis in Sufi Psychology*.
33 Corcoran, "Salman Rushdie's Satanic Narration," 157–8.
24 Said, *Orientalism*, 68–70.
35 Aravamudan, "'Being God's Postman,'" 14. Abedi and Fischer also observe that "Chamcha" connotes "toady" and "collaborator" as well as "a range of intercultural types." As examples of Chamcha's subservience they point to his bowler hat, his singing of "Rule Britannia," and his embarrassment at slipping back into an Indian accent (*Debating Muslims*, 339–440).
36 Milton, *Paradise Lost*, I, 61.

37 *Encyclopaedia of Islam*, Vol. III, 669.

38 This use of "picture" also anticipates Sisodia's movie based on Gibreel's anguished imagination.

39 Knönagel, *"The Satanic Verses,"* 71.

40 In his series of four books, *The Devil, Satan, Lucifer* and *Mephistopheles*, Jeffrey Russell illustrates the multifarious nature of the Devil in Western religion and literature.

41 Corcoran, "Salman Rushdie's Satanic Narration," 155–6.

42 Azazeel is distinct from Azraeel, the Angel of Death whom Saleem fears at the end of *Midnight's Children* and who Gibreel believes he has become in Chapter VII, "The Angel Azraeel." Before his fall, Iblis was known as Azazeel, who "was among the most industrious and dedicated" of spirits on Earth, and who moved "from heaven to heaven, until God raise[d] him to the Throne itself" (Awn, *Satan's Tragedy and Redemption*, 25–30).

43 Schimmel, *Mystical Dimensions of Islam*, 196.

44 Schimmel 194–5.

45 After having his eyes poked out, Gloucester tells his son, who is disguised as Poor Tom, "As flies to wanton boys, are we to th'Gods; / They kill us for their sport" (*King Lear* IV.i.36–7).

46 In Islamic cosmology it remains unclear whether Satan is a djinn or an angel. For discussions on Iblis's status as angel or djinn, see Awn, *Satan's Tragedy and Redemption*, 26–33, *The Encyclopaedia of Islam*, Vol. III, 668–9, and Russell, *Lucifer*, 55–56.

47 Pipes, *The Rushdie Affair: The Novel, the Ayatollah, and the West*, 58.

48 *Koran*, 372.

49 *Koran*, 238.

50 Pipes, *The Rushdie Affair*, 116–17.

51 I refer readers specifically to Pipes 113–20 for the insults caused by the title; to the same author at 53–69, for the blasphemous elements in the book; to Fischer and Abedi, *Debating Muslims*, 405–19, for the six main Muslim complaints and for an account and explanation of the satanic verses incident; to Ruthven, *A Satanic Affair: Salman Rushdie and the Rage of Islam*, 35–53, for information on the Orientalist context and on blasphemy in Islamic narrative.

52 Blake, *William Blake*, 102–4.

53 Ibid., 99, 95.

54 Ginsburg in Bulgakov, *The Master and Margarita*, xii.

55 Ibid., xii.

56 Ibid., xi.

57 Bulgakov, *The Master and Margarita*, 36–42.

58 Ibid., 381–9.

59 Ibid., 21.

60 *Rolling Stone Encyclopedia of Rock & Roll*, 477.

61 Awn, *Satan's Tragedy and Redemption*, 31.

62 Milton, *Paradise Lost*, II, 40–2.

63 Webster, *A Brief History of Blasphemy: Liberalism, Censorship and 'The Satanic Verses,'* 93.

64 Abedi and Fischer, *Debating Muslims* 413.

65 Ibid., 438.

66 Ruthven, *A Satanic Affair*, 35.

67 H. White, *Elements of Universal History*, 228.

68 Ibid., 227.

69 Koran, 238.

70 Akhtar, *Be Careful with Muhammad!; The Salman Rushdie Affair*, 20.

71 Webster, *A Brief History of Blasphemy*, 94.

72 Milton, *Paradise Lost*, I, 124, 114, 133.

73 Glassé, *The Concise Encyclopedia of Islam*, 370.

74 Abedi and Fischer, *Debating Muslims*, 419.

75 Milton, *Paradise Lost*, I, 45.

76 Mercantante, *The Facts on File Encyclopedia of World Mythology and Legend*, 208.

77 Corcoran, "Salman Rushdie's Satanic Narration," 164.

78 Schimmel, *Mystical Dimensions of Islam*, 14.

79 Kafi in Abdallah, *For Rushdie; Essays by Arab and Muslim Writers in Defense of Free Speech*, 188–90.

80 Abedi and Fischer, *Debating Muslims*, 420.

81 Syed, "Warped Mythologies: Salman Rushdie's *Grimus*," 139–40.

82 Myers, "From Satiric Farce to Tragic Epiphany: Salman Rushdie's *The Satanic Verses*," 145.

83 Suleri, "Contraband Histories: Salman Rushdie and the Embodiment of Blasphemy," 606, 609.

84 Ibid., 609.

CHAPTER SEVEN

1 Rushdie with Wachtel, 149.

2 Aklujkar, "*Haroun and the Sea of Stories*: Metamorphosis of an old Metaphor," 11.

3 Ibid., 3.

4 Ezekiel, *Hymns in Darkness*, 11.

5 Ezekiel, *Latter-Day Psalms*, 23.

6 1998 *Encyclopedia Britannica* cd rom, under "Ayodhya."

Bibliography

Abdallah, Anouar (et al.). *For Rushdie; Essays by Arab and Muslim Writers in Defense of Free Speech*. Translated from French by Kevin Anderson and Kenneth Whitehead. New York: George Braziller, 1994.

Abedi, Mehdi and Michael Fischer. *Debating Muslims: Cultural Dialogues in Postmodernity and Tradition*. Madison: University of Wisconsin Press, 1990.

Ahmed, Akbar. *Postmodernism and Islam: Predicament and Promise*. London: Routledge, 1992.

Akhtar, Shabbir. *Be Careful with Muhammad!; The Salman Rushdie Affair*. London: Bellew, 1989.

Aklujkar, Vidyut. "*Haroun and the Sea of Stories*: Metamorphosis of an old Metaphor." *Commonwealth Novel in English* 6: 1–2 (Spring-Fall 1993): 1–12.

Appignanesi, Lisa and Sara Maitland. *The Rushdie File*. London: Fourth Estate, 1989.

Aravamudam, Srinivas. "'Being God's Postman Is No Fun, Yaar': Salman Rushdie's *The Satanic Verses*." *Diacritics* 19.2 (Summer 1989): 3–20.

Ashcroft, Bill, Gareth Griffiths, and Helen Tiffin. *The Empire Writes Back*. London: Routledge, 1989.

Attar, Farid ud-Din. *The Conference of the Birds*. Translated from Persian and introduced by Afkhan Darbandi and Dick Davis. Harmondsworth: Penguin, 1984.

Awn, Peter. *Satan's Tragedy and Redemption: Iblis in Sufi Psychology*. Leiden: E.J. Brill, 1983.

Ball, John. Interview. "An Interview with Salman Rushdie." *Toronto South Asian Review* 10.1 (Summer 1991): 30–7.

Basham, A.L. *The Wonder That Was India*. Rupa: Calcutta, 1981.

Baudelaire, Charles. *Les Fleurs du Mal et autres poèmes*. Paris: Garnier-Flammarion, 1964.

Blake, William. *William Blake*, ed. J. Bronowski. Harmondsworth: Penguin, 1958.

Booker, Keith. "Beauty and the Beast: Dualism as Despotism in the Fiction of Salman Rushdie." *English Literary History* 57.4 (Winter 1990): 977–97.

– "*Finnegans Wake* and *The Satanic Verses*: Two Modern Myths of the Fall." *Critique: Studies in Contemporary Fiction* 32.3 (Spring 1991): 190–207.

Borges, Jorge Luis. *Labyrinths*, ed. James Irby and Donald Yates. New York: New Directions, 1962.

Brennan, Timothy. *Salman Rushdie and The Third World: Myths of the Nation*. London: Macmillan, 1989.

– "*Shame*'s Holy Book." *The Journal of Indian Writing in English* 16.2 (July 1988): 210–5.

Bulgakov, Mikhail. *The Master and Margarita*. Translated from Russian by Mirra Ginsburg. New York: Grove Weidenfeld, 1967.

Cambridge Encyclopedia of India, Pakistan, Bangladesh, Sri Lanka, Nepal, Bhutan and the Maldives, ed. Francis Robinson. Cambridge: Cambridge University Press, 1989.

Chaudhuri, Una. Interview. "Imaginative Maps; Excerpts from a Conversation with Salman Rushdie." *Turnstile* 2.1 (1990): 36–47.

– "Writing the Raj Away." *Turnstile* 2.1 (1990): 26–35.

Chaussee, Griffith. "A Textual Unicorn: Identity and Islamic Reference in Salman Rushdie's *Shame*." *Toronto South Asian Review* 8 (Spring 1990): 17–27.

Chuang Tze. *The Writings of Chuang Tze*. In *The Texts of Taoism*. Translated from Chinese by James Legge. New York: Julian, 1959.

Corcoran, Marlena. "Salman Rushdie's Satanic Narration." *The Iowa Review* 20.1 (Winter 1990): 155–67.

Cotterell, Arthur. *A Dictionary of World Mythology*. Oxford: Oxford University press, 1986.

Cronenberg, David. Interview. "Goodfellas: Two wise guys get together to fight the world's famous media battle." *Shift* (July-August 1995): 20–7.

Cundy, Catherine. " 'Rehearsing Voices': Salman Rushdie's *Grimus*." *The Journal of Commonwealth Literature* 27.1 (1992): 128–38.

– *Salman Rushdie*. Manchester: Manchester University Press, 1996.

Daniélou, Alain. *The Myths and Gods of India*. Rochester, Vermont: Iuner Traditions International, 1985.

Dante, Alighieri. *The Divine Comedy*. Translated from Italian by Allen Mandelbaum. New York: Bantam, 1986.

Dharker, Rani. Interview. "An Interview with Salman Rushdie." *New Quest* 42 (November-December 1983): 351–60.

Dipple, Elizabeth. *The Unresolvable Plot: Reading Contemporary Fiction*. New York: Routledge, 1988.

Durix, Jean-Pierre. "The Artistic Journey in Salman Rushdie's *Shame*." *World Literature Written in English* 23.2 (Spring 1984): 451–63.

– " 'The Gardener of Stories': Salman Rushdie's *Haroun and the Sea of Stories*." *Journal of Commonwealth Literature* 28.1 (1993): 114–22.

– "Magic Realism in *Midnight's Children*." *Commonwealth Essays and Studies* 8.1 (1985): 57–63.

– "The Magician of History: Salman Rushdie's *Midnight's Children*." In *The Writer Written: The Artist and Creation in the New Literatures in English*, 119–39. New York and Westport: Greenwood, 1987.

– "Salman Rushdie's Declaration of Kaleidoscopic Identity." In *Declarations of Cultural Independence in the English-Speaking World: A Symposium*, ed. Luigi Sampietro, 173–84. Milan: D'Imperio Editore Novara, 1989.

Eliade, Mircea. *A History of Religious Ideas; Vol. II: From Gautama Buddha to the Triumph of Christianity*. Translated from French by Willard Trask. Chicago: University of Chicago, 1982.

– *A History of Religious Ideas; Vol. III: From Muhammad to the Age of Reforms*. Translated from French by Willard Trask. Chicago: University of Chicago, 1985.

– *The Sacred and the Profane*. Translated from French by Willard Trask. New York: Harcourt Brace Jovanovich, 1959.

Eliot, T.S. *Collected Poems*. London: Faber & Faber, 1963.

Encyclopaedia Britannica 99. CD Rom, Multimedia edition, 1999.

Encyclopaedia of Islam. New Edition. Vol. III. London: Luzac & Co., 1971.

Esposito, John. *Islam: The Straight Path*. New York: Oxford, 1988.

Ezekiel, Nissim. *Hymns in Darkness*. Delhi: Oxford, 1976.

– *Latter-Day Psalms*. Delhi: Oxford, 1982.

Fletcher, M.D. "Rushdie's *Shame* as Apologue." *Journal of Commonwealth Literature* 21.1 (1986): 120–32.

Forster, E.M. *A Passage to India*. Harmondsworth: Penguin, 1978.

Glassé, Cyril. *The Concise Encyclopedia of Islam*. Harper: San Francisco, 1989.

Goonetilleke, D.C.R.A. *Salman Rushdie*. London: MacMillan, 1998.

Haffenden, John. Interview. "Salman Rushdie." In *Novelists in Interview*, 231–61. London: Methuen.

Hamilton, Ian. "The First Life of Salman Rushdie." *The New Yorker* (December 25, 1995-January 1, 1996): 90–113.

Harrison, James. "Reconstructing *Midnight's Children* and *Shame*." *University of Toronto Quarterly* 59.3 (Spring 1990): 399–412.

– *Salman Rushdie*. New York: Twayne, 1992.

Hesse, Hermann. *Magister Ludi*. Translated from German by Richard and Clara Wilson, and with a Foreword by Theodore Ziolkowski. New York: Bantam, 1970.

Hughes, Ted. *Crow: from the Life and Songs of the Crow*. London: Faber, 1970.

Hughes, Thomas. *Dictionary of Islam*. Rupa: Calcutta, 1988.

Hutchinson Encyclopedia. Oxford: Helicon, 1992.

Iyengar, Srinivasa. *Indian Writing in English.* Sixth edition. Delhi: Sterling, 1987.

Jasper, David. *The Study of Literature and Religion.* Minneapolis: Fortress, 1989.

Johansen, Ib. "The Flight from the Enchanter: Reflections on Salman Rushdie's *Grimus.*" *Kunapipi* 7.1 (1985): 20–32.

Joshi, Arun. *The Last Labyrinth.* Delhi: Orient, 1981.

Jussawalla, Feroza. "Rushdie's *Shame*: Problems in Communication." In *Studies in Indian Fiction in English,* ed. Balaram Gupta, 1–13. Gulbarga: JIWE Publications, 1987.

Kanaganayakam, C. "Myth and Fabulosity in *Midnight's Children.*" *Dalhousie Review* 67.1 (Spring 1987): 86–98.

Katrak, K.D. *Underworld.* Calcutta: Writers Workshop, 1979.

Keats, John. *The Complete Poems,* ed. John Barnard. Harmondsworth: Penguin, 1973.

Khayyam, Omar. *The Ruba'iyat* (illustrated edition). Translated from Persian by Peter Avery and John Heath-Stubbs. Harmondsworth: Penguin, 1981.

Kho'i, Esmail. "Letter to Salman Rushdie" (poem). *Toronto South Asian Review* 8 (Spring 1990): 1–10.

King, Bruce. "The New Internationalism: Shiva Naipaul, Salman Rushdie, Buchi Emecheta, Timothy Mo and Kazuo Ishiguro." In *The British and Irish Novel Since 1960,* ed. James Acheson, 192–211. New York: St. Martin's, 1991.

– "Who Wrote *The Satanic Verses*?" *World Literature Today* 63.3 (Summer 1989): 433–5.

Kinsley, David. *Hindu Goddesses: Visions of the Divine Feminine in the Hindu Religious Tradition.* Berkeley: University of California Press: 1936.

Kliever, Lonnie. "Polysymbolism and Modern Religiosity." *The Journal of Religion* 59 (1979): 169–94.

Knönagel, Alex. "*The Satanic Verses*: Narrative Structure and Islamic Doctrine." *The International Fiction Review* 18.2 (1991): 69–75.

Koran, The. Translated from Arabic by N.J. Dawood. Harmondsworth: Penguin, 1956.

Kunapipi. Interview. "*Midnight's Children* and *Shame.*" Vol. 7.1 (1985): 1–19.

Mann, Harveen. "'Being Borne Across': Translation and Salman Rushdie's *The Satanic Verses.*" *Criticism* 37 (Spring 1995): 281–308.

Marx, Karl. *Marx's Grundrisse.* Translated from German by David McLellan. Bungay, Suffolk: Paladin 1973.

Mathur, O.P. "Sense and Sensibility in *Shame.*" In *The Novels of Salman Rushdie,* ed. R.K. Dhawan and G.R. Taneja, 85–93. New Delhi: Indian Society for Commonwealth Studies, 1992.

Mazrui, Ali. "Is *The Satanic Verses* a Satanic Novel? Moral Dilemmas of the Rushdie Affair." *Michigan Quarterly Review* 28.3 (Summer 1989): 347–71.

Mercantante, Anthony. *The Facts on File Encyclopedia of World Mythology and Legend*. New York: Facts on File, 1988.

Milton, John. *Complete Poems and Major Prose*. Indianapolis: Odyssey, 1957.

Myers, David. "From Satiric Farce to Tragic Epiphany: Salman Rushdie's *The Satanic Verses*." *The Commonwealth Review* 2.1–2 (1990–1991): 144–67.

Nair, Sami. "Comment lire *Les Versets Sataniques*." *Esprit* 155 (October 1989): 20–4.

Newsweek. Interview. "An Exclusive Talk With Salman Rushdie." (February 12, 1990): 47–51.

O'Flaherty, Wendy. *Dreams, Illusions and Other Realities*. Chicago: Chicago University Press, 1984.

– *Hindu Myths*. Introduction to, translation of, and commentary on selected Sanskrit myths. Harmondsworth: Penguin Classics, 1975.

– *Shiva: The Erotic Ascetic*. London: Oxford University Press, 1981.

Parameswaran, Uma. *The Perforated Sheet: Essays on Salman Rushdie's Art*. Delhi: Affiliated East-West Press, 1988.

– "Salman Rushdie's *Shame*: An Overview of a Labyrinth." In *The New Indian Novel in English: A Study of the 1980s*, ed. Viney Kirpal, 121–30. New Delhi: Allied, 1990.

Pattanayak, Chandrabhanu. Interview. "Interview with Salman Rushdie." *Literary Criterion* 18.3 (1983): 19–22.

Petersson, Margareta. *Unending Metamorphoses: Myth, Satire and Religion in Salman Rushdie's Novels*. Lund, Sweden: Lund University Press, 1996.

Phillips, Caryl. Interview. "An Interview with Salman Rushdie." *Brick* 52 (Fall 1995): 15–21.

Pipes, Daniel. "The Ayatollah, the Novelist, and the West." *Commentary* 87.6 (June 1989): 9–17.

– *The Rushdie Affair: The Novel, the Ayatollah, and the West*. New York: Birch Lane, 1990.

The Poetic Edda. Translated from Old Norse, and introduced, by Lee Hollander. Austin: University of Texas Press, 1990.

Pourjavady, Nasrollah and Wilson, Peter. *The Drunken Universe; An Anthology of Persian Sufi Poetry*. Grand Rapids: Phanes, 1987.

Puhvel, Jaan, *Comparative Mythology*. Baltimore: John Hopkins, 1989.

Rao, Raja. *The Serpent and the Rope*. New Delhi: Orient 1960.

Rawson, Philip. *The Art of Tantra*. London: Thames and Hudson, 1978.

Reddy, P. Bayapa. "*Grimus*: An Analysis." In *The Novels of Salman Rushdie*, ed. R.K. Dhawan and G.R. Taneja, 5–9. New Delhi: Indian Society for Commonwealth Studies, 1992.

– "*Shame*: A Point of View." In *The Novels of Salman Rushdie*, ed. R.K. Dhawan and G.R. Taneja, 94–101. New Delhi: Indian Society for Commonwealth Studies, 1992.

Rig Veda. Selected and translated from Sanskrit by Wendy O'Flaherty. Harmondsworth: Penguin, 1981.

Rolling Stone Encyclopedia of Rock and Roll. ed. Jon Pareles and Patricia Romanowski. New York: Summit, 1983.

Rushdie, Salman. "After Midnight." *Vanity Fair* (September 1987): 88–94.

– *East, West.* Toronto: Knopf, 1994.

– "The Empire Writes Back with a Vengeance." *The Times* (July 3, 1982): 8.

– *Grimus.* London: Granta, 1975.

– *Haroun and the Sea of Stories.* London: Granta, 1990.

– *Imaginary Homelands; Essays and Criticism 1981–1991.* London: Granta, 1991.

– Introduction to *Home Front* (by Derek Dishton and John Reardon). London: Jonathan Cape, 1984.

– *The Jaguar Smile.* London: Picador, 1987.

– *Midnight's Children.* London: Picador, 1981.

– *The Moor's Last Sigh.* Toronto: Knopf, 1995.

– *The Satanic Verses.* London: Penguin, 1988.

– *Shame.* London: Picador, 1983.

– *The Wizard of Oz.* London: British Film Institute, 1992.

– "Zia Unmourned." *Nation* (September 19, 1988): 188–9.

Russell, Jeffrey. *The Devil: Perceptions of Evil from Antiquity to Primitive Christianity.* Ithaca: Cornell, 1977.

– *Lucifer: The Devil in the Middle Ages.* Ithaca: Cornell, 1984.

– *Mephistopheles: The Devil in the Modern World.* Ithaca: Cornell, 1986.

– *Satan: The Early Christian Tradition.* Ithaca: Cornell, 1981.

Ruthven, Malise. *A Satanic Affair; Salman Rushdie and the Rage of Islam.* London: Chatto & Windus, 1990.

Said, Edward. *Orientalism.* New York: Vintage, 1978.

Schimmel, Annemarie. *Mystical Dimensions of Islam.* Chapel Hill: University of North Carolina Press, 1975.

Scripsi. Interview. "An Interview With Salman Rushdie." Vol. 3.2–3 (1985): 107–26.

Shakespeare, William. *King Lear.* New York: Methuen, 1972.

– *Othello.* New York: Methuen, 1958.

Slemon, "Magic Realism as Postcolonial Discourse." In *Magic Realism; Theory, History, Community,* ed. Faris, Wendy and Lois Zamora, 407–26. Durham and London: Duke University Press, 1995.

Srivastava, Aruna. "'The Empire Writes Back': Language and History in *Shame* and *Midnight's Children.*" *Ariel* 20.4 (October 1989): 62–78.

Stutley, James and Margaret. *A Dictionary of Hinduism.* London: Routledge & Kegan Paul, 1977.

Suleri, Sara. "Contraband Histories: Salman Rushdie and the Embodiment of Blasphemy." *The Yale Review* 78.4 (Summer 1989): 604–24.

Swann, Joseph. " 'East Is East and West Is West'? Salman Rushdie's *Midnight's Children* as an Indian Novel." In *The New Indian Novel in English: A Study of the 1980s*, ed. Viney Kirpal, 251–62. New Delhi: Allied, 1990.

Syed, Mujeebuddin. "Warped Mythologies: Salman Rushdie's *Grimus.*" *Ariel* 25.4 (October 1994): 135–51.

Tales from The Thousand and One Nights. Selected and translated from Arabic by N.J. Dawood. Harmondsworth: Penguin, 1973.

Three Gothic Novels. Edited by Peter Fairclough. London: Penguin, 1968.

The Upanishads. Selected and translated from Sanskrit by Juan Mascaro. Harmondsworth: Penguin, 1965.

van Buitenen, J.A.B. *Tales of Ancient India*. Selected and translated from the Sanskrit collection, *Ocean of the Rivers of the Great Romance*. Chicago: University of Chicago, 1959.

Van der Veer, Peter. "Satanic or Angelic? The Politics of Religious and Literary Inspiration." *Public Culture* 2.1 (Fall 1989): 100–5.

Vitray-Meyerovitch, Eva de. *Rumi and Sufism*. Translated from French by Simone Fattal. Sausalito: Post-Apollo, 1987.

Wachtel, Eleanor. "Salman Rushdie." In *Writers & Company; In Conversation with CBC Radio's Eleanor Wachtel*, 138–58. Toronto: Alfred A. Knopf, 1993.

Wajsbrot, Cécile. "Salman Rushdie: Utiliser une technique qui permette à Dieu d'exister." *La Quinzaine Littéraire* 449 (16–31 October 1985): 22.

Walker, Bejamin. *The Hindu World*. Vol. 1. London: George Allen & Unwin, 1968.

Watson-Williams, Helen. "An Antique Land: Salman Rushdie's *Shame.*" *Westerly* 29.4 (December 1984): 37–45.

Weatherby, William. *Salman Rushdie: Sentenced to Death*. New York: Carroll & Graf, 1990.

Webster, Richard. *A Brief History of Blasphemy: Liberalism, Censorship and "The Satanic Verses."* Southwold: Orwell, 1990.

White, H. *Elements of Universal History, on a New and Systematic Plan, from the Earliest Times to the Middle of 1862*. Edinburgh: Oliver and Boyd, 1865.

Whitman, Walt. *Complete Poetry and Selected Prose*. Boston: Houghton Mifflin, 1959.

Zaehner, R.C. *Hindu & Muslim Mysticism*. Oxford: Oneworld, 1960.

Zakaria, Rafiq. *The Struggle Within Islam; the Conflict Between Religion and Politics*. London: Penguin, 1989.

Ziolkowski, Theodore. "Religion and Literature in a Secular Age: The Critic's Dilemma." *The Journal of Religion* 59 (1979): 18–34.

Index

This index contains selected ideas, mythological and religious figures, works, writers, philosophers, poets, places and historical incidents. It does not include characters in Rushdie's fiction. For instance, the entry on Shiva refers to the Hindu god and not the antagonist of *Midnight's Children*; the entry on Omar Khayyam refers to the Persian poet and not the peripheral hero of *Shame*. I have briefly glossed entries which may be obscure to some readers. Further information of a historical and contextual nature can be found in the text of my study and in the time-line, which is referred to below in small Roman numerals in bold print.